THE POLITICAL WRITINGS O|

GW00818901

THE POLITICAL WRITINGS

OF BHAGAT SINGH

EDITED AND WITH AN INTRODUCTION BY
CHAMAN LAL AND MICHAEL D. YATES

First published in December 2023

LeftWord Books
2254/2A, Shadi Khampur
New Ranjit Nagar
New Delhi 110008
INDIA

LeftWord Books and Vaam Prakashan are imprints of
    Naya Rasta Publishers Pvt. Ltd.

leftword.com

ISBN   978-93-92018-08-4 paperback
               978-93-92018-12-1 ebook

Printed and bound by Chaman Enterprises, Delhi.

DEDICATION

To the memory of Agnes Smedley, stalwart socialist feminist and early champion of Indian independence. Imprisoned in the United States in 1918 for her work with Indian revolutionaries, she later worked with the Chinese Communists in their long civil war and struggle for independence and socialism. A worthy role model for all who yearn and fight for a new world.

Contents

Publisher's Note

Each of the texts in this volume is prefaced by a short introduction by the editors. Some of the texts were written by Bhagat Singh originally in English. These have been lightly edited for punctuation and spelling. The texts translated from other Indian languages have been edited to a higher degree, but the attempt has been to keep the original flavour of the text intact.

The titles of these writings fall under the following categories:

a. Original English titles – they are as they appeared at the time of original publication.

b. Translated titles – they have been translated to English from various Indian languages.

c. Titles given by the editors, even though the English titles came out under a different title at the time of printing. In these cases, the original titles have been given in the body of the article.

d. Titles given by editors for unpublished articles and letters.

When writing in Punjabi or Hindustani, Bhagat Singh often left quotes from western authors in English. These have been indicated as such.

This edition is aimed as much at an international readership as Indian. We have provided a Glossary at the end of the volume to aid those not intimately familiar with India.

Chaman Lal and Michael D. Yates

Introduction:
The Life and Legend of Bhagat Singh

Anti-colonial and anti-imperialist struggles always produce young martyrs. During the efforts by Irish rebels to throw off the British yoke that had killed so many, Kevin Barry, age eighteen, was hanged by the occupying forces. He was a member of the Irish Republican Army and was arrested for an attack on a British Army lorry in which British soldiers were killed. Barry's death sentence elicited international condemnation. His hanging made him a martyr to the cause of Irish independence. A song in his memory titled 'Kevin Barry' has been recorded by numerous artists, from Paul Robeson to Tommy Makem.

There are many other examples we can give, from the Chen brothers in China, who were Communists murdered in the late 1920s, to Ahmed Timol, a Communist murdered by the South African authorities in 1971, to Nguyễn Văn Trỗi, a member of the National Liberation Front in Vietnam, executed after a failed attempt to assassinate the odious U.S. Secretary of Defence, Robert McNamara and the U.S. Ambassador, Henry Cabot Lodge Jr.

In this book, we will meet one of the greatest young revolutionary martyrs, Bhagat Singh. What makes him unique among the pantheon of young revolutionaries who died for a great cause is his precocity, in both his bold actions and his perspicacity. While still in his early teens, he showed a depth of understanding of Indian political reality. He read widely and became fluent in several Indian languages, as well as English. Moreover, he wrote insightful political essays, ones that a much older person would have been proud to have written. It is not only that his call to arms against the British imperialists inspired Indians – young and old. It is that his written works continue to stir the minds of all those who seek a world where everyone is equal, and all can fully develop their capacities. He is as much a part of the Indian radical tradition today as he was one hundred years ago.

Bhagat Singh is a legend, but how he became one needs to be understood. He was born on 28 September 1907 in the village of Chak No. 105, Lyallpur Bange, as it was called in those days, which is now in Faisalabad, Pakistan, which itself was formerly known as Lyallpur. Bhagat Singh died young, at twenty-three, on 23 March 1931. The British colonial government executed him in Lahore because he was a danger to the imperial power. Despite his tender years, his popularity soared so high that historian and activist in the Indian National Congress, Pattabhi Sitaramaiah, acknowledged that Bhagat Singh's popularity graph was at one time equal to that of Mahatma Gandhi, who himself was martyred like Bhagat Singh, though not by a foreign government, but by India's own rabid communal forces. Gandhi lived for seventy-eight years and had a long political life, greatly impacting South African and Indian societies. Bhagat Singh, on the other hand, had not even seven such years, and yet his effect on the Indian people has been remarkable, at times no less than that even of Gandhi and many other long-lived Indian leaders.

The legend surrounding the life of Bhagat Singh centres on the last two years and four months of his life, from 17 December 1928 to 23 March 1931.

The Deputy Superintendent of the Lahore police, John Saunders, was assassinated on 17 December 1928, in broad daylight, in front of the Senior Superintendent Police's office in Lahore. This assassination was claimed by the Hindustan Socialist Republican Army (HSRA), of which Singh was a member, with posters pasted on Lahore roads on 18 December. These posters read,

> JP Saunders is dead; Lala Lajpat Rai is avenged . . . . In this
> man has died an agent of the British authority in India . . . .
> Sorry for the bloodshed of the human being, but the sacrifice
> of individuals at the altar of revolution . . . is inevitable.

Newspapers the world over carried the sensational news from the next day onwards. The people of Lahore saw a similar HSRA notice, five days later, on 23 December. British colonial police frantically searched for the revolutionaries who killed Saunders, but to no avail. It took months for a breakthrough in the case.

Even before Saunders's death, the Indian political atmosphere was boiling over. In fact, this assassination itself was the result of the heated atmosphere, in which the (Sir John) Simon Commission had come to India to investigate the political situation. The Commission had no Indian members. This visit was boycotted everywhere, with anti-Simon processions led by national leaders. In Lahore, the youth had convinced Lala Lajpat Rai, the most important Punjabi leader of the Indian freedom struggle, to lead the anti-Simon commission protest, which he did on 30 October 1928. The police charged the march, and Rai became a victim of police brutality, hit repeatedly by the bamboo clubs known as lathis, wielded by DSP Saunders at the orders of Senior Superintendent of Police James A. Scott. Due to this beating, about which Bhagat Singh declared that 'every lathi on his body would prove to be the last nail in the coffin of British rule in India!', Lala Lajpat Rai died on 17 November 1928. Basanti Devi, the widow of radical nationalist, Chittranjan Das, had touched the raw nerve of the country's youth when in anguish, she questioned whether they were dead if they could not avenge the death of a great nationalist leader at the hands of a petty police official of the colonial raj.

The HSRA took up the challenge, despite leaving the path of pistol and violence three months earlier in its 8-9 September

1928 meeting at the grounds of the ancient Feroze Shah Kotla fortress in Delhi. Here the Hindustan Republican Association (HRA) rechristened itself the HSRA and decided to build mass organisations of peasants, youth, students, and workers to pursue the cause of socialist revolution in India.

Responding to the call of Basanti Devi, the HSRA decided to punish Scott. Bhagat Singh and Shivaram Rajguru were chosen to shoot him. Jai Gopal would identify Scott, and Chandra Shekhar Azad would provide cover. Bhagat Singh was supposed to shoot first, but at the signal given by Jai Gopal, Rajguru immediately shot him, while Bhagat Singh tried to call Azad, saying, 'Pandit Ji, he is not Scott. . .'. Before Bhagat Singh could complete his sentence, Saunders was already shot by Rajguru, who always wished to be at the forefront of every action. Bhagat Singh had no option but to pump more bullets into Saunders's fallen body to ensure he did not survive. While the target, Scott, was not killed, this could be justified, given that Saunders was equally responsible for Lalaji's death – in fact, it was he who struck Lala – and was as much a symbol of colonial power as Scott.

However, this action sealed the fate of Bhagat Singh, who clearly understood that he would be arrested by the British and then executed. So, with a clear grasp of the political climate, Bhagat Singh decided to perform as many spectacular revolutionary acts as possible in whatever time he had left. He carefully planned what he would do. His actions would trap the most powerful colonial authority in the world, putting the British themselves on trial for all of India to see and draw inspiration. This would guarantee his death, but it would make him a martyr for the cause of Indian independence and the creation of a radically new society. And the time and manner of what he was about to do would be decided by Bhagat Singh himself. This part of his life is a fascinating story, the creation of himself as the greatest symbol of the Indian revolutionary movement.

How did Bhagat Singh acquire such a mature political

perception? To understand this, it is necessary to examine his family, which was intensely committed to the national movement.

From infancy, Bhagat Singh drank deeply not just his mother's milk but also radical patriotism. In his home, the day of his birth brought the good news of the release orders from British prisons for his father, Kishan Singh, and two uncles –the revolutionary Ajit Singh and young Swarn Singh. Swarn Singh contracted tuberculosis in jail and died shortly after his release, still a young man in his early twenties. And his revolutionary uncle, Ajit Singh, a peasant organiser who had co-founded the Bharat Mata (Mother India) Society with Lala Lajpat Rai. Ajit Singh was forced to leave the country in 1909 when Bhagat Singh was two years old. He returned thirty-eight years later, just before India freed itself from British rule, dying in Dalhousie on the very day of independence, 15 August 1947.

Ajit Singh spent his exiled life, mostly in Latin America, in revolutionary activities for the freedom of the country. In fact, he tried to get Bhagat Singh out of the country as he knew about his revolutionary activities in India. According to Baba Bhagat Singh Bilga, the veteran Ghadarite (an expatriate movement dedicated to the overthrow of British rule) revolutionary who was living in Argentina in the 1930s – Ajit Singh often stayed with them – told one of this book's editors, Chaman Lal, that Ajit Singh had three letters of Bhagat Singh with him. These were given to someone for safe custody but were lost, as were some documents sent from jail by Bhagat Singh before his execution.

At the age of four, Bhagat Singh, as an innocent child talking to Mehta Anand Kishore, a well-known freedom fighter and friend of his father in the Congress, said that he 'would sow rifles in fields in order to reap a fruit of fulsome crop to drive British out of the country'. At age twelve, in April 1919, he visited Jallianwala Bagh (then a dry stretch of land used as a resting or meeting place but later a garden and memorial site) in Amritsar after the despicable massacre of people there by the British. He brought with him 'blood-soaked sand'. At age fourteen, while reading in school in Lahore, he informed his grandfather about the preparations by railway men to go on strike in 1921.

When he was fifteen, Bhagat Singh enrolled in the National College Lahore, founded two years earlier by Lala Lajpat Rai as an alternative to British-run schools. Singh had just passed his ninth class, which meant that he was very young to be attending the college.

Prior to this, he had welcomed the protesting Akali workers in his village. The Akali Movement aimed at community control of the Sikh Gurudwaras, which are both places of worship and community centres. The Akalis also were part of the Indian Independence movement. On 20 February 1921, more than 140 devout Sikhs were killed by Mahant Narain Dass, in collaboration with the British authorities, at Gurudwara Nankana Sahib; a Mahant serves as manager of a Gurudwara. Bhagat Singh visited Nankana Sahib in 1921 and wore a black turban in protest. Later, in 1924, he welcomed Akali workers in his village during another movement called Jaito Morcha.

This was also when Bhagat Singh learned the Gurmukhi script and the Punjabi Language. Since his grandfather, S. Arjan Singh, was a staunch Arya Samajist (Arya Samaj was a Hindu reform movement) despite being a Sikh, his emphasis was on learning the Sanskrit Language, which Bhagat Singh did learn in school along with Urdu, Hindi, and English. Worried about Bhagat's revolutionary traits and tendencies, the family, particularly his father, thought of 'controlling him through marriage.' There were already two young women in the house, the widow of Bhagat Singh's younger uncle Swarn Singh and Bibi Harnam Kaur, wife of his exiled revolutionary uncle Ajit Singh. However, if marriage could not control Ajit Singh, who had no children of his own, how could it control his nephew?

Besides, Bhagat Singh was too sensitive to the sufferings of his aunts. He was particularly attached to Harnam Kaur. According to the account of his schoolmate and close friend, Jaidev Gupta, available in the Nehru Memorial Museum and Library (NMML), Bhagat Singh was given to her as a 'son' due to her being childless, while Ajit Singh was living in uncertain exile.

From the point of view of political temperament, Bhagat Singh was like the son of Ajit Singh, with whom he was close despite never having lived with him. At the level of ideas, Ajit Singh was more advanced in terms of Indian freedom from British rule than was the dominant Congress. His was the revolutionary view. He wanted to awaken and organise the peasantry on the basis of their economic exploitation at the hands of the big feudal lords and the colonial system. Bhagat Singh took his uncle's thinking and pushed it further, eventually adopting the Marxist ideology of liberation.

At fifteen, Bhagat Singh questioned the termination of the non-cooperation movement by Mahatma Gandhi, who used the Chauri Chaura incident as a pretext. This movement was initiated by Gandhi in 1920. It urged his followers to stop participating in British rule by refusing to work in British enterprises, including schools, and boycotting British goods. On 4 February 1922, in the town of Chauri Chaura, in what is today the province of Uttar Pradesh, protesters in support of the movement were fired upon by British soldiers. The protesters retaliated, and in the end, more than twenty police officers were killed. Because this incident violated Gandhi's commitment to nonviolence, he halted the non-cooperation movement.

Gandhi's decision disillusioned many of the youth and revolutionaries across India. The young revolutionary, Chandra Shekhar Azad, who had once been flogged for shouting, '*Mahatma Gandhi Ki Jai*,' (Victory to Mahatma Gandhi), was among the youth who were bitter at this development and later, during their revolutionary activities, could never trust Gandhi. Instead, many had relations with leaders like C. R. Das, Moti Lal Nehru and his son Jawaharlal Nehru, Subhas Chandra Bose, Lala Lajpat Rai, and Madan Mohan Malviya. But no revolutionary claimed closeness to Gandhi, though some correspondence between Gandhi and radical leaders had taken place. Sukhdev Thapar, who was executed along with Bhagat Singh, wrote a letter to Gandhi before he was hanged, decrying Gandhi's disapproval of revolutionary tactics. Gandhi replied in his journal, *Young India*, but after Sukhdev died. To be fair, however, Gandhi received the letter, which had been written earlier, after Sukhdev's execution along with Bhagat Singh and Rajguru.

Ironically, the cessation of the non-cooperation movement gave impetus to a revolutionary movement throughout the country. Bhagat Singh reached Kanpur in 1923 after informing his father through a letter that he would dedicate his life to the nation – so he could not think of marrying – a remarkably mature and farsighted remark, given that he had not yet marked his sixteenth birthday.

His teacher in the National College, Jai Chander Vidyalankar, had given him an introduction letter to Ganesh Shankar Vidyarthi, editor of *Pratap*, in Kanpur, and a Congress leader of Uttar Pradesh (called United Province at that time) Bhagat Singh not only joined *Pratap*; he also joined the underground revolutionary organization, the Hindustan Republican Association (HRA), organised by Sachinder Nath Sanyal, the author of the autobiography, *Bandi Jivan* (A Prisoner's Life), who had already gone through one round of transportation to the notorious colonial prison in the Andaman and Nicobar Islands, located in the Bay of Bengal. This prison was constructed according to the plan for a panopticon by English philosopher Jeremy Bentham. Bhagat Singh had met Sanyal in Lahore. It was in Kanpur that Bhagat Singh met other revolutionary comrades of the HRA, Bejoy Kumar Sinha, Shiv Verma, Jaidev Kapoor, B.K. Dutt, Ajay Ghosh, along with Sukhdev and Bhagwati Charan Vohra. The latter two were in Lahore and part of the same group.

Bhagat Singh spent about six months in Kanpur, writing for *Pratap* under the pen name of Balwant, working some time for flood relief, and performing the duties of headmaster in a national school at Shadipur village near Aligarh. He then returned to Lahore upon hearing the news of his grandmother's illness and getting assurance that none in the house would talk about his marriage anymore.

By the age of sixteen, Bhagat Singh had matured so much that in 1923 he wrote an essay in Hindi on the language issue of Punjab, winning the prize in a writing competition. In 1924 and 1925, he wrote the essays '*Vishav Prem*' (Universal Love) and '*Yuvak*' (Young Boy or Youth), both published in the Calcutta Weekly, *Matwala*, under the assumed name of Balwant Singh. And then, at the execution of six Babbar Akali (a splinter group of militant Sikhs) revolutionaries in 1926, his article '*Holi ke din rakat ke chhinte*' (Blood drops on the festival of Holi) was published under the name of – One Punjabi Youth. And in 'Why I am an Atheist,' written in 1930, Bhagat Singh referred to the development of his ideas by saying that he had become an atheist by the end of 1926, when he was not yet nineteen. These developments in his personality had taken place against a backdrop of his reading of Marxist literature, going to the Dwarka Das Library in Lahore, where he had become a voracious reader from 1921.

Bhagat Singh did not stop at becoming an atheist. He was searching for the ultimate ideology of human liberation. By this time, he had become almost a committed Marxist, through his contacts with the *Kirti* (a leftist journal) group of Ghadarite revolutionaries of Punjab. He had regularly contributed articles to *Kirti*, written in Punjabi and Urdu, on various issues like 'Religion Oriented Riots and their Solution,' 'Issue of Untouchability,' and 'Religion and our Freedom Struggle.' If he had any differences with them, these were only about the program of the revolutionary party. Bhagat Singh and his comrades were convinced that to awaken the country from slumber, the youth needed to perform daring revolutionary nationalist actions and make sacrifices to advance the movement.

By 1928, Bhagat Singh and his comrades – Sukhdev and Bhagwati Charan Vohra in Punjab, along with Bejoy Kumar Sinha, Shiv Verma, and Jaidev Kapoor in Uttar Pradesh – saw the need for a socialist agenda in their revolutionary party. They gave practical shape to it by calling an urgent meeting of the central committee of the HRA on 8 and 9 September 1928 at the historic Feroze Shah Kotla ground in Delhi, where after lengthy deliberations and at the suggestion of Bhagat Singh, supported by Sukhdev, Bejoy Kumar Sinha, Shiv Verma, and Jaidev Kapoor, the HRA was rechristened the HSRA. The addition of the 'S' for Socialist was not simply ornamental as was the case when former Prime Minister Indira Gandhi, during the Emergency (1975-1977), had 'socialist' added to the preamble of the Indian constitution. It was a well-thought-out qualitative change of perception about the goal of the Indian revolution, and it had the sanction of Chander Shekher Azad, who, while not that well-read, trusted Bhagat Singh completely.

Prior to the formation of the HSRA, Bhagat Singh trained himself in mass organizational work. The Naujawan Bharat Sabha (NBS, Youth Society of India) was formed in 1926, patterned after the 'Young Italy' youth organization in Italy, inspired by Giuseppe Mazzini and Giuseppe Garibaldi. Bhagat Singh was its general secretary, and Bhagwati Charan Vohra was its propaganda secretary. NBS worked to organise lantern shows of the pictures of patriots. They were particularly inspired by the sacrifice of the Ghadarite revolutionary Kartar Singh Sarabha, who was executed in 1915 in Lahore at the young age of nineteen, and whose photograph Bhagat Singh always kept in his pocket. In all their public meetings, they garlanded Sarabha's picture and placed it on the dais.

During this period, Ghadarite revolutionaries returned from the Soviet Union, trained in Communist theory at the Eastern University of the Toilers in Moscow. They formed the Kirti group, and Santokh Singh began *Kirti*. Afterwards, Sohan Singh Josh became its editor after the untimely death of Santokh Singh.

Bhagat Singh formally worked on the *Kirti* editorial staff, as he was in touch with Sohan Singh Josh in connection with NBS activities.

Even before forming NBS in Lahore, Bhagat Singh was in contact with the earliest Indian Communists in Kanpur, a working-class city. Among his contacts were Satyabhakat, Radha Mohan Gokulji, Hasrat Mohani, and Shaukat Usmani. So, Bhagat Singh was part of the Communist movement in India from its very inception, and his later activities attest to this. Bhagat Singh did not become a member of the Communist Party, as it was still in its formative period, but he knew some of its leaders.

While Bhagat Singh had no reservations about joining the Communist Party, he and others were shaping their own revolutionary organization, the HSRA, as an elementary communist formation. Bhagat Singh was also clear, as is evident from his prison writings, that ultimately the HSRA had to commit to the mass organization of workers, peasants, students, and other potentially revolutionary sections of society. At the same time, he and his group were of the view that, given the relative backwardness of the Indian masses, some spectacular revolutionary actions, along with the sacrifices of young men that would awaken the masses from their slumber, were necessary to arouse an upsurge against British colonialism. Sohan Singh Josh aptly described this in his 'Four meetings with Bhagat Singh.' After the formation of the HSRA in September 1928, political developments took place that did not allow time for the HSRA to transform itself into a mass party. However, several mass organizations were formed, apart from NBS, such as the Lahore Students Union, the Bal Students Union, and Bal Bharat Sabha.

It is interesting to note that the NBS helped form Bal Bharat Sabha, an organization of school students between the ages of twelve and sixteen. Curiously, no historian has paid attention to this interesting aspect of the freedom struggle. The president of Bal Bharat Sabha Amritsar, Kahan Chand, age eleven, was awarded three months rigorous imprisonment. Yash, later a renowned editor of the Urdu daily *Milap* and son of Mahasha Khushal Chand, was secretary of the Bal Bharat Sabha. He was ten when he was prosecuted on three counts, including assisting the Lahore city Congress and the NBS. In those days, some 1,192 juveniles under the age of fifteen were convicted for political activities. Punjab accounted for 189 and Bengal 739 of these convictions.

Apart from Bal Bharat Sabha, the Bal Student Union was also active, showing the impact of Bhagat Singh. Not only the young but even the Lahore city Congress was affected by his magnetic personality. Lala Lajpat Rai's grandson, Baldev Raj, was secretary of the Bal Student Union, and Dyanat Rai was president. Such was the infectious impact of patriotic feelings that Singh and his comrades generated. Alarmed by Bhagat Singh's impact on the youth, the Lahore police arrested him in May 1927 on the pretext of his involvement in the October 1926 Dussehra festival bomb case. Bhagat Singh was jailed for about five weeks before being released on a bail bond of sixty thousand rupees (a reasonably large sum of money). The authorities withdrew the case a few months later. It was during this period that Bhagat Singh planned mass activities. Before he could bring these to fruition, the Simon Commission came to India.

NBS was very active in Punjab. It came into conflict with Lala Lajpat Rai because of his association with communal (religious) elements, which Bhagat Singh and the NBS openly opposed. As a result, Lala Lajpat Rai angrily shut the doors of his house to Bhagat Singh, Sukhdev, and Bhagwati Charan Vohra. Yet, as the most important independence leader in Punjab, Rai was asked to lead the demonstration against the Simon Commission when visiting Lahore on 30 October 1928.

Many comrades of the HSRA had gone underground for their involvement in the Kakori train robbery in 1925, particularly Chandra Shekhar Azad. After the Saunders murder, Bhagat Singh, Rajguru, Sukhdev, and others also went underground. Immediately after this, Bhagat Singh escaped to Calcutta along with Durga

Bhabhi. There he remained in touch with Congress delegates such as Sohan Singh Josh and also some Bengali revolutionaries, one of whom, Jatinder Nath Das (who died in prison after a prolonged hunger strike in 1929), agreed to come to Agra, home of the party headquarters, to train other comrades in bomb-making techniques.

At this point, the HSRA was in a fix. By adopting a socialist perspective on Indian liberation, its members wanted to concentrate on organising workers, peasants, students, and youth. However, the murder of Saunders and some earlier cases against them kept the young revolutionaries from working openly. Neither could they use the cover of the Congress for open political work, as they had serious and fundamental differences with it. There was little hope that they could allow the government to try them in their pending cases and, after getting cleared, participate in the process of organising the masses.

The only option Bhagat Singh could visualize in such a difficult situation was to awaken the people of his country through their revolutionary activities but with minimum loss of life and then sacrifice their own lives in such a manner that the whole country would become aware of their goals and ideas. Bhagat Singh also wanted to remove the terrorist tag from the HSRA, as well as from themselves. For this, they wished to utilize platforms that would allow their voices to reach millions.

Bhagat Singh understood that what they could not achieve by living longer, they could achieve by sacrificing their lives in the prime of youth, but in a manner such that their sacrifices would not go unnoticed. The HSRA moved earnestly in this direction by shooting Saunders in broad daylight. This incident inspired millions of Indians, including Lala Lajpat Rai. And Rai's death, the result of the brutal lathi charge by the colonial police at the Simon Commission demonstration, had engendered a simmering widespread humiliation.

By killing Saunders, the HSRA and Bhagat Singh became the

central focus of the nation's political scene, though Bhagat Singh made it clear in one of his court statements that they bore no personal grudge or malice against anyone. In his Session Court statement in the Delhi Assembly bombing case, he said, 'We hold human life sacred beyond words and would sooner lay our lives in the service of humanity than injure anyone else.'

Once Jatinder Nath Das arrived in Agra, he helped establish bomb factories in some rented houses. To reignite and steady the people's enthusiastic response to the assassination of Saunders, Bhagat Singh wanted another equally spectacular action. The British colonial government was bent upon passage of the Public Safety Bill and the Trade Disputes Bill despite stiff public opposition from the masses in demonstrations, as well as from members of the Central Assembly. So, Singh and others decided to throw harmless but loud bombs into the Central Assembly.

The issue was discussed in the central committee of the HSRA, with Sukhdev absent. The committee rejected Bhagat Singh's proposal to send himself for this action, as he was bound to be trapped in the Saunders murder, and the Party did not want to lose his leadership in such a crucial time. When Sukhdev learned of this decision, he became upset and angry at his close friend. He taunted him for 'trying to save his life', knowing full well that he was the best person for the job, since no one else could project the Party view as effectively as he.

The central committee met again, and Bhagat Singh insisted that not only would he go, but he, along with another comrade, B.K. Dutt and they would get themselves arrested after the act. The Party wanted them to escape after this but reluctantly agreed to Bhagat Singh's proposals. Along with Jaidev Kapoor, who was to accompany them to the Central Assembly, Bhagat Singh observed the entry and exit of the Assembly. They would throw the bombs after members exited the building. Despite his newly clean-shaven face, Dr Saifudin Kitchlew, an Assembly member, had recognized him there. Later, Kitchlew offered him support.

The bombing action was inspired by a similar act of French anarchist Auguste Vaillant at the Chamber of Deputies in 1893 to focus attention on the poverty of the people. At his trial for the bombing, Bhagat Singh, echoing Valliant, said, 'If the deaf are to hear, the sound has to be very loud.' This was the first sentence of the pamphlet that Bhagat Singh and B. K. Dutt threw into the Central Assembly after they had thrown two bombs over the empty benches. But the explosion created commotion in the room, and only a few members, such as Pandit Motilal Nehru, Madan Mohan Malviya, and Jinnah, could keep their calm by remaining standing on their seats. Others, including the home secretary, ran helter-skelter, some even hiding under the benches.

And here, two historic slogans came into existence on the Indian political horizon: *Inquilab Zindabad* (Long Live Revolution) and *Samrajyavad Ka Nash Ho* (Down with Imperialism). Over time, these slogans, particularly *Inquilab Zindabad*, became part not only of revolutionary groups but of all other organizations. It was even heard on Congress stages. Of course, right-wing Hindu Nationalist parties, such as Rashtriya Swayamsevak Sangh and Hindu Mahasabha, would never touch this slogan. (In the memoirs of some revolutionaries, it is mentioned that Bhagat Singh used to shout these two international slogans in English).

In fact, *Inquilab Zindabad* is the translation of 'Long Live Revolution,' an international slogan of the working-class movement. In India, there was an attempt to render it in Hindi as *Kranti Chirjivi Ho*, which has the same basic meaning, but it did not catch the imagination of the people. Only *Inquilab Zindabad* struck a deep chord in the minds of the Hindi-speaking people of India, and it also spread from Agartala to Chennai and from Srinagar to Mumbai, and across southern Asia. Bhagat Singh rightly felt proud that 'in his small life, he has made this slogan reach crores of Indians.' *Inquilab Zindabad* finally replaced *Bande Mataram* (Hail the Motherland), which was a popular slogan of the nationalist movement from 1905 to 8 April 1929, prior to

Bhagat Singh and Dutt raising their famous words in the Central Assembly. In any objective analysis of Bhagat Singh's contribution to the national movement, the most popular slogan of the masses, *Inquilab Zindabad*, would always shine with his name.

The revolutionaries planned this action with meticulous care. They had photographs of Bhagat Singh and Dutt made prior to it. Many copies of the statement issued were also prepared, and these were sent to the leading newspapers that same day, 8 April 1929. The *Hindustan Times* published the complete statement in its special edition. British police officers were afraid to arrest the two men because both were holding loaded pistols, although while shouting slogans, they laid these on the table, indicating to the police that they were ready to be arrested. Officers then moved forward and arrested them. Meanwhile, Jaidev Kapoor left the Assembly Hall. The HSRA had achieved its goal, and the next task was to spread the message of revolution to the people.

Bhagat Singh again had a well-thought-out plan. They would not defend themselves in the British courts; instead, they would use the courts as platforms, making political statements that would spread their *ideas and values*. They did not hire a lawyer for their defence but accepted the consultancy of advocates. So the nationalist advocate, Asaf Ali, was available to them for consultation. Ali read Bhagat Singh and B. K. Dutt's historic statement in the Sessions Court on 6 June 1929, where they were being tried in the Delhi bomb case. This statement is a political document that explains the aims and objectives of the revolutionary movement in lucid terms:

> We humbly claim to be no more than serious students of the history and the conditions of our country and her aspirations. We despise hypocrisy. Our practical protest was against the institution, which since its birth has eminently helped to display not only its worthlessness, but its far-reaching power for injustice. The more we have pondered, the more deeply we have been convinced that it exists only to demonstrate to the

world India's humiliation and helplessness, and it symbolizes the overriding domination of an irresistible and autocratic rule . . . Solemn resolutions passed by the house have been contemptuously trampled underfoot on the floor of so-called Indian Parliament.

Bhagat Singh and Dutt further clarified their aim:

We deliberately offered ourselves to bear the penalty for what we had done and to let the imperialist exploiters know that by crushing individuals, they cannot kill ideas. By crushing two insignificant units a nation cannot be crushed.

And they dared the colonialist power by putting forward the question,

Can ordinances and safety bills snuff out the flames of freedom in India? Conspiracy cases, trumped up or discovered, and the incarceration of all young men who cherish the vision of a great ideal, cannot check the march of a revolution. But a timely warning, if not unheeded, can help to prevent loss of life and general sufferings.

We took it upon ourselves to provide this warning, and our duty is done.

The main statement ends with these words. Bhagat Singh and Dutt had explained how thoughtfully they had thrown the harmless bombs in 'vacant spaces', in order not to injure anyone, not even the British, and the only damage these did was to the empty benches plus minor abrasions in less than half a dozen cases. And since each was asked in the lower court, 'what he meant by the word revolution,' in his statement in Sessions Court, he explained the concept of revolution almost in Marxist terminology. Both spoke of the knowledge of capitalism and the establishment of the dictatorship of the proletariat for the consummation of the ideal of revolution. But they also reminded the British colonial power of the Marxist epithet that 'peaceful transition is also possible if timely warning is heeded by the power that be.' The statement concludes again with the slogan 'Long live Revolution'!

The concept of revolution had become so engrossing for Bhagat Singh that all his attention and energy was focused upon clarifying it to himself as well as to his comrades and countrymen and the imperialist British power. When Ramanand Chatterjee, the editor of *Modern Review*, ridiculed the slogan 'Long Live Revolution,' Bhagat Singh and Dutt rebutted him in a letter published in *The Tribune* on 24 December 1929. 'Revolution did not necessarily involve sanguinary strife. It was not a cult of bomb and pistol. They may sometimes be mere means for its achievement. A rebellion is not a revolution. It may ultimately lead to that end.' Bhagat Singh defines revolution as the 'spirit of longing for change for the better,' and they wish that 'the spirit of revolution should always permeate the soul of humanity, so that the reactionary forces may not accumulate strength to check its eternal onward march.'

In his introduction to the *Selected Writings of Shaheed Bhagat Singh*, Shiv Verma has drawn attention to the ideology and development of the revolutionary movement 'From Chapekars to Bhagat Singh'. This is a significant analysis of the Indian revolutionary movement. There had been sporadic rebellions or revolutionary activities against British colonialism from 1757 when the British won the Battle of Plassey in Bengal and started controlling India step by step through the East India Company. There had been tribal revolts in Bihar, Jharkhand, like those of Tilka Manjhi, Sido-Kanu, and others, even prior to the first war of independence fought in 1857, after which direct British rule was established.

Shiv Verma traced the entry of revolutionaries in the freedom struggle to 1897 – when the Chapekar brothers in Poona fired the first shots. It was the time when Bal Gangadhar Tilak dominated the national scene, exposing the British colonial state machinery's oppression of the Indian people in his paper *Kesari*. The British called him the 'Father of the Indian unrest'. At that time, there was an outbreak of bubonic plague in Poona, and British officer Walter Charles Rand initiated draconian measures to deal with this, including public body searches. On 22 June 1897, Rand and his military escort, Charles Egerton Ayerst, were shot dead by the three Chapekar brothers. The brothers were arrested and sent to the gallows in May 1898.

The distinctive feature of these earliest revolutionaries was that they were inspired by strong Hindu religious sentiments. So, Shiv Verma calls the first period, from 1897 to 1913, the 'phase of the revolutionary movement inspired by Hindu religion'. The militant Anushilan Samiti movement in Bengal was also, in large part, influenced by Hindu philosophical concepts. The Bengal revolutionaries Khudi Ram Bose and Praful Chaki gave their lives in the cause of revolution in 1908. Both were convicted of murder. Chaki committed suicide, but Khudi Ram Bose, aged eighteen, was hanged. Tilak, Lala Lajpat Rai, Bipan Chandra Pal, and the philosopher Aurobindo Ghosh, like the earliest nationalists, also drew their inspiration from religion.

At the same time, however, there was another trend, particularly in foreign countries and in Punjab, to which Shiv Verma paid inadequate attention. Radicals like the lawyer and journalist Shyamji Krishan Verma and his comrade Madam Bhikaji Cama, Indian revolutionaries living abroad, were flying the flag of socialism as early as 1905. Lawyer and journalist Shyamji Krishna Varma founded and edited the journal, *The Indian Sociologist* in London in 1905, while Bhikaji Cama, who was associated with the international socialist movement, co-founded the Paris Indian Society also in 1905. In Punjab, Bhagat Singh's uncle, Ajit Singh, and others formed the Bharat Mata Society, which focused on issues like the exploitation of peasants. Punjabi nationalist poet and comrade of Ajit Singh, Lala Banke Dayal, wrote the song

'*Pagri Sambhal Jatta*' (Take care of your turban, O peasant), which became a war cry in Punjab. This song describes the exploitation of peasants and exhorts them to revolt. This song was first sung in March 1907. Banke Dayal was imprisoned for writing it. Both Aurobindo's brother, Barinder Kumar Ghosh, and Swami Vivekanand's brother, Dr Bhupender Nath Dutt, rejected a narrow religious vision of nationalism and adopted a more advanced and progressive socialist vision later in their lives.

Shiv Verma rightly focused on the formation of the Ghadar Movement by Indians living on the west coast of the United States as the beginning of a secular nationalist movement from 1914 onward, although the foundation for this movement had its roots in 1909 when Ajit Singh was forced to leave India and go into exile. He came in contact with the Ghadar Movement in 1918. Revolutionaries such as Lala Hardyal, Tarak Nath Das, and G.D. Kumar were either writing pamphlets or bringing out papers in India and abroad, which had finally led to the Ghadar Movement, which previously had been called The Hindi Association of the Pacific Coast, with Baba Sohan Singh Bhakna as president and Lala Hardyal as general secretary. The Association came into being in 1913, and its paper *Ghadar* began publishing that same year, on 1 November. The Association became popularly known as the Ghadar Party, and its foundation day came to be celebrated on 1 November. *Ghadar* was first published in Urdu, but later editions came out in Punjabi, Hindi, and Gujarati, with the paper's circulation climbing into the tens of thousands. The name Ghadar Party appropriated the legacy of the 1857 Ghadar movement, giving the word so long discredited by the British colonialists a new respectability. Its headquarters in San Francisco was named Yugantar Ashram, in honour of the Yugantar revolutionary movement of Bengal. The organization and movement had a large number of Punjabis, followed by Bengalis and a few members from Uttar Pradesh, the Central Province, and parts of southern India.

The Ghadar Party put out a call to liberate India through

armed struggle and even gave the date for its commencement, 21 February 1915, later changed to 19 February. While no armed struggle ensued on the appointed date, due to various factors, the movement revolutionized the tradition of radical nationalist movements in India, which for the first time, after 1857, became inclusive of people from all religious communities. It had a true all-India character and a modern secular perspective. Its martyrs came from all religions and parts of the country. This is why, after its attempt to overthrow the British colonial regime in 1915 was detected by the occupiers, the Party reorganised itself and took the shape of the first Communist groups in Punjab, those to which Bhagat Singh was directly related. In fact, Bhagat Singh's personal and political trajectory was shaped by the tradition of his uncle, Ajit Singh, and by the example of the Ghadar Party.

The Ghadar Movement began prior to the Bolshevik Revolution in Russia in 1917, but it was the first among the organizations worldwide that were deeply impressed by it. By 1922, Ghadarite revolutionaries had made their way to the newly-formed Soviet Union, seeking and receiving ideological training from the Communist University of the Toilers of the East, which was established in 1921. Rattan Singh and Santokh Singh, important Ghadarites, came to the Soviet Union in 1922. As we have seen, Santokh Singh later started the Punjabi journal *Kirti*, with which Bhagat Singh was deeply associated.

In this connection, Sreerajyam Sinha, in memoirs of her husband Bejoy Kumar Sinha, the close friend of and ideologically close to Bhagat Singh, mentioned that Shaukat Usmani, one of the founders of the Communist movement in India and frequent visitor to the Soviet Union, once contacted Bejoy on his return from Moscow to convey that Bhagat Singh and Bejoy should accompany him to Moscow. Bhagat Singh and Bejoy discussed the proposal and decided that the 'time was not opportune' for them to go, given that the revolutionary movement in India was at a crucial stage. However, they did wish that someone from the HSRA must visit. Later, Prithvi Singh Azad went as the HSRA representative.

Apart from the Ghadarites, there were many other Indian revolutionaries in the early years of the Soviet Union. Bhagat Singh was also in touch with the Kanpur group of Communists, including the writer Radha Mohan Gokulji, Satyabhakta (a co-founder of the Indian Communist Party in 1925), freedom fighter and noted poet Hasrat Mohani, and Shaukat Usmani (another co-founder of the Indian Communist Party). He also met Muzaffar Ahmad in Lahore earlier. Satyabhakta wrote a small book on Bhagat Singh in Hindi, *Krantiveer Bhagat Singh* (Brave Revolutionary Bhagat Singh), after Bhagat's martyrdom.

In his writing and through his close personal contact with him in prison, Shiv Verma discussed the growth of Bhagat Singh's thoughts about scientific socialism. In Bhagat Singh, he found the development of the idea of the need for a socialist revolution in India. This was an objective assessment, yet some later movements also need mention. The Chittagong revolt occurred in the early 1930s. It began with an assault on the armoury at Chittagong and was followed by a pitched battle with the British in which eight British soldiers and twelve revolutionaries were killed. Many more revolutionaries were killed later. Led by the legendary Master Surya Sen, inclusive of both Anushilan and Yugantar factions, the Chittagong revolt had issued the rallying cry, 'Do and Die,' years before Gandhi issued a similar call, but as 'Do or Die,' in 1942. Betrayed by an associate, Sen was captured in 1933 and brutally tortured before his hanging in 1934. Besides Sen, the Chittagong revolt led to the martyrdom of the young revolutionary woman, Preetilata Wadedar, who led a daring raid on the Pahartali European Club (which featured a sign that read, 'Dogs and Indians not allowed'). She was wounded in the attack and swallowed cyanide to avoid arrest. Many of the surviving Chittagong revolutionaries became committed Communists while in prison.

In March 1940, Udham Singh, inspired by Bhagat Singh, shot and killed Michael O' Dwyer, who was responsible for the

Jallianwala Bagh massacre and other oppressive actions in Punjab in 1919. For this, he was hanged in London four months later. The 'Quit India' movement of 1942, along with other radical actions of the 1940s, such as the 1946 Naval Uprising (which ultimately involved 20,000 sailors and numerous Indian police and civilians in opposition to the British), are part of the glorious legacy of India's revolutionary movements. But the distinctive feature of all revolutionary movements after Bhagat Singh and the HSRA is that they were secular, democratic, and broadly leftist in thought.

Returning to the life of Bhagat Singh, there were two things he sought to do while in prison:

1. Expose British colonialism through the courts by using them as platforms for the spread of their ideas.
2. Expose the brutalities of British colonialism while in prison by resorting to hunger strikes that would draw widespread public attention.

Bhagat Singh was successful in achieving both tasks. The British authorities were aware of his plans, but he was able to put the British rulers on trial through his self-sacrifice and that of his comrades.

Besides these undertakings, he also sought to deepen his own ideological development. It is amazing to see a man, about to go to the gallows, immersing himself deeply, under the most trying circumstances, in a serious study of world revolutionary history. He did not have the privilege of going every day to a library or a bookshop with a purse full of money to buy books and then visit a coffee house to discuss new ideas. He was preparing court statements (the preparation of which was aided by his serious study of Marxism), organising hunger strikes, and spending time with his comrades, while suffering brutal beatings in courts by the police and then nursing his wounds in jail. And with all of this, he managed to study and take notes from the books he was reading, and then write many perceptive essays and letters.

Bhagat Singh drafted four manuscripts in prison: 'The Ideal of Socialism,' 'Autobiography,' 'History of Revolutionary Movements in India,' and 'At the door of Death.' According to Shiv Verma, these manuscripts were smuggled out by the freedom fighter and teacher, Kumari Lajjawati of Jalandhar, who was active in the defence of Bhagat Singh. She handed these to Bejoy Kumar Sinha in 1938, after his release from the Circular Jail in the Andaman and Nicobar Islands. Sinha, in turn, transferred them to a friend for safekeeping, but this person destroyed the manuscripts in fear of a police raid. However, the manuscript of the *The Jail Notebook and Other Writings* was retrieved by a member of Bhagat Singh's family.

Kumari Lajjawati, secretary of the Bhagat Singh Defence Committee and a Congress activist, frequently visited the Lahore jail to discuss the legal aspects of the case. In an interview with the Nehru memorial museum and library's oral history cell, she said that she brought some papers given to her by Bhagat Singh, which she later showed to Feroze Chand, editor of *The People*, Lala Lajpat Rai's well-established paper in Lahore. Feroze Chand was given the freedom to select whatever he wanted for publication in *The People*. He did this and returned the rest to Lajjawati, who handed them over to Bejoy Kumar Sinha in 1938. From the papers he had, Feroze Chand published 'Why I am an Atheist' on 27 September 1931, Bhagat Singh's first birthday after his execution on 23 March of that same year. Prior to that, in its issue of 29 March, *The People* published extracts from the now famous 'Letter to Young Political Workers.' It appears that Chand selected some other papers, including Bhagat Singh's letter on his death sentence, given to his young revolutionary friend, Harikishan (himself executed in 1931 for attempting to assassinate the British governor of Punjab), which was also published in *The People*.

Bhagat Singh's father was keen to acquire or at least see those papers, but Lajjawati refused, obeying the instructions of Bhagat

Singh himself. The strange part of this saga of indifference to the documents, considered so valuable now, is that neither Kumari Lajjawati nor Feroze Chand, not even Bejoy Kumar Sinha, who was given the custodianship of those papers at the instructions of Bhagat Singh, took the trouble to look at them carefully and at least note down their contents. Fortunately, the essential aspects of Bhagat Singh's thought have since come to light, and the evaluation of it can be made on the basis of retrieved documents, which are quite substantial.

However, Bhagat Singh did plan to write a book on 'The Science of the State', for which he had taken detailed notes, which are included in his Jail Notebook. In this proposed book, he would attempt to trace the growth of the state from primitive communism to the modern socialist state. Had he been able to complete this project, it would very likely have been a significant contribution to the Marxist study of the state, as we can surmise from reading his notes.

The Jail Notebook manuscript was first published in 1994, edited and annotated by Bhupender Hooja. It is not like the prison notebooks of Gramsci, the philosophical notebooks of Lenin, or Che Guevara's diaries. Instead, Bhagat Singh's notebook is unique. It includes the notes of the books he read prior to his execution. Besides the significance of the books he chose to read, these notes objectively mirror the development of Bhagat Singh's worldview. They also reflect his aesthetic sensibilities, as many quotes are taken from the classics of world literature. These show that Bhagat Singh was a revolutionary with rare sensitivity. During his student days and after, his fondness for films was noticed by his close friends and comrades. He was a fan of Charlie Chaplin's movies, as well as films like *Uncle Tom's Cabin* and *The Three Musketeers*. He was a good singer and acted in college as part of the drama team, showing his involvement with literature and other art forms. That is why the older revolutionary, Ram Saran Das, asked for an introduction from Bhagat Singh to his poetry collection, *Dreamland*, which became one of the poets more important documents.

Interestingly, long before Bhagat Singh's jail notebooks of Bhagat Singh came to be read and studied in India, it was discussed in detail by the Soviet Indologist, L.V. Mitrokhin, in his 1981 book, *Lenin in India*, whose Hindi translation was published in 1990. An entire chapter is devoted to 'The last days of Bhagat Singh'. This book references even earlier documents, such as A.V. Raikov's 1971 article, 'Bhagat Singh and his ideological legacy', and Mitrokhin's own 'The books read by Bhagat Singh', included in the 1971 publication *India on Lenin*. In these Russian publications, an objective assessment of Bhagat Singh's ideological development was made, as well as his place in the tradition of Marxist thought. In his book *Lenin and Indian Freedom Fighters*, Mitrokhin wrote, 'Bhagat Singh had all the makings to become an important figure both nationally and internationally. His life was cut short at the point, when he became a Marxist.'

The jail notebooks of Bhagat Singh should be read in relation to his other significant works, such as 'Why I am an atheist', 'Court statements', 'Letter to young political workers', and the like, which by now have acquired the status of classic documents of revolutionary movements. In fact, in the notebooks, the quotes taken from books other than literary reference the significant books about the development of democratic political thought. These include books about ancient Greek thought and progress up to the latest Marxist classics of that time. The *Notebook* is also a mirror reflecting the ideological development of Bhagat Singh. It concludes with a partially read book, *Reminiscences of Lenin*, by Clara Zetkin, on 23 March 1931. The revolutionary Punjabi poet, Avtar Singh Sandhu, famously known as Pash, paid apt tribute to Bhagat Singh's last moments by saying that 'Indian youth need to read the next page of Lenin's book, folded by Bhagat Singh on the last day of his life.' And Mitrokhin, in *Lenin and Indian Freedom Fighters*, tells us something that is simply remarkable:

His University studies were taking place in a solitary death cell. Pran Nath Mehta, Bhagat Singh's lawyer, said, 'I went on 23rd March to give him a book on Lenin. No one was allowed to go. [But] I made an excuse of collecting his will as a lawyer[, which was] then allowed. Bhagat Singh asked whether I had the book? He said I will read it overnight (the formal execution date was 24th March morning). He could not know how he would finish. A Guard told relatives that Bhagat Singh was reading a book given by Pran Nath Mehta, when the door opened and he was told to be ready. Holding the book in his right hand, he did not even look up, raised his left hand and said, 'wait a minute, a revolutionary is meeting another revolutionary.' After reading a few more lines, he put the book down and said, 'let's go!'

Bhagat Singh's story continued in prison through indefinite hunger strikes, along with his comrades, in one of which their dear comrade Jatin Das gave his life on 13 September 1929, the sixty-third day of his fast unto death. His health was beyond redemption; forcible feeding of milk had burst his lungs, and despite appeals by his fellow prisoners to break the fast, Jatin Das refused to do so, with the clear understanding and declaration that he was consciously giving up his life for the nation. Bhagat Singh and Dutt continued their fast after Jatin Das's death, breaking it only in the first week of October, making it a record 111-day-long hunger strike. Bhagat Singh underwent another hunger strike against the tribunal hearing the Saunders murder case when they were brutally beaten upon the orders of presiding judge Coldstream. The Indian judge, Agha Haider, publicly disassociated himself from this egregious assault, for which he was removed from the tribunal. This second hunger strike by Bhagat Singh and his comrades was observed in February 1930, and it lasted sixteen days. Bhagat Singh undertook a third and final hunger strike from 28 July to 22 August 1930, which came to light only after his new letters were discovered in a Supreme Court exhibition of 'The Trial of Bhagat Singh.' These letters were first published by one of the editors of this book, Chaman Lal, on 15 August 2011, in *The Hindu*. Bhagat Singh and Dutt observed almost five months of hunger strike in less than two years of imprisonment, after which Bhagat Singh was executed.

Bhagat Singh and his comrades employed the political weapon of hunger striking most effectively. Historically, hunger strikes have a universal power to move people. This is because they compellingly demonstrate the moral strength of those who refuse to eat to achieve a just political end. The difference between a suicide bomber and a hunger striker is that the suicide bomber, while giving his life for a cause, takes away the lives of others as well, thereby losing public sympathy. Whereas hunger strikers, harming only their own health or even sacrificing their lives, pricks at the conscience of a nation. Bhagat Singh and his comrades were aware of this fact and used it dramatically, erasing the impression that they were killers or terrorists. This also shows the political maturity of Bhagat Singh.

Bhagat Singh and his comrades boycotted the Saunders murder trial, and with good reason. The way in which the tribunal declared the death sentence for Bhagat Singh, Rajguru, and Sukhdev was thoroughly exposed in lawyer A.G. Noorani's book, *The Trial of Bhagat Singh*. It was nothing but the murder of Indian revolutionaries committed by the British colonialists through judicial spectacle. Bhagat Singh had befittingly written to the Governor of Punjab on 20 March, three days prior to their execution, demanding that they be treated as prisoners of war, since they were waging war against British imperialism, and, as such, 'they should be shot dead' rather than hanged. But the British imperial power proved so cowardly that they did not even maintain their own protocol of capital punishment between 6 and 7 am. Against all international norms, they executed the three men at 7 pm on 23 March, the day a massive rally was held at Lahore, organised by the NBS, which had understood that the execution would take place on the morning of 24 March. Afraid of a huge gathering at the Lahore central jail, the British colonial officials executed them on the evening of 23 March instead.

However, the people of Lahore soon uncovered the truth. The rally was about to end when the news of the executions came. People rushed to the gates of the jail. Frightened British officials cut the still-warm bodies of the martyrs in pieces and, after filling these in sacks, took them away from the back gates of the jail to the banks of the Sutlej River at Ferozepur. It was an exercise that took the entire night. The British officials got some Granthi and Pandit (Sikh and Hindu religious officials) from Ferozepur to perform so-called religious rituals. They were not even shown the bodies, which were burnt in kerosene in an alarming hurry in the jungle near Ganda Singhwalla village. People from Ferozepur and Lahore followed in the night, searching for the place, and before the dawn of 24 March, they were able to locate the soft place at which unburnt and half-burnt bones, the smell of kerosene, and stains of blood were noticed. In anguish and anger, people collected these items and reached Lahore. The proper cremation of the three martyrs was done on the banks of the Ravi River, where earlier Lala Lajpat Rai had been cremated. Thousands of people joined the funeral procession, and a memorial meeting was held in Minto Park near the riverbank.

The Congress in Punjab formed a fact-finding committee to investigate the mistreatment of the dead bodies of the martyrs. Newspapers, particularly *Bhavishya* in Allahabad, highlighted the committee's hearing, but the report was either not released or remained filed away in Congress papers. Given that the Kanpur riots report of Congress after the execution of the martyrs, had drawn national attention and the National Book Trust has published its reprint, it is strange that no one refers to the Congress Party's fact-finding report about the disgraceful disposal of these great martyrs' bodies by the British colonial authorities. The Kanpur riots, which started after the execution of Bhagat Singh and his comrades, unfortunately, took on a communal (right-wing religious) colour and tragically took the life of Congress leader, nationalist journalist, and admirer of Bhagat Singh, Ganesh Shankar Vidyarthi.

The same disregard was shown for the condition of the martyrs' memorial. The NBS formed a committee to build a suitable memorial for the martyrs, which was sabotaged by Congress through the actions of Bhagat Singh's father, S. Kishan Singh, with the promise that Congress would build a national memorial. Later, in 1965, a memorial called Hussainiwala was built near Ferozepur, but it had no relevance at that time for the national revolutionary movement.

Lahore was the hub of the national movement. It was the place where Bhagat Singh and his comrades had spent their lives in political action. It was there that they were executed, and it was there where they were properly cremated and where earlier Lala Lajpat Rai had also been cremated. The most logical and appropriate thing would have been to build a memorial in memory of Lala Lajpat Rai, Bhagat Singh, Sukhdev, and Rajguru on the banks of the Ravi River. There it would have been a source of inspiration for Punjabi youth, and it might even have proved to be a deterrent to the eventual division of Punjab.

Looking back, nine decades later, one can only wonder why no memorial was built for these martyrs in Lahore or the birthplaces of Bhagat Singh and Sukhdev in Lyallpur, now called Faisalabad in Pakistan. Even today, it would be most desirable for the democratic peoples of Pakistan and India to erect a suitable memorial at Lahore, as well as at Faisalabad, in memory of Bhagat Singh. He is the one, and perhaps only, symbol who evokes respect among the Pakistani people as well. Bhagat Singh is the common thread between now divided Punjabis, a powerful symbol of resistance against colonialism and imperialism. Moreover, he could now become a common symbol of resistance against US imperialism.

There are other interesting aspects of Bhagat Singh's life and its place in Indian history. Bhagat Singh had an excellent rapport with national leaders, including Subhas Chandra Bose, Motilal Nehru, Jawaharlal Nehru, Lala Lajpat Rai, and Madan Mohan Malviya. Despite differences in approach, they remained in contact, while Chandra Shekhar Azad's meeting with Nehru at Allahabad, as described by Nehru himself, was not that pleasant. Nehru did not seem much impressed by Azad, who had helped reorganise the HRA. However, Nehru did pay one thousand rupees to help revolutionaries go to Russia, but such a trip never materialized due to Azad's death. Subhas Chandra Bose and Nehru were both much appreciative of Bhagat Singh's personality.

Congress leaders and revolutionary youth often worked at cross purposes due to their different political perceptions, but they frequently interacted with and supported one another. Seeing Lala Lajpat Rai moving waywardly toward the communal forces, Bhagat Singh and his comrades attacked him openly. Yet, they did not break with him. And Lala Lajpat Rai's grandson was the secretary of the Bal Students Union inspired by Bhagat Singh. Motilal Nehru, Madan Mohan Malviya, and Dewan Chaman Lal all condemned, in strong words, the bomb-throwing by Bhagat Singh in the Central Assembly. Gandhi declared it 'a mad act of two young men.' Bhagat Singh described trade union leader and politician Diwan Chaman Lal as a 'pseudo socialist' in his famous Sessions Court statement and politician and lawyer Tej Bahadur Sapru as no different from a British Viceroy. Yet, the same Pandit Motilal Nehru, Diwan Chaman Lal, Madan Mohan Malviya, and even Tej Bahadur Sapru, apart from Jawaharlal Nehru, Subhas Bose, and Jinnah, who stood for these revolutionary youth in courts, or when they were observing hunger strikes, still went to great lengths to save their lives. Advocates like Asaf Ali, Kailash Nath Katju, Chander Bhan Gupta, and Mohan Lal Saxena all stood by the youth. It was a spirit of nationalism that bound together these national leaders and revolutionary youth. They criticized each other bitterly yet joined together at the time of crisis, particularly against British oppression of the Indian people. This is something that must be learned by the present-day national leaders and youth of India.

An essential element in the ideology of Bhagat Singh and the revolutionary movement was total opposition to the caste system and communalism. Besides their champion, Dr B. R. Ambedkar (himself a Dalit), in the Dalit movements of today, one of the only national heroes accepted by the Dalit movements of today as their genuine supporter is Bhagat Singh. His writings and conduct earned him the love and support of the Dalit masses. In jail, before going to the gallows, Bhagat Singh was not only reading Lenin, he asked for food from *Bebe* (mother), the name given in affection by Bhagat Singh to the Dalit jail employee, Bogha. Just as a mother cleanses the defecation of her children, so too does the untouchable clean up the waste of grown-up people. So, Bhagat Singh treated the scavenger, the street sweeper, Bogha, like his mother. When Bhagat Singh, Sukhdev, and Rajguru were going to their deaths, laughing and singing, it was Charat Singh and other prisoners who were crying and also shouting *Inquilab Zindabad*, after Bhagat Singh.

And let this be underlined: none of the communal organizations of Hindus, Muslims, or Sikhs spoke a word in favour or defence of these revolutionaries. It is only the left movement in the country that has truly tried to uphold and imbibe the spirit of revolution in India. In contrast, the right-wing forces inside and outside Parliament have always only made idle noises about appropriating the legacy of this movement, whether on the issue of NCERT (National Council of Educational Research and Training) textbooks or the *Bande Mataram* controversy. In fact, rightist forces, during and after the freedom struggle, have always tried to divide the Indian people on narrow communal lines and have always played the role of agents of the imperialist powers, whether old or new. So, the left-wing forces of the country are the inheritors of the legacy of the revolutionary freedom struggles.

Though, ironically, they were dubbed as traitors by the agents of imperialism for not supporting the 1942 Quit India movement.

In this saga, two persons and an institution knew the exact ending of the whole scenario – Gandhi and Bhagat Singh. Because of their convictions and grasp of the political reality, both knew that nothing could stop the execution of revolutionaries. The institution of British colonialism, as embodied in those who constructed it and did what it demanded, also knew its finale, as it was bent upon finishing these young men, particularly Bhagat Singh, in whose personality it was observing the traits of a maturing Indian Lenin. The British could afford to deal with the Gandhian Congress. With it, at worst, the imperialists would have to shed their political power, but they would retain their economic interests. They could not afford to have Bhagat Singh, who, if he remained alive, would have struggled, with a good chance of success, for the complete overthrow of the system of imperialist and capitalist exploitation.

In the Introduction to his book, *They Lived Dangerously*, Manmath Nath Gupta makes evident how vital was the revolutionary and non-communal nationalism of Bhagat Singh: 'The greatest thing about these revolutionaries is that their movement . . . . [was] the first to adopt a socialistic philosophy under the leadership of Bhagat Singh and his valiant band of youths in 1927. Had Gandhi and Jinnah, Nehru and others followed the footsteps of Bhagat Singh, it is doubtless that the history of the subcontinent would have been different.'

Ironically, Bhagat Singh had his way vis-a-vis British colonial power. With a group of fewer than one hundred persons, he and his comrades unnerved and rattled the most powerful empire on earth. Through the HSRA, they struck their own path to martyrdom, inspiring and stirring millions of people. The success of this strategy was admitted by none other than Pattabhi Sitaramaya, the Congress historian and Gandhi's candidate against Subhas Chandra Bose in the 1939 Tripuri Congress. Not long after Bhagat Singh's hanging, Sitaramaya said, 'It is no exaggeration to say that at the moment Bhagat Singh's name was as widely known all over India and was as popular as Gandhi's.' This was no small achievement for a young man of twenty-three, with an active political career of just six or seven years.

After the pronouncement of his death sentence, Jaidev Kapoor asked Bhagat Singh, 'If he regretted dying so young'? Bhagat Singh first laughed at the question, then replied seriously,

> Stepping up on the path of revolution, I had thought that if I could spread the slogan of *Inquilab Zindabad* throughout the country, by giving away my life, I would feel that I have received the full value of my life. Today sitting behind the bars of the execution barracks, I hear the sound of the slogan from crores of people. I believe that this slogan of mine would attack imperialism as the driving force of the freedom struggle till the end. What more value can be of such a small life?

In his book, Shiv Verma mentioned an incident in July 1930, when Bhagat Singh had come to Lahore Burail prison from the Central jail to meet his comrades, with the excuse of discussing their court case. Jokingly, they pronounced judgments on one another, excepting Rajguru and Bhagat Singh, knowing they were the ones who would be hanged. And then Bhagat Singh said that we were afraid to face reality, as the sentence would be 'To be hanged by the neck till we are dead.' 'He was in form that day; he was speaking in a low pitch that was his style. Showing was not his habit, that was perhaps his strength also.' Then he quotes Bhagat Singh's words: 'This is the highest award for patriots and I am proud that I am going to get it. They may kill me, but they cannot kill my ideas. They may crush my body, but they will not be able to crush my spirits. My ideas will haunt the British like a curse till they are forced to run away from here.' Speaking with full passion, he continued,

Bhagat Singh dead will be more dangerous to the British enslavers than Bhagat Singh alive. After I am hanged, the fragrance of my revolutionary ideas will permeate the atmosphere of this beautiful land of ours. It will intoxicate the youth and make him mad for freedom and revolution, and that would bring the doom of the British imperialists nearer. This is my firm conviction. I am anxiously waiting for the day when I will receive the highest award for my services to the country, my love for my people.

Bhagat Singh's publications and actions during the last two-plus years of his life caused his popularity among the Indian people to skyrocket. He not only became popular, but he also achieved the status of a thinking revolutionary because of his letters, statements, and essays. An intellectual such as Jawaharlal Nehru would not have admired Bhagat Singh if he had not seen the spark of his intellectual quest for socialist ideas.

However, a few years after his martyrdom, social forces in Indian society conspired to limit him to a 'brave hero and martyr', while knowingly or unwittingly suppressing his ideas. He was painted with twitched moustaches, gun-toting with a yellow turban, making him look like a fearful person, frightening his colonial enemies. His ideas on socialism, ending exploitation, and social revolution were ignored, distorted, or suppressed. This continued for a long period, despite his comrades like Ajoy Ghosh, Sohan Singh Josh, Shiv Verma, and others writing about his ideas. However, their works were ignored, with the excuse that these were 'Communist writing'. All manner of trashy biographies were created, making him look like either a narrow and sectarian nationalist, as someone who fits into or was even supportive of the reactionary Hindutva (Hindu nationalist) agenda or as a gun-wielding Khalistani (a sometimes-violent Sikh separatist movement) warrior.

Credit goes to historian and professor Bipan Chandra for

resurrecting Bhagat Singh as a socialist intellectual through his publication, in 1970, of Singh's 'Why I am an Atheist.' His erudite introduction brought Bhagat Singh's ideas into focus again. Later, many of Bhagat Singh's writings came out in multiple publications in Hindi and other Indian languages, and some were brought out by one of this book's editors, Professor Chaman Lal.

Further understanding of Bhagat Singh's political depth began in his centenary year, 2007, when seminars, conferences, and public meetings were held throughout the country that focused on his ideas. After these, his publications became readily available in almost all Indian languages, and distorting his image became much more difficult. As a result, students, youth, and other left-oriented organizations appropriated the legacy of Bhagat Singh's ideas in earnestness. Now, many eminent historians, political scientists, and other scholars apart from Bipan Chandra, like professors Irfan Habib, J. S. Grewal, K M Panikkar, S. Irfan Habib, Sabyasachi Bhattacharya, and Mubarak Ali (from Pakistan) have begun to write about his role in the freedom struggle.

Finally, a more objective understanding of Bhagat Singh has come through studying his ideas through his writings. While almost all his writings have been available in many languages, only some were available in English. For the first time, all his documents/writings were made accessible in English through the yeoman work of Chaman Lal, who put together the monumental *The Bhagat Singh Reader*, published by HarperCollins India.

With this volume, *The Political Writings of Bhagat Singh*, we have concentrated on the major political works of a remarkable man, sophisticated and prescient in his thought. Had he lived longer, he indeed would have made even more outstanding contributions to the literature of politics and revolution.

The following sources are in English. It is not an exhaustive list, but the books noted will give readers an understanding of Bhagat Singh and Indian political history. Of course, there are a great number of books and essays about Bhagat Singh and Indian political history in the many languages of India. But given that one of the aims of this book is to introduce Bhagat Singh to those whose native language is English and who may know little about him, we thought it best to limit this note to works in English.

Chatterjee, Jogesh, *In Search of Freedom*. Calcutta: Firma KL 1967. Jogesh Chatterjee was one of the founders of the HRA. Bhagat Singh and his comrades had planned to rescue him from jail/ police custody, where he was serving life imprisonment in the Kakori case. Later, after his release, he wrote these memoirs of the revolutionary movement. He served as a member of the Indian Parliament as well.

Ghosh, Ajoy. *Bhagat Singh and His Comrades*. Bombay: People's Publishing House. 1945. Ajoy Ghosh was among the HSRA activists, but he was acquitted in the Lahore conspiracy case. He later served as General Secretary of the undivided Communist Party of India from 1951 until his death in 1962.

Gupta, Manmath Nath. *They Lived Dangerously*, Delhi: People's Publishing House. 1968. Manmath Nath Gupta was arrested for participating in the Kakori train robbery, which took place near Lucknow, in which one passenger was accidentally killed. The robbery was planned and executed by the HRA. Gupta was saved from the gallows only because he was not an adult when he was convicted. He was given life imprisonment, and after release, he became one of the best chroniclers of revolutionary movements in India. He wrote in Hindi, Bengali, and English and was a fiction writer too. He died at 93 years of age.

Habib, S. Irfan. *To Make the Deaf Hear*. Delhi: Three Essays

Collective. 2007. S. Irfan Habib is among the serious historians who have placed Bhagat Singh in his proper perspective.

Johar, K.L. Editor. *Martyr Bhagat Singh: An Intimate View*. Yamuna Nagar: Sneh Prakashan. 2008. K. L. Johar has collected a large number of memoirs and analytical writings on Bhagat Singh in this single volume.

Lal, Chaman. *Understanding Bhagat Singh*. Delhi, Aakar Books. 2013. This is a collection of analytical articles on Bhagat Singh and some original letters and documents of Bhagat Singh himself.

Lal, Chaman. Editor. *The Bhagat Singh Reader*. Delhi: HarperCollins India. 2019. An exhaustive collection of the complete 130 writings and the Jail Notebook, with many related materials. The bibliography contains entries in seventeen languages.

Maclean, Kama. *A Revolutionary History of Interwar India: Violence, Voice and Text*. London, Hurst and Company. 2015. Kama Maclean is a Professor of History at a prestigious University in Germany. She is an Australian scholar who has done well-documented research on India's revolutionary movements. In this book, she also examines the role of women in India's revolutionary struggles.

Mitrokhin, L.V. *Lenin in India*. Mumbai: Allied. 1981; *Lenin and Indian Freedom Fighters*. Delhi: Panchsheel Publishers. 1988. Bhagat Singh figures prominently in these books, which show the many connections between Soviet and Indian revolutionary movements.

Moffat, Chris. *India's Revolutionary Inheritance: Politics and Praise of Bhagat Singh*. London: Cambridge University Press. 1996. Chris Moffat is a UK scholar of Irish background who has done research with empathy for the Bhagat Singh phenomenon.

Nayar, Kuldip. *Without Fear*. 2007, Delhi: HarperCollins. 2007. This book was earlier published, in 2000, under a different title: *The Martyr Bhagat Singh: Experiments in Revolution*.

Noorani, A. G. *The Trial of Bhagat Singh*. 1st Edition. Delhi:

Kanishka. 1996. (2nd ed. Oxford: Oxford University Press. 2005). A.G. Noorani, a senior advocate and writer, has appeared as an attorney before the Supreme Court of India. In this pathbreaking book, he has exposed British colonial jurisprudence. A comment on the book says it all: 'With a lawyer's insight, Noorani unveils the facts of the case, arguing that Singh and comrades were the victims of a travesty of justice that amounted to judicial murder.'

Patnaik, Utsa and Prabhat Patnaik. *Capital and Imperialism: Theory, History, and the Present.* New York: Monthly Review Press. 2021. Political economists Utsa and Prabhat Patnaik show with great empirical detail how Great Britain drained India of its wealth during the period of Indian colonization. The flow of money and goods to England allowed Britain to become the world's leading capitalist power. This also ensured the incredible poverty and misery, with millions of premature deaths, of the Indian people.

Ram Chandra, Comrade. *Naujawan Bharat Sabha (NBS) and the Hindustan Socialist Republican Association/Army (HSRA).* Delhi. Self-published. 1986. Comrade Ram Chandra was one of the founders of Naujawan Bharat Sabha along with Bhagat Singh and remained a legislator in pre- and post-partition Punjab. On his own, he published three books on the revolutionary movement. This title is the most authentic history of the NBA and the HSRA.

Sanyal, Jitendra Nath. *Sardar Bhagat Singh.* Allahabad. Self-published. 1931. This book was initially self-published in the same year as Bhagat Singh's execution. It is the first good biography, and it was immediately banned by the British authorities. Sanyal, a comrade of Bhagat Singh, was acquitted in the main Lahore conspiracy case, but he was convicted to two years imprisonment for writing this biography. It could be reprinted only in 1946.

Singh, Ajit. *Buried Alive: Autobiography, Speeches and Writings of an Indian Revolutionary,* edited by Pardaman Singh and J.S. Dhanki. Delhi: Gitanjali Publishing House. 1984. Ajit Singh was the uncle of Bhagat Singh. He led the 1907 farmers' movement in Punjab and remained exiled in many countries for thirty-eight years, mainly in South America. He returned to India only in March 1947 and died in the early morning of 15 August 1947, the day of Indian independence.

Sinha, Srirajyam. *A Revolutionary's Quest for Sacrifice.* Bombay: Bhartiyta Vidya Bhavan. 1993. Bejoy Kumar Sinha was ideologically close to Bhagat Singh, and Singh left his jail papers to be handed over to Sinha, who was in the Cellular Jail at the time of Bhagat Singh's execution. He always wanted to write a biography of Bhagat Singh, but he could not. After Sinha's death, his wife, Srirajyam, wrote this biography of her husband based on his notes. However, it focuses on Bhagat Singh because Sinha's notes were mostly on him.

Verma, Shiv. Editor. *Selected Writings of Shaheed Bhagat Singh.* Delhi: National Book Centre.1986. The first collection of Bhagat Singh's writings in English. There are twenty-eight selections, along with a superb and enlightening Introduction. Verma was a close comrade of Bhagat Singh.

Waraich, M.J.S., G.S. Siddhu, et al. *The Hanging of Bhagat Singh.* Volumes I to V. Chandigarh: Unistar Books. 2007. In these edited volumes, parts of the proceedings of the two trials of Bhagat Singh and others have been assembled.

Lastly, let us note that oral history transcripts of many revolutionary comrades, classmates, and friends of Bhagat Singh can be found in the oral history cell of the Nehru Memorial Museum and Library in New Delhi. Of special interest are those of Jaidev Gupta, Kumari Lajjawati, Durga Bhabhi, Shiv Verma, Durga Das Khanna, Jaidev Kapoor, Pran Nath Mehta, and Principal Chhabil Das.

Chaman Lal and Michael D. Yates

Bhagat Singh's Political Writings

Bhagat Singh lived but twenty-three years, yet he is a legendary figure in India to this day. Much of his early fame was due to his brave political actions, his defiant stay in prison, his hunger strikes, and his death at the hands of a brutal British occupier. The way in which he consciously publicized his circumstances and that of the HSRA shows him to be a genius of effective revolutionary propaganda. He understood the power of images in moving a largely non-literate population. The famous photo of him – hair cut short, shaven face, and western-style clothing, with his trademark felt hat – was distributed across the length and breadth of India. It is probably difficult now to imagine how powerfully this image resonated with the Indian masses. In fact, his image in the 1930s was as prominent and well-known as that of Gandhi himself.

That would be remarkable enough if this were all we could say about him. But like another famous person, one with his own iconic photo, Che Guevara, there is much more to Bhagat Singh than his physical persona and flair for dramatic, self-sacrificing actions. Guevara was instrumental in the Cuban Revolution, second only to Fidel Castro among those who fought in the Sierra Maestra. But he was also an outstanding intellectual, writing, among many other essays and letters, the insightful 'Man and Socialism in Cuba'. As was Bhagat Singh, who wrote many sharp political analyses, a sample of which comprises the remainder of this book.

While Bhagat Singh's writing style is simple and direct, it does not lack depth or political sophistication. However, it is aimed at the masses of Indian workers and peasants and those radicals who champion their cause. It reminds the reader of the work of Mao Zedong. Mao's Liberation Army was comprised mainly of peasants and workers. The Army did much more than fight. It also produced food and educated its largely non-literate troops. Mao's writing might be best seen as directed towards newly literate people who have begun to grasp the larger social and economic circumstances in which their poverty and oppression have been lived. So too, Bhagat Singh's essays and articles, to some degree, must indeed have helped the workers and peasants of India grasp the causes of their conditions.

It is hard to overstate the importance of this kind of writing. It is a rare commodity, often enough disdained by the high-brow academic precisely because of its style. However, if those radicals who are educated, who have a great knowledge of a particular subject, cannot make what they know intelligible to those who must, by definition, be the agents of revolutionary change, then of what use is their knowledge?

These writings of Bhagat Singh continue to hold great relevance to the burning questions faced by the political revolts and struggles of today. These writings greatly helps find answers that would help us create a world of substantive democracy and equality.

WHAT IS THE ROLE OF YOUTH IN REVOLUTIONARY MOVEMENTS?

In the Indian anti-colonial efforts, youth played a critically substantial role. For someone like Bhagat Singh, who was well-educated and curious, it came naturally for him to sacrifice his life for his country's freedom and the emancipation of the oppressed. Today though, capital has gained enormous hegemony over every aspect of life, including education. For most young people, education is an exercise in the inculcation of ideas and values supporting the endless accumulation of capital. Even the labour unions, essential working-class organizations, seldom educate their members. This means educating the young must be a top priority of all organizations aiming to overthrow the existing order.

In the United States, the Democratic Socialists of America (DSA) has multiplied, with most of its new members being young people disgusted with the status quo of the US society. Yet, the DSA has a limited view of what socialism is, with the majority looking up to Scandinavian countries as role models. When youth learn that Sweden is the best we can do, with no grasp of the fact that the wealth inequality there is as great as it is in the US, capitalism will continue to rule.

One hopeful sign is the preponderance of young persons in the movements for a sustainable environment. Led by teenagers like Greta Thunberg, these efforts are increasingly directed toward *system change*, meaning that the capitalist system is the root cause of the theft and degradation of land, water, and air, each of which gives us life.

CAN NATIONALISM PLAY A PROGRESSIVE ROLE IN RADICAL MOVEMENTS?

Bhagat Singh and many other Indian revolutionaries were what Vijay Prashad terms 'international nationalists'. This means that while they wanted to free India from Great Britain's exploitive and murderous rule, they also wanted an India that was socialist. They understood that if independence meant that Indian oppressors replaced the British colonial power, Indians could not be truly free. This, indeed, is as true now as it was then. India's independence did not end the rule of capital, which today is buttressed by a Hindu nationalism that amounts to modern-day fascism.

Can this ever be avoided? The example of Cuba suggests that it can. However, for this to be true generally, any movement that uses national independence as a rallying cry – Palestine is a good example – must be motivated by a radical, socialist ideal if the retrograde power lurking underneath every nationalist movement is to be avoided.

SHOULD VIOLENCE BE A PART OF
ANY REVOLUTIONARY MOVEMENT?

Gandhi is the global icon of non-violence. Yet, as noted in the introduction, the more radical organizations, such as the HSRA, were not uniformly condemned by the Congress, which Gandhi headed.

One of the co-editors of this book, Michael D. Yates, once worked for the president of the United Farm Workers labour union in California, César Chávez. Chávez was a disciple of Gandhi and a sworn advocate of nonviolent protest. He famously undertook hunger strikes and long marches (sometimes bearing a cross like Jesus), was arrested in many peaceful protests, and always publicly opposed violence, even as the union faced violent enemies in the growers and the police. But again, the union was not always opposed to the use of violence, sometimes with the approval of Chávez himself. Refrigerated train cars carrying produce were sometimes shot at by union personnel. In the most notorious example, Chávez condoned the use of violence against undocumented immigrants along the US-Mexican border because they were taking union jobs in the fields.

In this regard, it is essential to ask a fundamental question: Has socialism ever been brought into being without violence? The answer is a resounding: No. Chile provides the best example of this. The coalition political party, *La Unidad Popular*, succeeded in getting its candidate, the socialist physician Salvador Allende, elected president of Chile in 1970. The Party's slogan was '*socialismo por medios pacíficos*' (socialism through peaceful means). Radical social and economic policies, widespread among the Chilean masses, were quickly enacted: nationalization of banks, the breakup of large rural estates owned by wealthy landowners and often kept idle, the expropriation of the foreign-owned copper mines, higher social welfare spending, and so on. However, unlike in Cuba, the Allende government did not control the military, which in collaboration with the United States, began to plan a military coup almost immediately. The Chilean people voted for increased support for *La Unidad Popular* in midterm elections, but this meant nothing to Chilean and foreign capital nor to the US government. The result is well-known. A violent coup occurred in 1973. Allende died during it, the fascist General Augusto Pinochet seized power, and a bloodbath of monstrous proportions ensued.

Wherever capitalism has been overthrown, violent revolution has been the means. In Russia, China, Vietnam, and Cuba, a revolutionary army supported by peasants and workers, took power and expropriated capitalist property and forced the capitalists to either leave the country or agree to submit to revolutionary authority. Capitalism is a system based on systematic violence and is unlikely to go away without some opposing violence.

We note that Bhagat Singh and his comrades often had close contact with Congress, and those influential within Congress were often ambivalent about violence. They sometimes supported the revolutionaries and refused to condemn them outright when they committed violent acts. The rigid separation between proponents of nonviolence and those who engaged in radical aggression that has been the standard wisdom of many historians does not hold up to close scrutiny.

IS ANARCHISM A VIABLE RADICAL POLITICAL PERSPECTIVE?

Humans have always resisted state authority. As philosopher István Mészáros has made clear, states from their beginning about 6,000 years ago have been deeply enmeshed in class rule. The primary purpose of all states is to maintain class power, whether it be that of enslavers, feudal lords, capitalists, or socialist bureaucrats. It has been common for people to try to evade state power by remaining outside its confines. However, this has become nearly impossible in the modern world, as global capitalism has infiltrated every aspect of our lives. Anarchists are opposed to all states, which means that they can be vital allies in revolutionary movements. As Marx put it, in a fully communist society, the state must have 'withered away'. That is, it will become unnecessary in terms of human flourishing as we organize ourselves in such a way that we democratically control life circumstances in the interest of everyone. However, there must, by definition, be a transition period in which a mass political movement seizes the state and begins to dismantle it. Here, the anarchists will have to decide whether to actively participate in forming entities that democratically begin to organize production and distribution from the ground up, building collective power from below. The communes formed in Venezuela, with the strong support of then-President Hugo Chávez, provide an excellent model for how this might be achieved.

WHAT GIVES COMMUNAL (RELIGIOUS) ALLEGIANCE ITS POWER?

In India, antagonisms among religious groups have a long history, as Bhagat Singh's essays make clear. The same is true in many other parts of the world. Communalism can never be a revolutionary force. In the United States, for example, evangelical Christians, who number in the millions, became diehard supporters of the neofascist regime of Donald Trump, supporting every reactionary policy Trump engineered. Profoundly patriarchal and racist, they are prime movers in dismantling what little democracy there is in the country. The same can be said, and probably worse, of the government of India, where Narendra Modi has actively fomented hatred and attacks by Hindus against Muslims. Extreme antisemitism was fundamental to the Nazi ideology of Adolph Hitler. Ironically, Jewish nationalism is used to justify the repression, theft of land, and murder of Palestinians in Israeli-occupied territories. The state of Israel was founded on the myths that the land was given to Jews by God and that it was 'a land without people for a people without land'. The second myth belied that there were more than one million non-Jews in Palestine in 1948, the year of the infamous *al Naqba* (Catastrophe), in which hundreds of thousands of Palestinian Arabs fled or were forced from their homes by Zionists.

It is clear that any revolutionary movement must be firmly opposed to communalism and do all it can to counter it and build a movement inclusive of all faiths. And what has been said about religion also applies to everything that divides the wage-earning and peasant classes, whether it be gender, race, ethnicity, sexual preference, or caste.

WHAT ACCOUNTS FOR THE STRENGTH OF ANTI-COMMUNISM?

The one matter that capital can never countenance is an attack upon private property and the 'freedom' to exploit the majority that allows a tiny minority of humans to accumulate riches. Thus, the British attacked those fighting for Indian independence as Bolsheviks. No matter how mild the opposition to capital is, it will always be condemned as socialist or communist. Endless propaganda from the media, schools, religious leaders, and even labour unions as well as social democratic politicians, about the evils of communism has usually succeeded in muting the voices of radical change.

Instead of pushing toward an end to exploitation by expropriating what should rightfully be everyone's property, liberal and social democratic movements invariably move to the right. They offer conspicuously unsubtle criticisms of countries with socialist revolutions as if this will mollify their enemies. It never does. Of course, we should examine with a careful eye all that exists, as Marx tells us.

But we should then make our rallying cry the building of a society with full democracy and substantive equality in all spheres of life. We should do this unabashedly and with complete confidence in the capacity of wage workers and peasants to comprehend and support our program. As Bhagat Singh put it, 'The real revolutionary armies are in the villages and in factories, the peasantry and the labourers'.

WHAT MIGHT THE IMPACT OF ANTI-COLONIAL AND ANTI-IMPERIAL MOVEMENTS BE ON ENVIRONMENTAL CATASTROPHES NOW UPON US?

Both colonialism and imperialism (colonialism-like oppression without physical colonies) always involve land theft. With the latter, there is a class of native oppressors who also steal land. The expropriated earth is used for mining, logging, and industrial agriculture, all of which wreak havoc on the environment. In addition, both forms of exploitation of the Global South by the countries of the Global North invariably mean an expansion of military operations, which are extraordinarily harmful to land, air, and water. Moreover, when peasant property is taken, we lose the knowledge that the proprietors have gained through centuries of careful husbandry. Peasants are the original agro-ecologists, the opposites of agri-businesses like Monsanto. Across the globe today, we see peasants, along with indigenous peoples, in revolt against the desecration and destruction of the habitats that gave them, and the world, life.

The following references will give readers some sources to deepen their understanding of the political writings of Bhagat Singh.

D'Mello, Bernard. *India after Naxalbari: Unfinished History.* New York: Monthly Review Press. 2018. This is a comprehensive study of the peasant movement inspired by Maoism.

Foster, John Bellamy, Hannah Holleman and Brett Clark, 'Imperialism in the Anthropocene', *Monthly Review.* Volume 61. Number 3 (July 2019). This article connects the dots between imperialism and environmental destruction.

Freire, Paulo. *Pedagogy of the Oppressed: 50th Anniversary Edition.* 4th Edition. New York: Bloomsbury Academic. 2018. The classic work on how best to educate those who have suffered colonial and imperial exploitation.

Ginger, Ann Fagan and David Christiano. *The Cold War Against Labor: An Anthology in Two Volumes.* Berkeley, CA. Meiklejohn Civil Liberties Institute. 1987. This collection vividly illustrates the power of anticommunism in combating labour unions in the United States.

Giroux, Henry. *America's Education Deficit and the War on Youth.* New York: Monthly Review Press. 2013. Giroux, a disciple of Pablo Freire, examines the failures of education systems and the need for a radical, critical pedagogy.

Krausz, Tamás. *Reconstructing Lenin: An Intellectual Biography.* New York: Monthly Review Press. 2015. This excellent biography of Lenin has a good discussion of the national question.

Lebowitz, Michael A. 'Proposing a Path to Socialism: Two Papers for Hugo Chávez.' *Monthly Review.* Volume 66. Number 10 (March 2014). This succinct description of a plausible path to socialism, with a corresponding withering away of the state.

Linebaugh, Peter. *Stop Thief!: The Commons, Enclosures, and Resistance*. Oakland, CA: PM Press. 2014. Essays on the need for 'the commons' and how peasants have resisted their destruction.

Mészáros, István. Edited and introduced by John Bellamy Foster, *Beyond Leviathan: Critique of the State* (New York: Monthly Review Press, 2022). The late Marxist philosopher writes here about the need to abolish the state as a prerequisite for the advent of communism. Hugo Chavez called him – 'the pathfinder of socialism'.

Nanda, Meera. *The God Market: How Globalization is Making India More Hindu*. New York: Monthly Review Press. 2011. Nanda examines the intertwining of Hindu nationalism and neoliberalism.

Prashad, Vijay. *The Darker Nations: A People's History of the Third World*. New York: The New Press. 2008. This book is a classic study of attempts by the nations of the Global South to liberate themselves from the clutches of imperial power. It is in this book that Prashad writes of the 'international nationalists'.

Scott. James C. *Against the Grain: A Deep History of the Earliest States*. New Haven, CT: Yale University Press. 2017. A scholarly anarchist take on state formation. Scott shows how people have always tried to evade state control of their lives.

Wald, Karen. *Children of Che: Childcare and education in Cuba*. Palo Alto, CA. 1978. An early book on Cuba's revolutionary system of educating youth.

Yates, Michael D. *Can the Working Class Change the World?* New York: Monthly Review Press. 2018. The author addresses most of the questions posed above.

The Political Writings
of Bhagat Singh

Youth

Originally written in Hindi and titled *Yuvak*, this essay was first published in *Matwala* on 16 May 1925 under the nom de plume Balwant Singh. Bhagat Singh was seventeen when he wrote this essay. This essay is a rousing discourse on the role of youth in revolutionary struggles.

While it is undoubtedly true that older people might direct armed struggles, the shock troops of armed revolts are the young. It is well to remember that Mao Zedong began his revolutionary path in his early twenties. Fidel Castro was twenty-six when he led the attack on the Moncada Barracks, for which he was imprisoned and where, at his trial, he made his famous *History Will Absolve Me* speech.

Youth is the spring season in human life. A person can go berserk during this time. He feels the intoxication of a thousand bottles. All the powers bestowed by the Creator spring like a thousand streams in this time. As uncontrollable as an elephant gone amok, as uncontainable as the dark clouds of the monsoon season, as furious as a strong hurricane in an age of annihilation, as tender as a jasmine bud of a new spring, as ungovernable as a volcano, and as sweet as a morning song, is the age of youth. The splendour of a radiant dawn, the lustre of a silken sunset, the sweet warmth of the full moon of autumn and the awful midnight of a hot moonless night in the sixth month of the year are contiguous in youth. The season of youth in a human body is like the bomb in the revolutionary's pocket, the loaded revolver under the Conspirator's belt, and the sword in the hand of a lover of war.

God fills in all possible tumult in a skin-and-bone box from sixteen to twenty-five years. This tumultuous boat tosses in the middle of a tempest for ten years. This age appears to be more attractive than the dark, passionate earth, but it is filled with the horror of an earthquake. That is why only two paths are available to a human being in youth – he can ascend the highest peak of progress or fall into the bottomless abyss. He can be an ascetic if he wants to, or he can become a philanderer. He can become an angel or a demon. He can destroy the world and offer it an assurance of shelter.

The world is ruled by the young. History is full of the exploits of the youth. The youth is the lines on the forehead of the war goddess. The youth is the excited war cry of drums proclaiming the glory of a free nation. The youth is the stuff of the banner of victory of freedom. He is as obstinate as the soaring waves of the ocean. He is as dreadful as the first war cry in the Bhishma chapter in the Mahabharata, ardent as the rich kiss of a first union, fearless as Ravana's arrogance, and steadfast and unflinching Prahlad's Satyagraha.

If you desire a brave man willing to sacrifice himself, ask the youth. It is to his share that the lusciousness of life has fallen. He holds sway over emotions. Despite being ignorant of poetics, he is a gifted poet. The poet, too, is the honeybee hovering over the secrets of his heart. He doesn't know the definition of the *rasas* but has a truly insightful understanding of it. The youth is a special problem of creation. He is an excellent example of the glory of God's creation. He can sit for hours by the banks of a river at sunset. He can go on gazing, enchanted, at the sun journeying with its crimson rays towards the horizon. He becomes immersed in the soft melody wafting across from beyond. Strange is his life. Marvellous is his courage. Unfailing is his enthusiasm.

He is free of worries, he is careful. If he gets involved in something, to keep awake the entire night is child's play to him, the sunlight in a summer afternoon is the moonlight of spring for him, the rains in the monsoons are showers of flowers in celebration, the stillness of the cremation grounds is the warbling of birds in a garden. If he desires, he can enlighten society and the community, keep the honour of the country, brighten the face of the nation, and even overset big imperial powers. The upliftment of the downtrodden and the redemption of the world are in his hands. He is the most skilled player on the vast stage of this world.

If blood sacrifice is needed, who but a youth can give it? If you want a sacrifice, you must look to youth for it. It is a youth who is the shaper of the destiny of any community. A western scholar rightly said, 'It is an established truism that young men of today are the countrymen of tomorrow holding in their hands the high destinies of the Land. They are the seeds that spring and bear fruit'.[1] It means that the youth of today is the maker of a country's destiny. The young are the seeds of the success of the future.

Open the pages of the history of the world; it is full of immortal messages written in the blood of the young. Sift through the descriptions of revolutionary transformations in the world, and one will find only such young people, whom the wise have called 'mad boys' and 'misguided'. But what cynics can understand what men of steel those Japanese youths were who, fired by patriotism, built bridges over moats of forts with their corpses! A true youth embraces death without hesitation, digs in his feet with this chest thrust out in front of rifles, smiles even as he sits on the mouth of cannon, bursts into the national song to the jangle of iron cuffs, and swings on the gallows with a mocking laugh. It is the youth who gains weight on the day he is to be hanged, it is the youth who hums an inspiring mantra as he grinds the millstone in the jail and lifts his country out of the darkness only by sinking in the darkness of the jail cell. Patrick Henry, the leader of the American youth, once said in one of his passionate speeches, 'Life is dearer within

1 Quotation originally in English.

the prison cell, where it is the price paid for the freedom's fight'.[2,3] He meant that though life outside the jail was precious, life within the four walls of a jail was priceless because it is paid as the price of the freedom struggle.

Since the leader is so inspiring, the youth of America have the courage to give this rousing declaration, 'We believe that when a Government becomes destructive of the natural right of man, it is the man's duty to destroy that Government'.[4] This means that the youth of America believe that it is mankind's duty to destroy a government that denies fundamental rights to people.

O, the youth of India! Why do you lie slumbering in this haze of ignorance? Wake up, open your eyes and look around. The sun is ready to dawn in the eastern sky. Now don't keep sleeping. If you have to sleep, then sleep in the arms of eternal sleep. Why sleep in the bosom of cowardice? Renounce worldly ties of love and affection and declare:

Farewell! Farewell, my true Love
The army is on the move
And if I stayed with you, Love
A coward, I shall prove.[5]

Your mother, worthy of your reverence, the most adored, Goddess Durga, giver of food and nourishment, your goddess with a trident, your goddess on a lion, the verdant deity of abundance, is weeping bitterly today. Does her distress not disturb you even a tiny bit? May your supineness be damned! Even your ancestors bow their heads in shame at this

---

2 Quotation originally in English.
3 Patrick Henry (29 May 1736–6 June 1799) was a Founding Father of the United States, an attorney, planter, politician and orator known for declaring to the Second Virginia Convention (1775): 'Give me liberty, or give me death!'
4 This quotation from the 'The Declaration of Independence of the United States of America' originally in English.
5 Quotation originally in English.

impotence. If there is any shame in any part of your body, then get up and honour your mother's milk, pick up the challenge of redeeming her honour, take a pledge for every teardrop that she sheds, address her sorrow, and with a free throat, utter – *Vande Mataram*!

Students and Politics

Originally titled *Vidyarthi Ate Rajneeti,* this article was published in the Punjabi newspaper *Kirti* in July 1928, when Bhagat Singh was twenty years old. Here he notes the weaknesses of the colonial education system in India, where students are urged to abstain from politics and focus on their studies, presumably with a narrow view of the political. Its relevance today is evident from the fact that the youth is still advised to be 'apolitical' while exploitative and oppressive structures continue to thrive. Here Bhagat Singh's message of study and struggle resists these thought processes, complementing the previous article, 'Youth'.

A lot of noise is being made, saying students should not participate in political activities. The Punjab government's stand is most peculiar. Students are being made to sign an agreement that, as a condition for admission to the college, they would not engage in political activities. On top of this, it is our misfortune that Manohar Lal, elected by the people, is now the Education Minister, who sends a circular to schools and colleges, decreeing that anyone studying or teaching shall not participate in political activities. A few days ago in Lahore, where the students' union was celebrating Student Week, Sir Abdul Qadir and Professor Ishwar Chandra Nanda emphasized that students should not get involved in politics.

Punjab is known negatively as the most backward in the political field. What is the reason for this?

Have the sacrifices made by Punjab been too few? The reason is clear our educated people are complete fools. Today after reading the proceedings of the Punjab Council meeting, one has no doubts that our education system is rotten and useless, and young students, uncaring about the world around them, do not participate in national events. Nor do the students have any knowledge about such things.

After completing their college education, only a few of them study further, but they talk so immaturely that one has no option but to bemoan such childishness. An attempt is being made today itself to make idiots out of the youth who will hold the reins of the country in the future. We should be able to understand the consequence of this. We agree that the primary purpose for a student is to gain an education; they should direct all their energies to it, but is it not a part of education to develop the capacity to reflect upon the conditions in the country and think of ways to improve it? If not, then we consider such education useless, which should be acquired only to get a clerical job. What is the use of such education? Some over-clever people say: 'Kaka, you may certainly study and think about politics, but don't take any practical part in it. You will prove to be more beneficial to your nation by getting greater competence.'[1]

This sounds beautiful, but we tell you, this is only superficial talk. The following anecdote makes it clear. One day a student was reading a book, *An Appeal to the Young,* by Prince Kropotkin. A learned Professor asked, 'Which is this book? And this seems to be some Bengali name'. The boy answered, 'Prince Kropotkin is very well known. He was a scholar in Economics'. It was essential for every Professor to be familiar with this name. The student even laughed at the Professor's lack of knowledge. And then he added, 'He was a Russian'. That was enough. 'Russian!' Catastrophic! The Professor said, 'You are a Bolshevik because you read political books. I will immediately report to the Principal!'

Look at the Professor's ability. Now, what is there for those

---

1 *Kaka*: Punjabi for a young boy.

poor students to learn from such people? What can those youths learn in such a situation?

The other thing is – what is practical politics? To welcome and listen to the speeches of Mahatma Gandhi, Jawaharlal Nehru, and Subhas Chandra Bose is practical politics, but what about welcoming the Commission or the Viceroy? Is that not the other side of politics? Anything concerned with governments and nations would be considered a part of the political field. Would this be politics or not? Will it be said that the government would be pleased with this but displeased with that? Then the question is of the pleasure or displeasure of the government. Should students be taught the lesson of sycophancy right from birth? We think that until foreign thugs rule Hindustan, the loyal are not loyal but traitors, not human beings, but beasts, slaves to their bellies. So how can we say that the students should learn the lesson of loyalty?

Everyone agrees that at this time, Hindustan needs people who will sacrifice everything they have – body, mind, and soul – for the country and shower everything in life like madmen upon their country. But can we find such people among older people? Will people entangled in family and worldly affairs be able to come out? Only those young people can get involved who are not caught in any webs. Students and young people can think of this before getting entangled, only if they have acquired practical knowledge and have done more than just cramming for the maths and geography exams.

Was it not politics, when all the students in England left colleges to fight against Germany? Were our advisors then to instruct them, 'Go, go and get an education'. Today, will the national college Ahmedabad students helping the Bardoli satyagrahis remain immature? Let us see how many competent people Punjab University produces compared to them. It is the youth in all countries, who wins freedom for their country. Can the youth of Hindustan save their identity and that of their country by staying indifferent? The youth cannot forget the tyrannies inflicted upon the students in 1919. They also understand that there is a need for a great revolution. Let them study; certainly, let them study. But let them also learn about politics and jump into the fray and devote their lives to it when needed. Offer their lives to this cause. There seems to be no other way.

Universal Love

This article, titled *Vishwa Prem*, was published in the Hindi magazine *Matwala* in November 1924, when Bhagat Singh was seventeen. The essay begins in a tone reminiscent of John Lennon's song *Imagine*. Then it turns sharply toward condemning those who speak of a world of peace and equality but refuse to act to make it so. It is a tour de force argument for the propaganda of the deed.

It is impossible for humanity to describe the greatness of the king of poetry who envisioned the invaluable idea of *Vasudev Kutumbakam*! It is the aspiration of one who has experienced such universal love.

'World Fraternity!' – I consider equality in the world (Communism, worldwide equality in the true sense).[1]

How noble is this ideal! Let everyone be one's own. No one should be a stranger. How beautiful would that time be when alienation is forever destroyed? The day this ideal is brought into practice – that day, one can claim that the world has reached its zenith. How will the day look when each individual can internalize this ideal in his heart? Just imagine!

That day there will be so much strength that even shouting 'Peace! Peace!' will not be able to break the peace. That day no hungry soul will need to scream for food. Trade will be at the zenith of progress, but France and Germany will no longer go to horrible war in the name of trade. America and Japan will be there, but there will be no East or West. Black and white races will be there, but the Americans will not be able to burn the native black people

---

1 Words in parentheses originally in English.

alive.[2] There will be peace but no need for the Penal Code. There will be the British and the Indians, but there will be no division into master and slave. That day Mahatma Tolstoy's principle of 'Resist not the Evil' will not need to be shouted from the roof-tops, but there will be no evil in the world.[3] That is when we shall have complete freedom. What will such a time be like? Just imagine!

Looking at the present situation, who can believe such a day will dawn when no one will be afraid of anyone? In fact, people will desist from committing sins because of the voice of their conscience. If we yearn for some imaginary heaven even on such a day, then we shall say that such heaven does not exist. Can such a day dawn? This is a problem – a big problem. It is not easy. But I wish to know if people are interested in bringing about such a day. Are the people who talk so stridently about 'Universal Brotherhood' or 'Cosmopolitanism' concerned?[4] It is not enough to say 'Yes'. This is not the proposal that Congress has. This issue needs serious consideration. Are people prepared to offer a sacrifice for it? We will have to have an extreme present for such an imagined future. For such imagined peace, we will have to spread discord. We will have to sacrifice everything for such castles in the air. We will have to spread total anarchy to establish such a peaceful rule. To draw that blissful world towards us, we will have to inflict tyranny. For that happy time; no, no, for the mere hope of it, we will have to lay down our lives. Are people prepared for that?

We will have to spread the word of equality and egalitarianism. We will have to inflict oppression on those who oppose this. We will have to spread anarchy in those places where rules and empires have been blinded by power and are causing misery to crores of people. Are people prepared for that?

We will have to prepare the entire world to be ready to welcome this ideal. To reap such a good harvest, we shall have to weed out

---

2 He means Native Americans.
3 Words in quotes originally in English.
4 Words in quotes originally in English.

everything from the fields. The thorny bushes will have to be consigned to the pyre of peace. Stones and pebbles will have to be crushed. We will have to toil very hard. We will have to help the poor rise. The crushed will need to be shown the path of progress. These false powers will have to be dragged and compelled to stand with us. The arrogance of the arrogant will have to be crushed, and they will have to be taught the lesson of humility. We will have to give strength to the weak, freedom to the slaves, education to the illiterate, a ray of hope to the despairing, food to the hungry, homes to the homeless, faith to the unbelievers, and vision to the superstitious.

Will people be willing to do all this? O Votaries of Universal Brotherhood! Are you prepared to do this? If not, then stop your pretence. We will have to offer you as a sacrifice at the feet of the Goddess of Universal Brotherhood because you are deceivers. If you are prepared, step into the *karmkshetra*, and you shall be tested. Don't hide behind this noble principle sitting at home, crouching in corners, trembling at the mere thought of the terrible images of the battlefield, avoiding the light of the truth. If you truly desire to bring about this imagined time, then come forward. The first task will be to raise this fallen Bharat. The shackles of slavery will have to be shattered. Tyranny will have to be destroyed. Lack of freedom will have to be trampled into the dust because it lures humanity that the Almighty moulded in His own image, away from the path of justice because of its own weakness.

If the fear of being jailed or hanged still prevents you from following this path despite acknowledging the truth of it, then give up this pretence henceforth. If the fear that this revolution will lead to great anarchy and great bloodshed, and total strife prevents you from taking this path, even then, you are craven, weak, and cowardly. Abandon this pretence.

If discord spreads, so be it; at least there won't be any subjugation. If anarchy spreads, so be it. At least slavery will be abolished. Ah! This conflict will crush the weak. The daily whining will come to an end. No weak shall remain; the mighty will become friends. There will be amity among the strong people. They will feel love for each other, and the message of universal love will be carried forward.

Yes! Yes! The weak will have to be crushed in one blow. They are accountable to the entire world. They are the ones who are responsible for the spread of conflict. Let everyone be strong, or else they will be ground in the millstone.

Oh! Who is the true son of the soil who wants universal brotherhood with his whole heart? Who is willing to give up his happiness for the sake of the entire world?

No slave race has the right even to mention this noble ideal. These words lose their significance the moment the lips of an enslaved person utter them. If a disgraced man, crushed under his feet, grounded in the dust, says, 'I am a follower of Universal Brotherhood, a believer in this ideal, so I do not avenge these tyrannies', what value can his words have? Who will heed his cowardly words? Yes – if you have strength, if you have energy, if you have the power to trample the great and mighty underfoot, if you are able to lift a finger and grind the arrogance of people to dust, you can put to sleep great ruling powers, can crush them into the dust. And then you say, 'We believe in Universal Love, so please don't do this', then your words will hold weight – then each sentence you utter will have value. Then the words *Vasudev Kutumbakam* will also become significant.

Today you are enslaved, under foreign rule, not free, and your words seem a sham, pretence, rubbish. Do you want to propagate them? If yes, then you will have to follow the one who said – 'He who loveth Humanity loveth God', 'God is love and love is God' – who embraced the gallows under the crime of sedition; are you prepared to propagate universal love as courageously as he did?[5] The day you become a true propagator of this unique ideal, you will

5 Words in quotes originally in English.

have to step into the battlefield like the faithful son, Guru Gobind Singh. Who, like a true devotee of universal love, saying 'All are the sons of the same Father', like the great soul who sacrificed all of his four beloved sons for the nation, and upon being questioned by the mother, replying simply this; you will have to show patience like him. Can you bear to see someone sacrifice him or herself, or endure unspeakable torture, someone you hold the dearest to your heart, thinking of whom makes your heartbeat race, which you want to keep hidden in your heart? And can you climb onto a burning pyre with a smile before the same dear one and bid goodbye to the world with a compassionate look? If yes, then come forward for the test; it is time. If there is the slightest hesitation in your heart, give up this pretence for God's sake.

How can universal brotherhood and universal love flourish until this vocabulary of black-white, civilized-savage, ruler-ruled, rich-poor, high caste-untouchable, etc., continues to be used? This message can be delivered only by free people. An enslaved people like the Indians cannot even mention it.

Then how will the message spread? You will have to muster power. To muster power, you must spend all the strength earned till now. You will have to endure a lifetime of obstacles like Rana Pratap; only then may you pass the exam. Don't you see a true propagator of universal brotherhood, Mazzini, who stays incarcerated at one place alone for twenty years? Lenin was his supporter; he endured untold hardships. George Washington – the giver of freedom to America –was a believer in Universal Brotherhood; the revolutionaries of France were staunch believers –how much blood they shed! The idealistic Brutus was a follower of universal brotherhood, who even assassinated his beloved Caesar because of his love for his motherland and committed suicide afterwards. Happily and skillfully fighting wars was Garibaldi, who can also get credit for a belief in universal love.

A lover of universal love is the brave individual whom we have no hesitation in calling an awesome rebel, an uncompromising anarchist – the same Veer Savarkar, who pacing in his lawn thinking about universal love, would stop walking on the grass, lest he crushed the tender grass under his feet.

The brave MacSwiney, who passed away after 75 days of fasting, can take the credit for treading this path; who used to say:[6]

It is the love of the country that inspires us and not the hate of the enemy and the desire for full satisfaction for the past.[7]

A devotee of the Goddess of Universal Love was the author of *Gita Rahasya*, the revered Lokmanya Tilak.[8] Do you want more? That thin, scrawny man in the loincloth who could give a delighted chuckle upon being sentenced and say, 'the punishment given to me is too mild, and I cannot hope for more courteous behaviour that I have met with', whose poignant tale will have no effect on your stony hearts – a believer in the ideal, he is a Mahatma.[9]

And Lord Rama, who destroyed Ravan and Bali, demonstrated universal love by eating the berries which were first tasted by the Bhil woman, demonstrated Universal love. The one who brought cousins to fight a war with each other, who completely erased the injustice from the world–Lord Krishna–demonstrated his universal love by gobbling up the uncooked rice that Sudama had brought for him.

Do you also assert universal love? First, learn to stand on your feet. Develop the capability to stand with your head held high with pride among the people of the free nations. Till the time unfortunate incidents like the Kamagata Maru ship keep

---

6   Terence James MacSwiney (28 March 1879–25 October 1920) was an Irish playwright, author and politician. He was arrested by the British Government on charges of sedition and imprisoned in Brixton Prison. His death there in October 1920 after 74 days on hunger strike brought him and the Irish Republican campaign to international attention.

7   Quotation originally in English.

8   *Gita Rahasya*: Translated from Hindi as 'The secret of the Gita'.

9   Reference to Mahatama Gandhi.

on happening, till the time you continue to be called 'Damn black man', till the Jallianwala Bagh-like horrible tragedies keep happening in your country, till the time you don't react to brave women being dishonoured, till then this pretence has no meaning. What peace, what happiness, and what kind of universal love is it?

If you genuinely desire to propagate the ideal of peace and happiness in the entire world, then first learn to react to the insults thrown at you. Be ready to die to cut loose the shackles of your motherland. Be prepared to serve a life sentence at the Cellular Jail across the black seas, if you want to set your mother free. Be ready to die to keep your sobbing mother alive. Only then will our country be free! We shall be strong. We shall be able to proclaim the ideal of universal love proudly. Will be able to compel the world to follow the path of peace.

Drops of Blood on the Day of Holi

This essay, published in the Hindi weekly *Pratap* on 15 March 1926, was written from Kanpur by Bhagat Singh when he was eighteen, under the name *Ek Punjabi Yuvak* (A Punjabi Youth). He wrote this from Kanpur, where he had come three years earlier after running away from his home. He participated in many activities there and met many Indian nationalists and revolutionaries. He also read widely. And he had already come under suspicion by the police.

The Babbar Akali Agitation had been underway in Punjab. This essay describes the agitation and the hanging of six Akali activists. It shows the growing political consciousness of the young Bhagat Singh and his anger with British imperialism.

And it also shows the brutality of the British, who might have claimed to be 'civilizing' the Indian people but, in reality, were exploiting them to transfer the wealth of the country to Britain.

Finally, this essay illustrates the profound irony of people celebrating the day of Holi, a festival celebrating the arrival of Spring, while young people are being tortured and hanged for trying to liberate these very people from the yoke of British rule.

The festival of Holi celebrates the triumph of good over evil, which is exactly what these young people represented.

On the 27th of February, 1926, on the day of Holi, when the rest of us were busy in our merriment, a terrible event unfolded in one corner of this vast province. When you hear of it, you will tremble! You will shudder! Six brave Babbar Akali men were hanged to death that day in the Lahore Central Jail. The contempt and light-heartedness that these people had demonstrated for the past nearly two years during their trial proved how earnestly Shri Kishan Singh ji Gadgajj, Shri Santa Singh ji, Shri Dilip Singh ji, Shri Nand Singh ji, Shri Karam Singh ji, and Shri Dharam Singh ji had been waiting for just such a day. The Honorable Judge pronounced his verdict after months. The verdict was death by hanging for five, exile and long sentences in the Cellular Jail in the Andaman Islands for many others. The brave defendants thundered. The sky reverberated with their enthusiastic victory cries. An appeal was filed. Six, instead of five, became the recipient of the death sentence. That day the news came that a mercy petition had been filed, and the Punjab Secretary declared that the hanging would not occur immediately.

There was a waiting period, but suddenly we saw a small group of people accompanying the dead bodies to the cremation ground on Holi. Quietly their last rites were conducted.

The city was filled with festivities. People were throwing colour at passers-by as usual. What terrible disregard! If they were misguided, so be it; if they were crazy, so be it. They were fearless patriots. Whatever they did was for this unfortunate country. They could not endure injustice, could not see the country in this fallen state, the oppression inflicted upon the weak became intolerable for them, and they could not bear the exploitation of the people – they challenged it and jumped into the fray. They were alive, and they were visionaries. O, the mercilessness of the battlefield! Blessed are you! All friends and foes are equal after death; this is the principle of human beings. Even if they had done anything unpleasant, they should be worshipped because they sacrificed their lives for the country bravely and unhesitatingly. Despite being in the opposition, Mr Teggart could offer condolences upon the death of Jatin Mukherjee, a brave Bengali revolutionary, and praise his courage, patriotism and commitment; but we cowardly, beastly men cannot pause in our pursuit of pleasure even for a moment to dare to heave a sigh at the martyrdom of such brave men. How disappointing this is! These poor souls got 'adequate' punishment for their crime in the eyes of bureaucracy; another chapter in this tragic play came to a close. But the climax is still to come. Some more terrible scenes are yet to be played out. It is a long story; one must go back in time to hear the story.

The Non-Cooperation Movement was at its peak, and Punjab was not to be left behind. The Sikhs also rose in Punjab; they awoke from deep slumber and rose with a mighty roar. The Akali Agitation began. A string of sacrifices was made. The Ex-Schoolmaster, Master Mota Singh of Khalsa Middle School, Mahalpur, in the Hoshiarpur district, gave a speech. A warrant was issued for him. But the Emperor's 'hospitality' was not acceptable to him. Even otherwise, they were opposed to going to jail. He continued to give speeches. A huge meeting occurred in Kot Fatuhi; the police surrounded it, but Master Mota Singh continued to speak. With the President's permission, the audience rose to their feet at the end. No one knew where Masterji had disappeared. This hide-and-seek went on for a long time. The government was unable to handle this. Ultimately, an associate betrayed him, and after a year and a half, Master Sahib was caught. This was the first scene of this horrible play.

The agitation for *Guru Ka Bagh* began. Hired goons would fall upon unarmed brave men and beat them to a pulp. Could anyone who witnessed or heard about it remain unaffected? All around, there was a spate of arrests. A warrant was issued for Sardar Kishan Singh Gadgajj too. But he, too, belonged to the same group of people who did not believe in voluntary arrest. The police pursued him relentlessly, but he kept managing to evade arrest. He had also organized a small revolutionary band. He could not bear the brutal attacks on unarmed crowds. Along with pursuing peaceful ways of agitation, he also considered using weapons necessary.

On one side, police dogs were set to sniff him out. On the other side, it was decided that the sycophants be 'reformed'.

Sardar Kishan Singh ji felt that though they needed to be armed for their own protection, they should try not to precipitate the issue. But the majority was of the other opinion. Finally, it was decided that three people would announce their names, and take the entire responsibility upon themselves and begin to 'reform' the sycophants.[1] Shri Karam Singh, Shri Dhanna Singh and Shri Uday Singh ji came forward. For a moment, keep aside the issue of whether this was appropriate or inappropriate and try to imagine the scene when these brave men took the oath:

We shall sacrifice everything for the love of our country; we take an oath that we shall die fighting, but never go to jail.

It must have been a beautiful, sacred scene in which these people who had sacrificed their families took their oaths! What is the limit of self-sacrifice? Is there any limit to courage and fearlessness? Can one ever reach the peak of idealism?

A *subedar* was the first victim near a Sham Churasi, Hoshiarpur railway branch line station. After that, these three people announced their names. The government tried very hard to arrest them but could not succeed. In Rurki Kalan, Sardar Kishan Singh Gadagajj was surrounded. Another youth who was with him was also injured and arrested.

But Kishan Singh managed to escape with the help of his weapons. He met an ascetic on the way, who told him he had a unique herb with which anything he wanted could be done. He fell into his trap and went to see the ascetic, leaving his weapons behind. The ascetic gave him some medicine to grind and left, ostensibly to fetch the herb. He brought the police back with him. Sardar Sahib was arrested. That ascetic was a Sub-Inspector in the C.I.D.

Babbar Akali braves had started their work in earnest. Several police informers were killed. The area between Doaba-Beas and Sutlej, Jalandhar and Hoshiarpur districts had been well known on

1 'Reform the sycophants' refers to annihilating the British.

the political map of India even earlier. Even in 1915, most of the martyrs had been from this region. This is where the maximum action was taking place now as well. The police department expended all its energy but could not touch anyone.

A small stream is a little distance away from Jalandhar, Chaunta Sahib Gurudwara is located in a village on its banks. Shri Karam Singh ji, Shri Dhanna Singh ji, Shri Uday Singh ji, and Shri Anoop Singh ji were sitting with a few other people while tea was being made. Shri Dhanna Singh said, 'Baba Karam Singh ji! We should leave this place this very instant. I feel something bad is going to happen'. The 75-year-old Karam Singh did not pay heed to this. But Shri Dhanna Singh and the 18-year-old Dilip Singh left. Baba Karam Singh carefully approached Shri Anoop Singh and said, 'Anoop Singh, you are not a good man'. But he did not pay too much attention to his own words. They were conversing when the police landed there. All the bombs were in Shri Anoop Singh's custody. All these people hid themselves in the village. The police searched everywhere, but it was futile. Finally, the police made an announcement: 'Hand over the traitors, or the village will be set on fire'. But still, the villagers did not weaken.

Baba Karam Singh himself came forward when he realized the situation. Anoop Singh ran towards the police with all the bombs and surrendered. The other four people stood surrounded. The English police officer said, 'Karam Singh! Surrender, and you shall be pardoned'. The brave man challenged the police, 'We will die for our country like true revolutionaries but will never surrender'. He encouraged the other three comrades as well with his words. All of them roared like lions. Both sides began to fire. When the ammunition of the patriots was exhausted, they jumped into the river. But the heavy firing went on, and finally, these four were martyred.

Shri Karam Singh was 75 years old. He had lived in Canada. He had an unblemished and pious character. The government thought they had finished off Babbar Akalis, but they were rising steadily. The 18-year-old Dilip Singh was an extremely handsome, determined, robust, but illiterate youth who had joined a band of robbers. Dhanna Singh ji's education turned him from a robber into a true revolutionary. Moreover, Sardar Banta Singh and Waryam Singh and several other dreaded robbers also abandoned robbery and became revolutionaries.

None of them feared death. They wished to cleanse their past sins. Their numbers rose steadily. One day while Dhanna Singh was sitting in village Manhaana, the police were called in. Dhanna Singh was heavily intoxicated and was arrested. His loaded pistol was snatched, and he was handcuffed and brought out. Twelve plainclothes policemen and two English officers surrounded him. That very moment, a bomb exploded. It was Dhanna Singh's handiwork. He died, along with an English officer and ten soldiers. The others were injured badly.

Similarly, in village Munder, Banta Singh, Jwala Singh and several others were besieged. They were sitting on a terrace. There was an exchange of fire for some time, and then the police sprinkled kerosene oil with a pump and set the house on fire. Even so, Waryam Singh escaped, but Banta Singh was killed.

It would not be inappropriate to mention a couple of incidents that occurred earlier. Banta Singh was a very courageous man. Once, perhaps in Jalandhar Cantt, he had snatched a horse and a rifle from a soldier standing guard. During this time, when police parties would be searching for him high and low, he accidentally bumped into one such search party in the jungle. Sardar Banta Singh immediately challenged them. 'Come and fight if you dare!' On one side were mercenaries; on this side, a person willing to do or die. How could there be any comparison? The police party left quietly.

A special force had been appointed to deal with these people. And this was the state of affairs! Anyway, there were plenty of arrests. In village after village, police posts were set up. Gradually the power of the Babbar Akalis began to wane. So far, they had ruled virtually unchallenged. They were welcomed happily and affectionately wherever they went, albeit with a little fear and dread. The informers of the government were defeated. They dared not even step out of their houses before dawn or after sunset. These people were regarded as heroes. They were brave, and it was considered auspicious to worship them. But gradually, their influence began to ebb. Hundreds were arrested, and cases were filed against them.

Only Waryam Singh managed to stay alive. Upon realizing there was a greater police presence in Jalandhar and Hoshiarpur, he decided to leave for Lyallpur. One day, he was completely surrounded but he managed to escape by fighting heroically. However, the fight had exhausted him. And he had no companion. It was a difficult situation. One day he went to the village of Desiyan to visit his maternal uncle. His weapons were kept outside. After his evening meal, he was just about to pick up his weapons when the police arrived. He was surrounded again. The English officer caught him from behind. But Waryam Singh managed to wound him grievously with his *kirpan*. Then he fell down on the ground. All attempts to handcuff him were in vain. After two full years of attempts to suppress the Akali group, it ended. A case was filed, the result of which has already been written above. That day these people had expressed a desire to be hanged quickly. Their wish was granted. They were granted eternal peace.

The Religious Riots and Their Solution

The original essay, *Dharmvar Fasad Teunha De Iilaj* was written in Punjabi and published in the June 1927 issue of *Kirti*, when Bhagat Singh was not yet twenty years old.

In the wake of the 1919 Jallianwala Bagh tragedy, the British intentionally incited communal riots. This resulted in inhuman riots between the Hindus and Muslims in 1924 in Kohat. After this, there was considerable debate on religious riots in the national political arena. Everyone felt the need to end these, but the Congress leaders tried to get Hindu and Muslim leaders to sign a pact to stop them. Bhagat Singh sees clearly that religious conflict deters radical change and that the root causes of it, mainly economic, must be addressed. Given India's current situation, these causes have yet to be dealt with and eliminated.

The condition of Bharatvarsha/India is indeed pitiable today. The devotees of one religion are sworn enemies of the devotees of another religion. Merely belonging to one religion is now considered enough reason to be the enemy of another religion. If we find this difficult to believe, let us look at the fresh outbreaks of violence in Lahore. How the Muslims killed innocent Sikhs and Hindus, and how even the Sikhs did their worst when the opportunity came. This butchering was not done because a particular man committed a crime, but because a particular man is a Hindu or a Sikh or a Muslim. Just the fact of a person being a Sikh or a Hindu is enough for him to be killed by a Muslim, and in the same way, merely being a Muslim is a sufficient reason to take his life. If this is the situation, then may God help Hindustan!

Under these conditions, the future of Hindustan seems very bleak. These 'religions' have ruined the country. And one has no idea how long these religious riots will plague Hindustan. These riots have shamed Hindustan in the eyes of the world. And we have seen how everyone is carried on the tide of blind faith. It is a rare Hindu, Muslim or Sikh who can keep a cool head; the rest of them take sticks and staffs, swords and knives and kill each other. Those who escape death go to the gallows or are thrown into jail. After so much bloodshed, these 'religious' folk are subjected to the baton of the English government, and only then do they come to their senses.

As far as we've seen, communal leaders and newspapers are behind these riots. These days Indian leaders exhibit such shameful conduct that it is better not to say anything. The same leaders who have taken upon themselves the challenge of winning independence for their country and who don't tire of shouting slogans of 'Common Nationality' and 'Self Rule . . . Self-Rule . . .' are hiding themselves and are flowing on this tide of religious blindness. The number of people hiding themselves is much less. But leaders who join communal agitations can be found in hundreds when one scratches the surface. There are very few leaders who wish for the welfare of people from the bottom of their hearts. Communalism has become such a great deluge that they cannot stem it. It appears as if the leadership of Bharat/India has gone bankrupt.

The other people who have played a special role in igniting communal riots are the newspaper people. The profession of journalism, which was, at one point in time, accorded a very high status, has become very filthy now. These people print prominent, provocative headlines and rouse the passions of people against one another, which leads to rioting. Not just in one or two places, but riots have taken place in many places because the local papers have written outrageous essays. Few writers have been able to maintain their sanity and keep calm on such days.

The real duty of the newspapers was to impart education,

eradicate narrow-mindedness in people, put an end to communal feelings, encourage mutual understanding, and create a common Indian nationalism. But they have turned their main business to spreading ignorance, preaching narrowness, creating prejudice, leading to rioting, and destroying Indian common nationalism. This is the reason that tears of blood flow from our eyes at Bharat's present state, and the question that rises in our hearts is, 'What will become of Hindustan?'

The people familiar with the enthusiasm and awakening of the times during the Non-Cooperation movement feel like crying in this present state. What days they were when they could glimpse independence in front of them – and today! The idea of Home Rule seems like a mere dream now. That is the advantage that the tyrants have gotten from communal riots. The bureaucracy that had begun to fear for its very existence has dug in its roots so deeply that it is not easy to shake it.

If we look for the roots of these communal riots, the reason seems to be economic. Leaders and journalists went through untold sacrifices during the days of the Non-Cooperation Movement. They suffered financially as well. When the movement ebbed, it led to a lack of confidence in the leaders, which led to the collapse of the business of a lot of these religious leaders. The question of filling one's belly is at the bottom of whatever work is done in this world. This is one of the three principal maxims of Karl Marx. It is due to this maxim that practices like the *Tabligh, Tanzeem,* and *Shuddhi* were initiated, and it is because of this we are in such a terrible state; in this mess.

If there is to be any lasting solution to all these communal riots, it lies only in the improvement in the economic condition of Hindustan; because the financial condition of the common people is so degraded in Hindustan that anyone can pay four annas to get another person insulted. Tormented by hunger and sorrow, a person can abandon all principles. It becomes a matter of survival.

But economic reforms are too difficult in the present

circumstances because the government is foreign and does not allow any improvement in the condition of the people. That is why people must concentrate all their energy on attacking it and not rest till it is completely transformed.

Class consciousness is crucial to stop people from fighting each other. The poor workers and peasants should be made to understand that their real enemies are the capitalists clearly, so they must be careful not to fall into their trap. All the poor people of the world – whatever their caste, race, religion or nation – have the same rights. It is in your interest that all discrimination on account of religion, colour, race, and nationality is eliminated and the power of the government be taken in your hands. These efforts will not harm you in any way but will one day cut off your shackles, and you will get economic freedom.

The people who are familiar with the history of Russia know that similar conditions prevailed there during the rule of the Tsar. Several groups kept dragging each other down. But from the day the Workers' Revolution took place, the very map of the place changed. Now there are never any riots there. Now everyone is considered to be a 'human being' there, not 'a member of a religious group'. The economic condition of the people was very pathetic during the times of the Tsar, leading to rioting. But now, when the economic condition of the Russians has improved, and they have developed class consciousness, there is no news from there about any riots.

Though one hears heart-rending accounts of such riots, yet one hears something positive about the Calcutta riots. The workers of the trade unions did not participate in the riots, nor did they come to blows with each other; on the other hand, all the Hindus and Muslims behaved normally towards each other in the mills and even tried to stop the riots. This is because there was class consciousness in them, and they fully recognized what would benefit their class. This is the beautiful path of class consciousness that can stop communal rioting.

We have received this bit of happy news that the youth of Bharat is now tired of religions that teach mutual hatred and war and are washing their hands off such religions, and there is so much progressiveness in them now that they look upon the people of Bharat, not from the point of view of religion – as Hindu, Muslim or Sikh – but human beings first, and then as citizens of one country. The birth of such feelings in the youth of Bharat gives us hope for a golden future, and the people of Bharat should not worry about these riots; they should rather hold themselves in a state of readiness and always attempt to ensure that such an environment is not created; there are no riots ever.

In 1914-15 the martyrs separated religion from politics. They believed religion was an individual's personal matter and no one else should interfere. Nor should one let religion push itself into politics because it does not unite everyone or make them work together. That is why movements like the Ghadar Party were strong and had a single soul in which the Sikhs were at the forefront for going to the gallows, and even the Hindus and the Muslims didn't lag behind.

At present, some Indian leaders also want to separate religion from politics. This is also a beautiful remedy to eliminate quarrels, and we support it.

If religion is separated from politics, we can all come together in politics, even if we belong to different religions.

We think that the real sympathizers of Hindustan will ponder over our prescribed remedy and that we will save India from self-destruction.

We hope that class consciousness shall also emerge among the workers and peasants of organizations that the Congress party has adopted, because this will hasten the elimination of communal riots.

The Issue of Untouchability

The caste system in India greatly complicates the analysis of the society's class structure. One of the editors had a colleague at his college, a man born in Calcutta, who was going to be married. His wife's parents were communists, but they disapproved of the marriage because he was born into a 'lower' caste. 'Untouchables', known today as Dalits, are those born outside of, and beneath, the caste system.

In this essay, Bhagat Singh deals radically and compassionately with caste, as with so many aspects of modern society, as something irrational and unconscionable. Titled *Achhoot Ka Sawal*, it was published in *Kirti* in June 1928 under the pen name of *Vidrohi* (Rebel).

In no other country except ours does such a bad state of affairs prevail. Strange and peculiar questions keep arising here. One crucial question is that of the untouchables. The problem is that in a population of 30 crores, there are 6 crores people called 'untouchable', i.e. their mere touch will pollute the dharma of the rest. Their entry into temples would displease the Gods. Drawing water from wells would make the water of these wells impure. These questions are being raised in the twentieth century, and one is ashamed even to listen to these questions.

Our country is very spiritual, yet we hesitate to give the status of a human being to a person, while the West, referred to as entirely materialistic, has been raising the banner of oneness for centuries. They declared equality as a principle in the American and French Revolutions. Today Russia has resolved to eradicate every kind of discrimination, fulfilling the ideals of the first May. We are forever bothered about the being of soul and God and involved in a strident debate about whether we should grant the *janeyu*, to the untouchable or do they have the right to study the Vedas and the scriptures or not. We complain that we are not treated well in other countries. The English government does not consider us at par with the English, but do we have the right to make this complaint?

A Muslim gentleman from Sindh, Shri Noor Mohammed, a member of the Bombay Council spoke at length about this in 1926,

> If the Hindu Society refuses to allow other human beings, fellow creatures so that, to attend public schools, and if . . . the president of local board representing so many lakhs of people in this house refuses to allow his fellows and brothers the elementary human right of having water to drink, what right have they to ask for more rights from the bureaucracy? Before we accuse people coming from other lands, we should see how we ourselves behave toward our own people . . . How can we ask for greater political rights when (we ourselves) deny elementary rights to human beings?[1]

What he says is absolutely right, but because a Muslim has said it, the Hindus will say, 'Look! He wants to convert the untouchables to Islam and assimilate them in their fold'.

If you consider them worse than beasts, they will certainly embrace other religions where they will be given better rights and treated like human beings. Then, lamenting, 'Just see, the Christians and the Muslims are harming the Hindu community!' would be futile.

How true this statement but everyone is enraged at it. Exactly this anxiety gripped the Hindus as well. Even the Sanatan Dharam scholars have begun to ponder over this problem. At times, those who were known as great revolutionaries joined in. In the

---

1 Excerpt originally in English.

conference of the Hindu Mahasabha in Patna, which was held under the aegis of Lala Lajpat Rai as President – an old supporter of the untouchables – a sharp debate began. There were a lot of clashes.

The problem was whether the untouchables had the right or not to perform *yagyopavit*. And did they have the right to study the scriptures and the Vedas or not? Great, well-known social reformers were incensed, but Lala ji made everyone concur; redeemed Hindu dharma by accepting both. Otherwise, just think how shameful it would have been. A dog can sit on our lap. He can roam freely in our kitchen, but we become polluted if a human being touches us!

Now a great social reformer like Pandit Malviya ji, a great champion of the untouchables, and what not, can be garlanded by a scavenger but considers himself to be impure unless he has a bath with his clothes on afterwards. What a great swindle! Make a temple to worship the God who loves everyone, but it becomes defiled if an untouchable enters it. God becomes angry. If this is the state of affairs at home, is it seemly to fight for equal rights abroad? Then our behaviour reveals only an extremity of ingratitude. We shun the very people who do the lowliest of work to provide us with facilities. We can worship beasts but cannot make a human being sit next to us.

Today there is a great deal of hue and cry over this issue. Those ideas are being especially discussed these days. The communal feelings may or may not have done any good to enhance the freedom struggle in the country, but at least it has given one advantage. Everyone is anxious to increase the numbers of their community to ask for better rights. The Muslims made a little extra effort. They converted the untouchables to Islam and gave them equal rights. This hurt the pride of the Hindus. Hostility grew, which even led to riots. Gradually even the Sikhs thought that they should not be left behind. They also began to baptize them. Hindus and Sikhs fought over the taking off of the *janeyu* and the cutting of hair. Now all three communities are drawing the untouchables into their fold. So there is a lot of hue and cry. On the other side, the Christians are quietly enhancing their status. Anyway, all this activity is erasing this slur on the country.

And when the untouchables saw how everyone was fighting over them and thought of them as fodder, they reflected on why they should not unite by themselves. Whether the English had any hand in this idea is not clear, but there was considerable use of government machinery in the propagation of this idea. Organizations like Adi Dharma Mandal are a result of this idea.

Now another question is what the correct solution to this problem should be. The answer to this is very simple. First, it should be decided that all human beings are equal and none is different either at birth or through the division of labour. That is, just because a man has been born in the house of a poor sweeper, he will spend the rest of his life cleaning the toilets of others and have no right in the world to progress – all this is rubbish. This is the cruel manner in which our Aryan ancestors treated them, stigmatizing them as low-caste and making them do lowly tasks.

Along with this, there was an anxiety lest they revolt. Then the philosophy of reincarnation was propagated to show that it was the fruit of their sins in past lives. So what can be done? Spend your days quietly. By preaching patience to them in this manner, they managed to silence the unprivileged for a long time. But they committed a grave sin. They erased humanity from human beings. A lot of oppression and cruelty were inflicted. Now is the time to atone for our sins.

Another problem arose along with this. Abhorrence for essential tasks arose in the minds of the people. We spurned the weaver. Today even weavers are considered untouchables. In the region of the United Provinces, even pallbearers are considered untouchable. This has led to a lot of mess being created. This is proving to be detrimental to the process of progress.

Keeping these communities in mind, we need to neither call

them untouchable nor think of them as being so. And the problem would be solved! The strategy that Naujawan Bharat Sabha and the youth conference have adopted is quite good. We should ask for forgiveness of those who have been called untouchables and consider them to be equal human beings like us, without being given *amrit*, without reciting the *kalma* or being purified, and count them among ourselves, to take water from their hands; that is the right course. And to fight amongst ourselves and not give them any rights is not the correct approach.

When the propagation of labour rights began in villages, the government officials tried to mislead the Jat peasants by saying that pampering the low castes would adversely affect their work. And that was enough! The Jat peasants were incensed. They must remember that their condition cannot improve until they want to keep these poor people by terming them as low-born and mean under their thumb. It is often said that they are not clean. The answer is clear – they are poor. Treat poverty. The poor in the high castes also don't stay clean. Even the pretext of doing dirty work cannot be taken because mothers clean the shit of their children and don't become untouchable or of low caste.

But this cannot be accomplished till the time the untouchables organize themselves. We consider it a very positive movement that they are organizing themselves voluntarily or because they are equal in numbers to the Muslims and thus asking for equal rights. Either end this problem of communal discrimination or give them their separate rights. The Councils and the Assemblies must ensure complete freedom for these people to use schools, colleges, wells, and roads, not just by lip service but by taking them to the wells. Get their children admitted to schools. But in the Legislature, where the Bill against child marriage and religion creates such public outrage, how can they muster the courage to assimilate the untouchables within the community?

So we say that they must have their representatives. They must demand more rights for themselves. We clearly say, 'Rise, brothers who are called Untouchables and are the real servants of the people! Rise, look at your history'. You were the real strength of Guru Gobind Singh's army. It was due to you that Shivaji was able to do so much; due to you that his name lives on today. Your sacrifices are etched in golden letters. You are doing us a great favour by rendering your services daily, adding to the comfort of the life of the public and making life possible, and we people do not understand that. According to the Land Alienation Act, you cannot buy land by saving money. You are so much oppressed that American Miss Mayo describes you as less than a man. Rise, recognize your strength. Get organized. In reality, without making your efforts, you will get nothing. *Those who would be free must themselves strike the blow.*[2] Those who want freedom must fight for independence. Gradually human beings have developed a habit of wanting greater rights for themselves, but keeping those under them, to remain suppressed. So those who understand the language of punches don't understand words. That is, organize, stand on your own feet, and challenge the world. Then you will see that no one will dare to deny you your rights. Don't become fodder for others. Don't look to others for help. But beware, don't be trapped by bureaucracy. They don't want to help you but make you their pawns. This capitalist bureaucracy is the real reason behind your slavery and poverty. So make sure that you never join them. Be wary of their wiles. Everything will become all right then. You are the real working class. Workers unite. You have nothing to lose except chains. Rise and rebel against the present system. Gradual, slow reforms will lead you nowhere. Create a revolution with social agitation and tighten your belts for a political and economic revolution. You are the foundation of the country, the real strength. Awake the sleeping lions! Rise and revolt!

2 Sentence originally in English.

Satyagraha and Strikes

These editorial notes were published as *Satiagrahi Ate Haratlan* in *Kirti* in June 1928. Bhagat Singh was then on the editorial board of *Kirti*. Unlike many others who focused on the fight for independence alone, Bhagat Singh was also dedicated to the struggle of workers. The original was written in Punjabi.

SATYAGRAHA

Life again seems to have been infused into Hindustan in 1928. On the one hand, there are general strikes; on the other, preparations are underfoot for Satyagraha. These are very good signs. The biggest Satyagraha is being held by the peasants of Bardoli in Gujarat. After every thirty years, taxes are revised, and the tax on the land is raised every time. The same thing happened this year, and the tax has been hiked. What are people to do? In any case, the poor peasant cannot fill his belly, and how can he pay 22 per cent more tax than before?

Preparations were made for Satyagraha. Mahatma Gandhi corresponded with the Governor of Punjab to try and get the tax reduced, but Sir, this government is not about to bend only through letters. It had no effect. The people had to go on a Satyagraha. Even earlier, on a few occasions, the peasants had gone on a Satyagraha in Gujarat and defeated the government. In 1917–18, the crop had rotted due to excessive rains and was not even worth one-fourth of the price of the normal crop. The law stated that tax would not be collected if the crop was less than six annas worth in a rupee, and it would be collected along with the next year's tax in the next year. When the people protested that they did not have even four annas worth of crop, the government did not heed their word that year. Then Mahatma Gandhi ji took the matter into his hands and held a meeting. He explained to the people that if they refused to pay the tax, their land would be confiscated and asked them if they were prepared for that. The people kept quiet, and the Satyagraha leaders from Bombay became upset and got up to leave. But then an old farmer got up and said they would endure everything, and the others also began to concur with him. Satyagraha began. The government also began to confiscate the land and property, but after two months, the government was forced to blink first and accede to the conditions set by the landlords.

The second Satyagraha took place in 1923–24 when Mahatma ji was in jail. The first time 600 villages had taken part. This time the tax of 94 villages was raised, and these villages went on Satyagraha. A punitive tax was imposed on them. There was a law that no property could be attached after sunset, and the peasants would lock up their houses early in the morning and leave, so the police would not find a single person as a witness. Finally, the government got fed up and revoked the tax.

This time the Satyagraha has begun in Bardoli. In 1921-22 intense preparations were made in Bardoli to Satyagraha for freedom. All a game of chance! All preparations went to nought.[1] Anyway, why brood over the past now? Now the government fixed the tax in that area. The poor farmers! Land tax was raised by 22 per cent. Many protests took place, but was the government about to listen? Work began under the leadership of Shri Vallabh Bhai Patel, and the farmers refused to pay the tax. Now all the Recovery Officers and government officials have gathered together in the Bardoli area. They are doing whatever they can to misguide these people. Property is being attached; orders are being given to confiscate land. But there is no one to carry the stuff. These

---

1 The reference here seems to be to the withdrawal of the 1921 massive non-cooperation movement by Mahatma Gandhi after the Chauri-Chaura incident.

days there is a lot of activity there, but one interesting thing is that everything is being done very peacefully. The officers, who had come to trouble the farmers, are being dealt with very cordially. Earlier, they did not get food and water. Now, the Headman said that they must be given food and water. One day four containers were impounded from the liquor shop, but no one was carrying them. When the officer said, 'I'm very thirsty; at least give me some water', a volunteer satyagrahi immediately brought a bottle of soda for him. So the action is on at great speed, but very peacefully. There are high hopes that the government will bow down finally.

The other place where the Satyagraha is to take place is Kanpur. There were Hindu-Muslim riots in the last few days in Kanpur. Later a disciplinary force was put on duty. A few days ago, Shri Ganesh Shankar ji Vidyarthi, a member of the Kanpur Council and the editor of the newspaper, *Pratap*, received a letter from a magistrate that he should prepare a list of all employees with details of their designations and salary, because a punitive tax was to be collected. But Vidyarthi ji wrote back to say that he was not prepared to pay any tax; nor would he render any assistance in this task because it was the police that were responsible for the riots. The people should not be punished for the police's crime. The people asked Vidyarthi ji, 'What should we do?' and he answered, 'There will be trouble, a lot of damage will be done, but we should not pay this unreasonable tax'. Processions were held. Seven thousand people signed a petition that they would not pay the tax and sent it to the government. Preparations are being made.

The third place is Meerut. There also, the land tax was revised, and the tax was raised. Satyagraha has been proclaimed there as well.

Even in Punjab, signs of something similar are visible. The crops in Sheikhupura and Lahore districts have been ruined due to hailstorms. There is hardly any harvest, so how can they pay the tax? But the wise and intelligent people of this region speak a different language: 'Let not the "disreputable" people of the Congress give speeches to the farmers, lest the government gets annoyed'. Such things are happening, but it should be remembered that 'those who understand the language of punches, don't understand words'. The British understand only the language of money and to expect that they would voluntarily take back the tax! Till when will this illusion remain?

STRIKES

On the one hand, Satyagraha is making waves; on the other, strikes are playing a no less important role. It is very happy that there is life again in the nation, and the war between the peasants and the workers has begun for the first time. This will impact the forthcoming movement. These are the people who deserve freedom. The peasant and the worker demand food, and their demand will not be met till one has attained complete freedom. They cannot stop at the Round Table Conference or other such thing. Anyway!

These days, the Liluah Railway Workshop, the Tata Mills in Jamshedpur, the sweeper class in Jamshedpur and the textile mills in Bombay have gone on strike. In fact, the main demands of most people are the same: the struggle against low wages, gruelling work, and bad treatment. The poor eke out an existence as best they can under the circumstances, but it finally becomes unendurable. Today there are about a lakh to a lakh and a half people on strike in Bombay. Only one mill is functioning.

The fact is that new looms have been bought, in which one person has to work on two looms and thus has to put in double the effort. The demands include raising the wages of such workers specially, but also ask for an increase in the salaries of all the workers and a stipulation of not more than 8 hours of work. These days, strikes are popular. The Jamshedpur mill workers have similar demands. The strikes are on the rise there as well. The scavengers are on strike, and the entire city is in a mess. If we do not allow these brothers who serve us the maximum to come close to us, cast them off, calling them 'scavenger-scavenger' and take advantage of their poverty, and make them work for very low wages, and even without wages! Great! Finally, these people, too, would finally rise against this. They can bring people, especially in the cities, to their knees in just a few days. Their awakening is a happy development. Some people were fired from the Liluah Workshop, and there was some issue regarding wages, so they went on strike. Later it was declared that the posts of several thousands of workers would be abolished, and they would not be taken back even after the end of the strike. This created a sensation. But the strike is going strong. Gentlemen like Spratt are working very hard. People should support them in every way and put an end to the efforts being made to break the strike. We want all peasants and workers to unite and fight for their rights.

What is Anarchism?

This essay is originally in three parts. We have added a fourth part, which is Bhagat Singh's article on Nihilism, focusing on Russian Nihilists. Lenin's older brother, Aleksandr Ulyanov, was part of the Nihilist movement in Russia. He was hanged in 1887 at the age of twenty-one for plotting to kill Czar Alexander III.

Bhagat Singh, like the Ghadarites, was influenced by European and Russian anarchist thought, such as that of Peter Kropotkin. He was not an anarchist, though the term, anarcho-communist, would not be an unreasonable description of his political philosophy. That is, he was a communist in arguing for the abolition of private ownership of the means of production and the establishment of full collective provision of goods and services. However, he was justifiably suspicious of the state, irrespective of who wielded political power. Socialism from the ground up would indeed have been his ideal had he lived longer.

In part II of this essay, note the reference to the U.S. anarchists Nicola Sacco and Bartolomeo Vanzetti, executed by the state of Massachusetts in 1927. The words of Bhagat Singh just before death, given in the introduction, are comparable to those of Bartolomeo Vanzetti to Judge Thayer, who ordered their deaths: 'If it had not been for these things, I might have lived out my life talking at street corners to scorning men. I might have died, unmarked, unknown, a failure. Now we are not a failure. This our career and our triumph. Never in our full life could we hope to do such work for tolerance, for justice, for man's understanding of man as now we do by accident. Our words – our lives – our pain – nothing! The taking of our lives – lives of a good shoemaker and a poor fish peddler – all! That last moment belongs to us – that agony is our triumph.'

Today, there is a lot of unrest in the world. Well-known scholars are engaged in establishing peace in the world; however, the peace that is sought to be established is not a temporary one, but something that can be everlasting. Several great souls have sacrificed their lives to achieve it, and people continue to do so. But today, we are slaves. Our eyesight is weak; our brains are dull. Our heart is weak and weeping over its weakness. How can we worry about world peace when we are not able to do anything for our own country? We can only call it our misfortune. We are being ruined by our own conservative ideas. We are trapped in the illusion of finding God and heaven and seek redemption for our souls. We don't take more than an instant to refer to Europe as materialistic. We pay no attention to their great ideas. Because we are more inclined towards spiritual thought! Because we believe in renunciation! We should not even speak of this material world! We have come to such a pass that one wants to weep at the condition of the world, but the situation is improving in the twentieth century. European thought is beginning to make an impact on the youth's thinking. And the youth that wants to progress in the world should study the great and noble ideas of the modern age.

A person's knowledge is incomplete without understanding fully what voices are being raised in society today against oppression, or the ideas are being born for the establishment of permanent peace in the world. Today we are listening to summarized versions of a lot many ideas of communism and socialism etc. Anarchism is thought to be the highest ideal among all these. This essay is being written regarding anarchism.

The people fear the word 'anarchist'. When a person rises to fight for his freedom, armed with a pistol or a bomb, then all the 'bureaucrats' and their underlings scream 'Anarchist-Anarchist!' and try to frighten the world. An anarchist is considered to be a very terrible person, who has no mercy in his heart, who sucks blood, who is delirious with joy at destruction and ruin. The word 'anarchist' has been given such a bad name that even the revolutionaries of India are referred to as anarchists to make people hate them.

Dr Bhupindra Nath Dutt has mentioned this in the first part of his Bengali book, *Unpublished Political History*, saying that even if the government called them 'anarchist' to defame them, in truth they were a group of people who sought to usher in a new order. And anarchism is a very noble ideal. How was it possible for our common people to think of such a noble ideal, because they could not think of being revolutionaries[1] of ushering in a new age. These people were merely rebels. Anyway![2]

As we mentioned earlier, the word 'anarchist' was given a bad name. This word was slandered in the same way that selfish capitalists slandered words like 'Bolshevik', 'socialist', etc. Yet anarchists are the most sensitive and ardent well-wishers of the entire world. Even if we disagree with their views, sobriety, love for the people, spirit of sacrifice and genuineness cannot be doubted.

The word 'anarchist', for which the Hindi word *araajk* is used, is derived from a Greek word which means (an = not, arche = rule), that is, no government of any kind (negation of government).[3] Human beings have always had the desire to be as free as possible, and from time to time, the idea of complete freedom, which is the principle of anarchism, has been mooted. For example, a long time ago, a Greek philosopher said, 'We wish neither to belong to the governing class nor to the governed'.[4]

I consider that the feeling of world fraternity in India and the

1 Insert: beyond rebelling
2 The Punjabi words *Raj-paltau* and *jug-paltau* can both be translated as 'revolutionary', but there is an important distinction between them. *Jug-paltau*, composed of '*jug*' meaning 'world' and '*paltau*' meaning 'complete change', connotes people who have the ideal of societal/system revolution. *Raj-paltau* ('*raj*' meaning government or state) are people who wish to overthrow the government/state only.
3 Sentence originally in English.
4 Quotation originally in English.

Sanskrit phrase *Vasudhev Kutumbkam* conveys the same sense. Even if we cannot reach any conclusive proposition based on our ancient beliefs, we still have to believe that these thoughts were placed before and openly propagated in the world at the beginning of the nineteenth century by the French philosopher Proudhon. That is why he is called the father of anarchism. He began to propagate anarchism, and later one brave Russian man Bakunin, did a lot of work to make it successful. Later several anarchists like Johann Most and Prince Kropotkin were born. These days, Mrs Emma Goldman and Alexander Berkman propagate this in America. About anarchism, Mrs Goldman writes:

> Anarchism: The philosophy of a new social order based on liberty unrestricted by man-made law. The theory that all forms of Government rest on violence, and are therefore wrong and harmful, as well as unnecessary.[5]

This tells us that anarchists do not wish for any kind of government, and this is true. But such a thought scares us. Several bogies are raised in our minds. We should remain fearful of the ghosts of the preceding English rule even after setting up our government and keep on trembling in fear – this is the policy of our rulers. Under such circumstances, how can we think even for one moment that such a day will dawn when we can live happily and freely without a government? But this is, in fact, our own weakness. The ideal or the feeling is not to be blamed.

The ideal freedom that is imagined in anarchism is a complete liberation, according to which neither God nor religion should oppress our minds, nor should the temptation of money or material world overtake us, or the body could be shackled or controlled by any kind of governmental structure. This means that broadly, they wished to eradicate three things from this world completely:

5 Quotation originally in English.

1. The Church, God (and religion)
2. The State (Government)
3. Private Property

This subject is very interesting and vast, and much can be written about it, but we cannot stretch this essay too much due to the paucity of space. So we shall discuss the issues only broadly.

GOD AND RELIGION

Let us first consider God and religion. Now even in Hindustan, voices are being raised against both these demons, but in Europe, a revolution had risen in the last century itself. They begin with reference to the age when people were ignorant; in those times, they were afraid of everything, especially supernatural powers. They completely lacked self-confidence and called themselves 'puppets of dust'. They say that religion, the supernatural and God are the result of the same ignorance, and that is why the illusion of their entity must be eliminated. Also that from their very childhood, children are taught that – God is everything, man is nothing.[6] Man is merely a statue of clay. Such thoughts crowding a person's mind erode his self-confidence. He begins to feel that he is very feeble. In this way, he is always fearful. Till the time this fear remains, complete happiness and peace cannot be attained.

In Hindustan, it was Gautam Buddha who first denied the existence of God. He had no belief in God. Even now there are a few ascetics who do not believe in the existence of God. Sohom Swami of Bengal is one such example. These days is Niralamba Swami. Recently, a book by Sohom Swami called *Common Sense* has been published in English. He has written robustly against the existence of God, trying to prove his proposition, but he does not become an anarchist. He does not wander about aimlessly using

6 Originally in English.

'renunciation' and 'yoga' as pretexts. In this manner, the existence of God is being brought to an end in this scientific age, which will eradicate the very name of religion. In fact, the leader of the anarchists, Bakunin, has thoroughly insulted God in his book, *God and the State*. He placed the Biblical story and said that God made the world and man in his own image. Thank you very much! But he also warned against tasting the fruit of the forbidden tree of knowledge. Actually, God did create Adam and Eve for his own amusement, but he wanted them to remain his slaves forever and to never raise their head before him. So he gave them the gifts of the entire world but no intelligence. This state of affairs encouraged Satan to move forward – 'but here steps in Satan, the eternal rebel, the first free thinker and the emancipator of the world'.[7] He stepped forward, taught man to rebel and offered the fruit of the forbidden tree of knowledge. And that was enough for the omnipotent, omniscient God to lose his temper with a low-class, mean-minded mentality and he began to curse the world he himself had created. Wonderful!

The question that arises is why God made a world full of such sorrow. To enjoy the spectacle? In that case, he is crueler than the Roman tyrant, Nero. Is that his miracle? What is the need for such a miraculous God? The debate is growing. So we'll conclude it right here by stating that religion has always been used by the selfish, the capitalists for their personal good. History bears witness to that. 'Have patience!', 'Look at your own deeds!' The havoc that such a philosophy has brought to mankind is evident for all to see.

People ask what would happen if we deny the existence of God? Sin would grow in the world. Chaos would reign. But the anarchists say that man would then grow to such a stature that without the greed of heaven and the fear of hell, he would shun bad deeds and begin to do good things. In actual fact, the reality is that in Hindustan, in the *Gita*, a world-famous book, Shri Krishna,

---

7 Quotation originally in English.

even while inspiring Arjuna to work selflessly without expectation
of fruit lures him with visions of heaven after death and the crown
of a king after victory in the battle. But today when we look at
the sacrifices made by the anarchists, one wishes to kiss their
feet. Sacco and Vanzetti's stories have been read by our readers.
There is neither any desire to flatter God nor any avariciousness
to enjoy the pleasures of heaven, nor any expectation of the bliss
of reincarnation. To sacrifice one's life for the people and for truth
with a smile on one's face is no small thing. The anarchists say
that once people become completely liberated, their character will
become very noble. Anyway, there can be long debates on each
and every question, but we do not have enough space.

PART II

The next thing they wish is to do away with the government.
If we look for the roots of political power, we arrive at two
conclusions. Some people believe that the caveman's intelligence
evolved gradually, and people began to live together in groups.
Political power was born in this way. This is called the theory of
evolution. The other theory is that people needed to get together
and to organize in order to fight off wild animals and to fulfill
other needs. Then these groups began to fight with each other
and each one of them was afraid of the more powerful enemy.
So people cooperated to establish a political order. This is called
Utilitarianism. We may pick both. The evolutionists can be asked
why only now evolution has come to an end. Panchayati Raj is
followed by anarchism, and the answer to the others is that now
there is no need for any government. This debate has taken place
earlier. Even if we pay little attention to this or other such things,
we shall have to agree that the people had agreed to a contract,
which the famous French thinker, Rousseau, called a Social
Contract. According to the contract, a person would surrender a

part of his freedom, a part of his income, in return for which he would be provided with security and peace.

After all this, what is worth considering is whether this contract was fulfilled. After establishing the government, the State and the Church hatched a conspiracy. People were told that these persons, the rulers, had been sent by God.[8] People were afraid of God, and the king was able to carry out willful oppression. The Tsar in Russia and Louis in France are good examples to reveal the truth of this matter, because this conspiracy could not be carried out for too long; Pope Gregory and King Henry fell out with each other. The Pope incited the people against King Henry's rule, and Henry shattered the bogey of religion. The meaning is that selfish people fought, and these misconceptions were destroyed. Anyway, people rose in rebellion again and killed the cruel Louis. The entire world was in a state of chaos. Democratic governments were established, but complete freedom was still not won. On one side, when the Austrian minister, Metternich, was oppressing people and thus disillusioning them through autocratic royal rule, on the other side in America, the poor slaves were in a miserable condition in democracy. The French masses were struggling time and again to raise themselves from the morass of poverty. Even today France has democracy but people do not have complete freedom. That is the reason the anarchists say that no government is required. In every other thing, they are similar to the communists, but one or two things differ. The eminent communist, Karl Marx's well-known friend, Friedrich Engels, has written about his own and Marx's communism; and it is our ideal as well: 'Communism also looks forward to a period in the evolution of the society when the State will become superfluous and having no longer any function to perform, will die away'.[9]

This means that political power should disappear and people

8 Theory of divine right of kings.
9 Quotation originally in English.

should have a sense of fraternity. Italy's famous political thinker, Machiavelli, believed that some form of rule should always prevail, whether it is a democracy or a monarchy. He believed in strong rule; like an iron fist. But the anarchists ask what is soft or hard. They want neither a soft nor a strong government. They say: 'Undermine the whole conception of a State and then and then only we have Liberty worth having'.[10]

People would say that that is absurd; if there is no government, there would be no law, no police to enforce the law, and this would lead to chaos. But they say this view is also wrong. The famous political philosopher, David Thoreau, said, 'Law never made a man whit more just, and by means of their respect for it even the well disposed are daily made gents of injustice'.[11]

There doesn't seem to be any untruth in this. We can see that as law becomes more rigid, corruption also increases. It is an ordinary complaint that earlier without any written agreement, thousands of rupees would be exchanged and no one would cheat. Now agreements have signatures, thumb impressions, witnesses and are registered. But fraud is on the rise. Then the solution they suggest is that the needs of every person should be met, everything should go according to his wish, and there would be no sin or crime.

'Crime is naught but misdirected energy. So long as every institution of today, economic, political, social and moral conspires to misdirect human energy into wrong channels, so long as most people are out of place doing the things they loathe to do, living a life they hate to live, crime will be inevitable and all the laws on the statutes can only increase but never do away with crime'.[12] (Originally in English)

If a person has complete freedom, then he would be able to do things according to his own will. There would be no injustice.

---

10 Quotation originally in English.
11 Quotation originally in English.
12 Quotation originally in English.

If the exploitation by the capitalists does not end, even the most stringent of laws would not help. People say that human nature is such that it cannot survive without some government. Human beings can cause a great deal of harm if they are not kept on a leash. Commenting on human nature in his book, *The Principles of Politics*, the author, Lord says that ants can live in a group; animals can live in a group, but not human beings.[13] Man is greedy, inhuman and idle by nature. Hearing such talk, Emma Goldman lost her temper and in *Anarchism and Other Essays*, she wrote, 'Every fool from king to policeman, from a flat-headed person to the visionless dabbler in science presumes to speak authoritatively of human nature'.[14] She says that the bigger a fool a person is, the more stridently his opinion in this matter is expressed. Have human beings ever been tested by giving them complete freedom, that one is forever crying over their flaws? She feels that small elected bodies should be made and the work be carried out freely.

PRIVATE PROPERTY

The third most important thing is Private Property. In fact, it is the question of filling one's belly that makes the world goes round. It is for this that sermons preaching patience, contentment, etc. are crafted. Till now everything in life was done for the sake of property; now the anarchists, communists, socialists are all against property. They say, "Property is robbery"[15] . . . 'but without risk or danger to the robber'.[16]

The notion of amassing property makes a person greedy. Then he becomes increasingly more stone-hearted. Mercy and humanity begin to fade from his heart. A government is required for the security of property. This again leads to an escalation of

13 The author is Arthur Ritchie Lord.
14 Quotation originally in English.
15 Proudhon.
16 Emma Goldman. Quotation originally in English.

greed and the ultimate end of that is – first, imperialism, and then war. Bloodshed and a lot of destruction. There would be no greed if everything becomes common property. Everyone would work together. There would be no fear of theft or robbery. There would be no need for the police, jail, court, or army. And those with fat bellies and the parasites would also work. Production will be more even with fewer hours of work. People can have good education as well. There would be spontaneous peace, and prosperity would increase. That is, they emphasize how very important it is to eradicate ignorance from the world.

In fact, property is the most important issue; that is why another essay is required to debate this issue. The real issue arises from bread; Karl Manning averred clearly, 'Ask for work and if they don't give you work, ask for bread and if they do not give you work or bread, then take bread'.[17] Meaning that if one doesn't get either work or food, then steal food. What right does one have to gorge on cakes when others may not even get dry crumbs of bread? He also asked why a person born in a destitute household should be forced to scrimp and save, whereas a person born in a prosperous household should grow fat on idleness. The precept 'Let riches add to riches' should be stopped. It is for these reasons that they shattered the illusion of the sanctity of private property for the sake of the principle of equal opportunity. They say that property is attached to corruption, and law is needed to protect it which in turn requires government. In fact, this is at the root of all evil. As soon as this is removed, everything will be all right. What do they really want; how will it really work? This is a vast question.

It has been stated above that anarchists are anti-God and religion because these cause mental slavery. Secondly, they are against the government, because this is physical slavery. They say that it is wrong to inspire human beings to do good by the lure of heaven or fear of hell, or by wielding the stick of law. And it is an

17 Quotation originally in English.

insult to the nobility of man. One should attain knowledge freely and then work according to one's will and spend one's life happily. People say that this would mean that we wish to keep mankind in a state of wildness; as we were at the beginning. This is a false interpretation; in olden days, due to ignorance, people could not go far away. But now with full awareness, establishing mutual relations in the world, man should live free. There should be no greed for money. And the issue of money should be eradicated.

In the next essay, we shall write about some other things regarding this philosophy, different viewpoints, history and the reasons for its unpopularity, and the reason for the inclusion of violence in this.

PART III

In the previous two essays, we have presented the popular notions regarding anarchy. The curiosity of the public cannot be assuaged merely with these two essays about such an important topic that has recently emerged before the world as a reaction to the world's trite thoughts and traditions. Several doubts raise their heads. Even so, we are placing the broad principles before the readers so that they may understand the main ideas. Now, similarly, we shall write about the ideology of Communism, Socialism and Nihilism so that Hindustan becomes familiar with the ideologies currently prevalent in the world. But before writing about any other topic, the intention is to write down several important and interesting facts about Anarchism, which also touches upon the history of Nihilism; that is, what have the Anarchists done so far? How did they acquire such an unsavoury reputation?

We have presented their thoughts above. Now we want to discuss what they did to give a practical shape to their ideas and how they confronted very powerful governments with the use of force and even staked their lives in that conflict.

The fact is that when oppression and exploitation cross a

certain limit, when peaceful and free movement is crushed, then those who are always doers begin their work secretly and are ready to fight oppression as soon as they see it. When the poor working class was being exploited appallingly in Europe, all their efforts were crushed or were being crushed, at that time, Mikhail Bakunin, who belonged to a prosperous family in Russia and was a top officer in an arms factory, was sent to Poland to deal with the revolt. There the manner in which the rebels were being brutally crushed brought about a change in his mindset, and he became a revolutionary. Ultimately, his thoughts turned towards anarchism. He resigned from his job in 1834. Subsequently, he reached Paris through Berlin and Switzerland. Those days, most of the governments were against him due to his views. Till 1864, he evolved his beliefs and propagated them among the working class.

Later he gained control over the International Workingmen's Association, and from 1860 to 1870, he consolidated his group. On the 4th of September, 1870, an announcement was made to establish the Third Republic in Paris. There was unrest and riots in several places in France against the capitalist government. Bakunin was involved in these. They were the stronger side. But in a few days, they lost and left the place.

In 1873, there was a revolt in Spain. He joined in and fought. For some time the matter was really hot, then it finally ended in a defeat. When they returned from there, a fight was raging in Italy. He went there and took the reins of the battle in his hands. After some initial differences, Garibaldi also joined him. After a few days of opposition, they lost there as well. In this manner, his entire life was spent in waging battles. When he grew old, he wrote a letter to his compatriots saying that he would relinquish the leadership, so that their work did not suffer. Finally, in 1876, he died due to an illness.

Later, four very strong people got ready for this task with great determination. They were Carlo Cafiero, an Italian, belonging to quite a prosperous family. The second was Malatesta; he was a great doctor. But he renounced everything to become a revolutionary. The third was Paul Brousse, who was also a famous doctor. The fourth was Peter Kropotkin. He was from a Russian royal family. It was often said jokingly that he was to become the Tsar. They were all devotees of Bakunin. He said that they had propagated enough with the tongue but it had had no effect. They were tired of hearing about newfangled ideologies. These hadn't had any effect on the public. So now it was time to propagate action. Kropotkin said,

A single deed makes more propaganda in a few days than a thousand pamphlets. The Government defends itself. It rages pitilessly, but by this, it only caused further deeds to be committed by one or more persons and drives the insurgents to heroism. One deed brings forth another, opponent's join the mutiny, the Government splits into fractions, harshness intensifies the conflict, concessions come too late, the revolution breaks out.[18]

Peter Kropotkin was one of the Russian revolutionaries. After being arrested, Peter was incarcerated in the Peter and Paul Fortress. He escaped from this very strongly guarded prison and began to disseminate his ideas in Europe. These things tell us his state of mind in those days.

First of all, he celebrated the anniversary of the establishment of the rule of the workers in Berne city in France. This was the 18th of March, 1876. He took out a procession of workers on that day and got into a scuffle with the police in the streets. A riot ensued when the policemen tried to uproot their red flag. Several policemen were seriously injured. In the end, all these people were arrested and sentenced for 10 to 40 days in jail.

In the month of April, they incited the peasants of Italy and set off riots in several parts of the country. Even there, their

18 Quotation originally in English.

companions were arrested, out of whom several were released. Now their strategy was a kind of publicity. That is why they used to say, 'Neither money nor organizations nor literature was needed any longer [for their propaganda work]. One human being in revolt with torch or dynamite was off to instruct the world'. [19]

From the next year onwards in 1868, such activities were on the rise. An attempt was made to assassinate the Italian emperor Umberto when he was travelling in a motorcar with his daughter. Emperor Wilhelm I of Germany was shot at by an ordinary youth. After three weeks, Dr Karl Nobiling also tried to shoot at the Emperor from a window. In those days in Germany, the movements of the poor working classes were silenced brutally. After that, it was decided in a meeting that the corrupt capitalist class and the government and the police that colluded with it, should be made frightened in whatever way it was possible.

On the 15th of December, 1833, a notorious police officer by the name of Ulubek was killed in Willirid Floridsdorf. On the 23rd of June, 1884, Rouget was hanged for this crime. The very next day, Blatik, a police officer, was killed to avenge the hanging. The Austrian government was enraged, and in Vienna, the police besieged several people and arrested them; and two of them were hanged. There were strikes in Leon. One of the striking men, Fournier, shot his capitalist owner. He was awarded a pistol in a ceremony held to honour him. In 1888, there was a lot of unrest there, and the silk workers were starving. At that time, the capitalist's newspaper-owning friends and other rich friends were busy living it up elsewhere. A bomb was thrown there. The rich were terrified. Sixty anarchists were held. Only 3 were acquitted. But still the search for the actual bomb thrower did not come to an end. He was finally caught and hanged. And in this way, this line of thinking gained momentum. And then, wherever there were strikes, murders would take place. The anarchists were blamed for

---

19 Quotation originally in English.

all this, and as a result, people would shudder at the very mention of them.

A German anarchist, Johann Most, who had worked in an office, went to America in 1882. He also began to place his ideas before the people. He was a very good orator and impressed his audience in America. In 1886, several strikes were called in Chicago and other places. In one paper factory, an anarchist called Spies was giving a speech. The owners of the factory tried to shut the factory. A riot erupted. The police were called in, and they began firing as soon as they came. Six men were killed, and several were injured. Spies was furious. He himself composed a notice and decreed that the workers should unite to avenge the murder of their innocent comrades. The next day, on the 4th of May, 1886, the Haymarket procession was to be taken out. The Mayor of the city had come to watch it. He saw nothing objectionable going on. So he went there. Later the police came and, without any provocation, began to beat up people and asked them to stop the procession. Just then a bomb was thrown at the police and many policemen were killed. Several people were arrested and hanged. As he was leaving, one of them said,

I repeat, I am a sworn enemy of this present state of affairs. I want this political establishment to be destroyed, and we should be able to wield political power ourselves. You may laugh that I shall no longer be able to throw bombs, but let me tell you that your oppression has forced every worker to handle and throw a bomb. You should know that after I am hanged, another one will be born. I see you with revulsion in my eyes and want to trample your State. Hang me.

Anyway, several such incidents happened. But there are a couple of other famous incidents. The American President, McKinley, was shot at, and then there was a strike in the Carnegie steel company. The workers were being brutalized here. The owner,

Henry C. Frick, was injured by an anarchist, Alexander, who was sentenced for life.[20] Anyway, this is how anarchism spread to America and began to be practiced.

In Europe, too, things were bad. The anarchists' feud with the police and the government had intensified. Finally, a youth named Vaillant threw a bomb in the Assembly, but a woman caught his hand and stopped him, as a result of which nothing much happened, except that some Deputies were injured. He offered an explanation in a ringing voice, 'It takes a loud voice to make the deaf hear.[21] Now you will punish me, but I have no fear because I have struck at your hearts. You, who oppress the poor and those who work hard, starve, and you suck their blood and take pleasure in life. I have hurt you. Now it is your turn'.

Several appeals were made on his behalf. Even the most seriously injured member of the Assembly requested the jury to show mercy to him, but the jury, presided over by a person named Carnot, refused to pay any attention and sentenced him to death by hanging. Later an Italian boy stabbed Carnot with a knife with the name Vaillant written on it.

In this manner, unable to endure any more oppression, bombs were set off even in Spain, and finally, an Italian killed a minister. In a similar manner, the Emperor of Greece and the Empress of Austria were also attacked. In 1900, Gaetano Bresci killed the Emperor of Italy, Umberto. In this manner, these people smilingly gave up their lives for the sake of the poor . . . kissed the gallows joyfully. That is why; even those opposed to them could do nothing against them. Their last martyrs, Sacco and Vanzetti, have been hanged only last year. The courage with which these people went to the gallows is known to everyone.

And this is the brief history of anarchism and its activities. Next time we shall write an essay about Communism.

---

20 Alexander Berkman.
21 Quotation originally in English.

Russia has given birth to a very great novelist – Ivan Turgenev. In 1862 he wrote a novel, *Fathers and Sons*. There was a great hue and cry over the publication of this novel because it depicted the modern views of the youth. It was Turgenev who first used the word 'nihilism'. Nihilism means not to believe in anything (*nihil* – nothing); the literal meaning is one who believes in nothing. Though in reality, these people were the opponents of the traditional rituals and customs and bad practices. These people were fed up with the country's mental slavery, so they protested against it. They not only spoke against it but practiced what they preached. Turgenev says that the hero of his novel is not a fictional character, on the other hand, he was a real person with such ideas, and these ideas had become quite common. He says that the idea of the novel occurred to him one day while he was lazing in the sun. And he wrote the book by expanding the ideas a bit. The hero is Bazarov. He is a kind of atheist; completely opposed to conventional rituals. He does not find verbal sycophancy very attractive. He is blunt. What he says, he does. He says everything to one's face, immediately and clearly, so much so that at times, he appears to be very brash. He is an opponent of poetry. He does not like music. But he is a lover of freedom. He is a big supporter of freedom for the common people. He fights the prevailing mindset of the people.

The picture of a real nihilist is a little different from this because the hero of the novel has some fictional elements along with reality. The true picture of nihilism is delineated in quite another manner. 'The Nihilism of 1861 – a philosophical system especially dealing with what Mr Herbert Spencer would call religious, governmental and social fetishism'.[22]

The Russian revolutionary prince, Kropotkin, uttered these words while referring to nihilism in 1861, which means that

---

22 Quotation originally in English.

nihilism was just one of the philosophies of those times, which was in relation to religious superstition, social injustice, narrow-mindedness, and the excesses of the government, and preached against the superstitions created to perpetuate such things. The fact is that the youth had jumped into the fray to protest against the conditions of the times. They believed that it was necessary to destroy every existing thing completely. Even without a complete answer to what would happen later or should happen, they believed that they would be able to build a beautiful world.

'Nihilism was destructive because it wanted a wholesale destruction but with a pleasure of building up.'[23]

Gradually these ideas became more popular and a large number of young people became enamored of them. They wanted 'to liberate the people from the chains of tradition and autocracy of the Tsar'.

These were the kinds of things being propagated then. Conditions changed. In those days, a large number of slaves had been freed, but most of them had not been given any land to till and earn, or at least, escape starvation. Whatever little land had been allotted to them was taxed so heavily that people starved, and there was a terrible famine in 1867. Those days Government arrangements were unspeakably bad. There was so much oppression that the public could bear it no longer. Harassed by official excesses, even big government officials became revolutionaries. Ossinsky and Kviatkovsky, who were hanged in 1880, had been government servants earlier. Similarly, many other well-known officers, even judges, became revolutionaries.

The oppression on the people became unbearable. Good books were not allowed to be propagated among the youth. There were some associations that would pick up good books from the publishers and distribute them free of cost or at cost price. All these books were censored by the government. But when the

23 Quotation originally in English.

government realized that they were being used for propaganda, they decided to destroy all book publishers and distributors and began to repress these people. From 1861 to 1870, every possible and appropriate way to improve the condition of the people and show the right way to the government was tried, but it had no impact.

In such a situation, a lot of people would sit twiddling their thumbs, waiting for times to change by themselves. How they would improve – nobody knew. People remained passive, just placing trust in God. But a fire had been lit in the hearts of the youth. There was no trust in God in their hearts. It had become difficult for them to sit quietly, without doing anything.

Prince Kropotkin writes in an essay:

> There are periods when some generations are penetrated with the noblest feelings of altruism and self-sacrifice, when life becomes utterly impossible – morally and physically impossible – for the man and woman who feels that he is not doing duty; and so it was with the youth in Russia.[24]

In 1871, a large number of young men and women ran away to Western Europe. They studied there. Most of them were in Switzerland. They got permission to return to their country. They returned with new ideas of community and unity. They began propaganda immediately upon their return and the Tsar got all of them arrested and they were exiled to Siberia. Their movement then assumed a covert shape.

At that time, three parties were working. Their leaders were Chernyshevsky, Ishutin, and Nechaif. Earlier, the slogan was that they should be with the public, that is, they should sympathize with the public and try to uplift them. But now a new voice was heard that said that they should all become the public, that is, blend

---

24 Quotation originally in English.

with it. As soon as this voice was heard, people were inspired to set such amazing examples of sacrifice that, even today, the world cannot find anything to match them.

But first, it is necessary to discuss why this voice rose? Prince Kropotkin writes:

> Until of late – however the Russian peasant has always regarded the man who wears broad cloth and neither ploughs, nor hews, nor hammers, nor digs side by side with him, as an enemy. We wanted faith and love from him; and to obtain them it was necessary to live their life. [Originally in English]

Ah! Today we make exaggerated claims to liberate Hindustan, but how many people are ready to make such sacrifices? How many will leave their cities and be prepared to go to the villages and live in unhygienic conditions like peasants? There a unique situation had been created.

> Young men left their classrooms, their regiments and their desks, learned the smith's trade, or the cobbler's or the ploughman's, and went to work among the villages. Highborn and wealthy ladies betook themselves to factories, worked fifteen or sixteen hours a day at machine, slept in dog holes with peasants, went barefoot as our working women go, bringing water from the river for the house.[25]

Just one passion. One obsession. To make those poor workers aware of their miserable condition and to offer a solution. What a big sacrifice it is! The young women did a marvellous job. Madam Catherine Breshkovsky, the woman known as the grandmother of the Russian Revolution, was a wealthy and beautiful lady. She also joined them. First, she threw acid on herself to destroy her beauty

---

25 Quotation originally in English.

so that it did not hinder her work among the common people. Oh! How many people would have the courage to do that in Hindustan today? In Russia, young men and women run away from home and spend their lives in this kind of work. But how many young people in Hindustan have this yearning to liberate their country? One sees quite intelligent people around, but everyone is concerned only with his or her individual life and happiness. How can we then hope to improve our condition and that of our country? The youth of Russia spent the last part of the previous century in this kind of propaganda work. There are several beautiful anecdotes about women being inspired to come out of their homes.

Sonia was a priest's daughter. Revolutionary women had just joined her school as teachers. Listening to their teachings, Sonia was inspired to do patriotic work. One day she ran away from home. But her father caught her after a few days. Then the party made arrangements to liberate her from home. A young man posed as her boyfriend and went to her house. He convinced her father and married her. The story is very interesting and has been published in *The Heroes and Heroines of Russia*. We shall present the story to our readers if we get a chance. Anyway, readers shall get an idea about the kind of work underfoot in Russia through this brief description.

At first, the work was done openly, but then the government cracked down brutally on them, and several thousands of people were sent to Siberia. Thousands were arrested without warrants. They were locked in dark cells for four or five years. Later, cases were filed against about a hundred people. Some were sentenced. One among these thousands of cases became famous by the name of 'the Trial of the Hundred and Ninety-Three'. To be brief, as per the government figures, thousands of people were arrested and kept in dark, dingy cells for four to five years. Three hundred were kept in jail for a very long time out of which 11 died of tuberculosis, four slashed their own throats, and many others also tried to kill themselves like this. Cases were filed against 193 people. An extremely unjust court sentenced them to ten years imprisonment just because they were the propagators, even though there was very little evidence against them. 90 were acquitted and the rest were given rigorous punishment from 7 to 10 years and then exile to Siberia for the rest of their lives. In a related matter, a woman was given 9 to 10 years of rigorous punishment only for giving a communist pamphlet to a worker.

Faced with this level of oppression, the work took a more covert and prudent form. And the feeling of revenge grew. More often than not, some wicked secret service officer would arrest and exile anyone he wished to. He would be given a reward, but this endangered the life of the youth. Harassed by this, these people also thought of eliminating these tyrants.

It is said that on the 16th of April, 1866, when Karakozoff shot at the Tsar, it was the work of nihilists. And the shooting at the Tsar the next year in Paris by a Polish gentleman, Berezovsky, was also a party action. But about the present situation, Kropotkin has written that the Tsar was never more secure as he was in the initial stages of their work. They thought of using force only in the end when they had exhausted other avenues. At first, they always tried to protect the Tsar. Once when some young man reached St Petersburg to kill the Tsar, the members of the party prevented him from doing so.

But later, the work started with gusto. In 1879, one of the arrested persons, who still had not been charge-sheeted formally, was caned because he did not rise and greet the police officer, and the rest of the arrested people who supported him were beaten badly on the orders of General Trepov. At this, a young woman, Vera Zasulich, shot at General Trepov. He did not die, and a case was filed against the young woman. She was acquitted. The police tried to arrest her again, but the public snatched her away.

When the Russian revolutionaries realized that no one helped them and that there was no law to protect them, they began to take care of their own protection. The police would encircle the houses of people early in the morning; they even stripped the women of their clothes to search them. The people were harassed. Murmuring began that this did not happen in other countries. They would also not let it happen. Kovalsky was the first one to do this in Odessa. He confronted the police. The oppression grew more intense. And then, the taking of revenge began. The use of force for self-protection began to be considered appropriate. First, five spies, then three officers were murdered, in return for which seventeen young people were hanged. Then this chain reaction continued – revenge, then gallows, then . . ..

In 1879, the word 'nihilism' came to connote only the bursting of bombs and the shooting of guns. The Tsar also finally lost his patience and decided to teach them a lesson.

And this was the catalyst needed to set all of them to complete this task. On the 14th of April, 1879, Solovioff had shot at the Tsar, but the Tsar escaped. The same year the Winter Palace of the Tsar was bombed with dynamite, but the Tsar still escaped. The next year, when the Tsar was going from St. Petersburg to Moscow, the train on which he was travelling was bombed. Several compartments were destroyed, but the Tsar escaped yet again. On the 13th of March, 1881, when the Tsar was returning with his special squad after inspecting the parade of his horses and platoon, a bomb was hurled at him. The carriage was smashed, and the Tsar got off to take a look at the servant, saying, 'thank God, I'm saved'. But another young man, Grinevizky, moved forward, and said as he hurled another bomb, 'Tsar, it is too early to thank God'. The bomb exploded, and the Tsar was killed. Thousands of people were arrested. Many were sent to the gallows. Five people were hanged publicly. The most famous among them was a woman called Sophia Perovskya.

The party was suppressed at that time. Then several other parties rose. But the history of the Nihilist Party is just this much. The Nihilists were judged unfairly by the people and given a bad name like the anarchists. An English newspaper drew a cartoon in which two nihilists stand with bombs and dynamite amid destruction. One asks, 'Brother, does anything remain?' and the other answers, 'Just the globe of the earth'. The first says, 'Let me put dynamite on that too'. This is complete misrepresentation. Oscar Wilde wrote a play titled *Vera the Nihilist*, which depicted the nihilists in a positive light, but there are several errors. Another book, *The Career of a Nihilist*, was published. This is a readable account. It is an accurate book about nihilists. In Hindi, *Bolshevikon ki Kartoot* (The Action of Bolsheviks) and *Nihilist Rahasya* (Mystery of the Nihilist) have been published. The first has been written by the martyr of Kakori, Shri Ram Prasad Bismil. He has delineated a very pitiful picture of Nihilists. But they have been shown as being only destructive, which is not accurate. They were sincere servants of the people. They were very sacrificing and loved the common people. They were great souls.

Why I am an Atheist

This extended and trenchant essay originated from a request by Bhagat Singh to meet in the Lahore jail with Bhai Randhir Singh, imprisoned for his participation in the 1915 Ghadar party revolt.

Bhai Randhir Singh was a Ghadarite in Lahore Central Jail in 1930–31. Shiv Verma's annotation: 'Baba Randhir Singh . . . was a God-fearing religious man. It pained him to learn that Bhagat Singh was a non-believer. He somehow managed to see Bhagat Singh in the condemned cell and tried to convince him about the existence of God, but failed. Baba lost his temper and said tauntingly: 'You are giddy with fame and have developed an ego which is standing like a black curtain between you and the God'. It was in reply to that remark that Bhagat Singh wrote this article.'

Bhagat Singh wrote an impassioned letter to Bhai Randir Singh, and the latter agreed to meet. However, he implored the young revolutionary to renounce his atheism and embrace the religion in which he was raised. He claimed his word convinced Bhagat Singh to repent and return to the religious fold. But Bhagat Singh, understanding that what he said could be distorted after his death, soon wrote this famous essay, so that people would know what he really believed. This was done in October 1930, and the essay was published in *The People* on 27 September 1931, the first birth anniversary of Bhagat Singh after his execution.[1]

Although believers in many religions have fought for radical change, it remains difficult to reconcile religious beliefs and primarily the actions taken by those who are at the top of religious hierarchies with socialist revolution. In a

---

1 Bhagat Singh's birth anniversary is now widely accepted to fall on 28 September.

straightforward, rational, and impassioned manner, Bhagat Singh puts forth the case for atheism and a foundation for social transformation.

A new question has cropped up. Is it due to vanity that I do not believe in the existence of an omnipotent, omnipresent and omniscient God? I had never imagined that I would ever have to confront such a question. But conversation with some friends has given me a hint that certain of my friends – if I am not claiming too much in thinking them to be so – are inclined to conclude from the brief contact they have had with me, that it was too much on my part to deny the existence of God and that there was a certain amount of vanity that actuated my disbelief. Well, the problem is a serious one. I do not boast to be quite above these human traits. I am a man and nothing more. None can claim to be more. I also have this weakness in me. Vanity does form a part of my nature. Amongst my comrades I was called an autocrat. Even my friend Mr. B.K. Dutt sometimes called me so. On certain occasions I was decried as a despot. Some friends do complain, and very seriously too, that I involuntarily thrust my opinions upon others and get my proposals accepted. That this is true up to a certain extent, I do not deny. This may amount to egotism. There is vanity in me inasmuch as our cult as opposed to other popular creeds is concerned. But that is not personal. It may be, it is only legitimate pride in our cult and does not amount to vanity. Vanity, or to be more precise 'ahankar', is the excess of undue pride in one's self. Whether it is such an undue pride that has led me to atheism or whether it is after very careful study of the subject and after much consideration that I have come to disbelieve in God, is a question that I intend to discuss here. Let me first make it clear that egotism and vanity are two different things.

In the first place, I have altogether failed to comprehend as to how undue pride or vaingloriousness could ever stand in the way of a man in believing in God. I can refuse to recognize the greatness of a really great man, provided I have also achieved a certain amount of popularity without deserving it or without having possessed the qualities really essential or indispensable for the same purpose. That much is conceivable. But in what way can a man believing in God cease believing due to his personal vanity? There are only two ways. The man should either begin to think himself a rival of God or he may begin to believe himself to be God. In neither case can he become a genuine atheist. In the first case he does not even deny the existence of his rival. In the second case as well, he admits the existence of a conscious being behind the screen guiding all the movements of nature. It is of no importance to us whether he thinks himself to be that Supreme Being or whether he thinks the supreme conscious being to be somebody apart from himself. The fundamental is there. His belief is there. He is, by no means an atheist. Well, here I am. I neither belong to the first category nor to the second. I deny the very existence of that Almighty Supreme Being. Why I deny it, shall be dealt with later on. Here I want to clear one thing, that it is not vanity that has actuated me to adopt the doctrines of atheism. I am neither a rival a rival nor an incarnation, nor the Supreme Being Himself. One point is decided, that it is not vanity that has led me to this mode of thinking. Let me examine the facts to disprove this allegation. According to these friends of mine I have grown vainglorious perhaps due to the undue popularity gained during the trials – both Delhi Bomb and Lahore Conspiracy Cases. Well, let us see if their premises are correct. My atheism is not of so recent origin. I had stopped believing in God when I was an obscure young man, of whose existence my above-mentioned friends were not even aware. At least a college student cannot cherish any short of undue pride, which may lead him to atheism. Thought a favourite with some professors and disliked by certain others.

I was never an industrious or a studious boy. I could not get any chance of indulging in such feelings as vanity. I was rather a boy with a very shy nature, who had certain pessimistic dispositions about the future career. And in those days, I was not a perfect atheist. My grandfather under whose influence I was brought up is an orthodox Arya Samajist. An Arya Samajist is anything but an atheist. After finishing my primary education, I joined the D.A.V. School of Lahore and stayed in its Boarding House for full one year. There, apart from morning and evening prayers, I used to recite the 'Gayatri Mantra' for hours and hours. I was a perfect devotee in those days. Later on, I began to live with my father. He is a liberal in as much as the orthodoxy of religions is concerned. It was through his teachings that I aspired to devote my life to the cause of freedom. But he is not an atheist. He is a firm believer. He used to encourage me for offering prayers daily. So this is how I was brought up. In the Non-Cooperation days, I joined the National College. It was there that I began to think liberally and discuss and criticize all the religious problem, even about God. But still I was a devout believer. By that time I had begun to preserve the unshorn and unclipped long hair, but I could never believe in the mythology and doctrines of Sikhism or any other religion. But I had a firm faith in God's existence.

Later on I joined the revolutionary party. The first leader with whom I came in contact, though not convinced, could not dare to deny the existence of God. On my persistent inquiries about God, he used to say: 'Pray whenever you want to'. Now this is atheism less courage required for the adoption of that creed. The second leader with whom I came in contact was a firm believer. Let me mention his name – respected Comrade Sachindra Nath Sanyal, now undergoing life transportation in connection with the Kakori Conspiracy Case. From the very first page of his famous and only book, *Bandi Jivan* (Incarcerated Life), the Glory of God is sung vehemently. On the last page of the second part of that beautiful book, his mystic – because of vedantism –praises showered upon God form a very conspicuous part of his thoughts. 'The Revolutionary' distributed throughout India on January 28th, 1925, was, according to the prosecution story, the result of his intellectual labour. Now, as is inevitable in the secret work, the prominent leader expresses his own views, which are very dear to his person, and the rest of the workers have to acquiesce in them, in spite of differences which they might have. In that leaflet, one full paragraph was devoted to praise the Almighty and His rejoicings and doing. That is all mysticism. What I wanted to point out was that the idea of disbelief had not even germinated in the revolutionary party. The famous Kakori martyrs – all four of them – passed their last days in prayers. Ram Prasad Bismil was an orthodox Arya Samajist. Despite his wide studies in the field of socialism and communism, Rajen Lahiri could not suppress his desire of reciting hymns of the Upanishads and the Gita. I saw only one man amongst them, who never prayed and used to say:

'Philosophy is the outcome of human weakness or limitation of knowledge.' He is also undergoing a sentence of transportation for life. But he also never dared to deny the existence of God.

Up to that period I was only a romantic idealist revolutionary. Up till then we were to follow. Now came the time to shoulder the whole responsibility. Due to the inevitable reaction for some time, the very existence of the party seemed impossible. Enthusiastic comrades – nay, leaders –began to jeer at us. For some time, I was afraid that someday I also might not be convinced of the futility of our own program. That was a turning point in my revolutionary career. *Study* was the cry that reverberated in the corridors of my mind. Study to enable yourself with arguments in favour of your cult. I began to study. My previous faith and convictions underwent a remarkable modification. The romance of the violent methods alone which was so prominent amongst our predecessors, was replaced by serious ideas. No more mysticism, no more blind faith. Realism became our cult. Use of force justifiable when resorted to as a matter of terrible necessity: non-violence as policy indispensable for all mass movements. So much about methods. The most important thing was the clear conception of the ideal for which we were to fight. As there were no important activities in the field of action, I got ample opportunity to study various ideals of the world revolution. I studied Bakunin, the anarchist leader, something of Marx, the father of communism, and much of Lenin, Trotsky and others – the men who had successfully carried out a revolution in their country. They were all atheists. Bakunin's *God and State*, though only fragmentary, is an interesting study of the subject. Later still, I came across a book entitled *Common Sense* by Nirlamba Swami. It was only a sort of mystic atheism. This subject became of utmost interest to me. By the end of 1926, I had been convinced as to the baselessness of the theory of the existence of an almighty supreme being who created, guided and controlled the universe. I had given out this disbelief of mine. I began discussion on the subjects with my friends. I had become a pronounced atheist. But what it meant will presently be discussed.

In May 1927, I was arrested at Lahore. The arrest was a surprise. I was quite unaware of the fact that the police wanted me. All of a sudden, while passing through a garden, I found myself surrounded by police. To my own surprise, I was very calm at that time. I did not feel any sensation, nor did I experience any excitement. I was taken into police custody. Next day I was taken to the Railway Police lock-up, where I was to pass full one month. After many days of conversation with the police officials, I guessed that they had some information regarding my connection with the Kakori party and my other activities in connection with the revolutionary movement. They told me that I had been to Lucknow while the trial was going on there, that I had negotiated a certain scheme about their rescue, that after obtaining their approval, we had procured some bombs, that by way of test one of the bombs was thrown in the crowd on the occasion of Dussehra 1926. They further informed me, in my interest, that if I could give any statement throwing some light on the activities of the revolutionary party, I was not to be imprisoned but, on the contrary, set free and rewarded, even without being produced as an approver in the court.

I laughed at the proposal. It was all humbug. People holding ideas like ours do not throw bombs on their own innocent people. One fine morning Mr. Newman, the then Senior Superintendent of C.I.D., came to me. And after much sympathetic talk with me, imparted – to him the extremely sad – news that if I did not give any statement as demanded by them, they would be forced to send me up for trial for conspiracy to wage war in connection with Kakori Case and for brutal murders in connection with Dussehra bomb outrage. And he further informed me that they had evidence enough to get me convicted and hanged. In those days, I believed – though I was quite innocent – the police could do it if they desired. That very day certain police officials began to persuade me to offer my prayers to God regularly, both the times.

Now I was an atheist. I wanted to settle for myself, whether it was in the days of peace and enjoyment alone that I could boast of being an atheist or whether, during such hard times as well; I could stick to those principles of mine. After great consideration, I decided that I could not lead myself to believe in and pray to God. No, I never did. That was the real test, and I came out successful. Never for a moment did I desire to save my neck at the cost of certain other things. So I was a staunch disbeliever; and have ever since been. It was not an easy job to stand that test. 'Belief' softens the hardships, even can make them pleasant. In God man can find very strong consolation and support. Without Him man has to depend upon himself. To stand upon one's own legs amid storms and hurricanes is not a child's play. At such testing moments, vanity – if any – evaporates and man cannot dare to defy the general beliefs. If he does, then we must conclude that he has got certain other strength than mere vanity.

This is exactly the situation now. Judgment is already too well known. Within a week it is to be pronounced. What is the consolation with the exception of the idea that I am going to sacrifice my life for a cause? A God-believing Hindu might be expecting to be reborn as a king, a Muslim or a Christian might dream of the luxuries to be enjoyed in paradise and the reward he is to get for his suffering and sacrifices. But, what am I to expect? I know the moment the rope is fitted around my neck and rafters removed under my feet, that will be the final moment – that will be the last moment. I, or to be more precise, my soul, as interpreted in the metaphysical terminology, shall all be finished there. Nothing further. A short life of struggle with no such magnificent end, shall in itself be the reward, if I have the courage to take it in that light. That is all. With no selfish motive or desire to be awarded here or hereafter, quite disinterestedly, have I devoted my life to the cause of independence, because I could not do otherwise.

The day we find a great number of men and women with this psychology, who cannot devote themselves to anything else than the service of mankind and emancipation of the suffering humanity, that day shall inaugurate the era of liberty. Not to become a king, nor to gain any other rewards here, or in the next birth or after death in paradise, shall they be inspired to challenge the oppressors, exploiters, and tyrants, but to cast off the yoke of serfdom from the neck of humanity and to establish liberty and peace shall they tread this – to their individual selves perilous and to their noble selves the only glorious imaginable – path. Is the pride in their noble cause to be misinterpreted as vanity? Who dares to utter such an abominable epithet? To him I say either he is a fool or a knave. Let us forgive him for he cannot realise the depth, the emotion, the sentiment and the noble feelings that surge in that heart. His heart is dead as a mere lump of flesh, his eyes are weak, the evils of other interests having been cast over them. Self-reliance is always liable to be interpreted as vanity. It is sad and miserable, but there is no help.

You go and oppose the prevailing faith, you go and criticize a hero, a great man who is generally believed to be above criticism because he is thought to be infallible, the strength of your argument shall force the multitude to decry you as vainglorious. This is due to the mental stagnation. Criticism and independent thinking are the two indispensable qualities of a revolutionary. Because Mahatamaji is great, therefore none should criticize him. Because he has risen above, therefore everything he says – maybe in the field of Politics or Religion, Economics or Ethics – is right. Whether you are convinced or not, you must say: 'Yes, that's true'. This mentality does not lead towards progress. It is rather too obviously reactionary.

Because our forefathers had set up a faith in some Supreme Being – the Almighty God –therefore, any man who dares to challenge the validity of that faith, or the very existence of that Supreme Being, he shall have to be called an apostate, a renegade. If his argument are too sound to be refuted by counter-arguments and spirit too strong to be cowed down by the threat of misfortunes that may befall him by the wrath of the Almighty, he shall be decried as vainglorious, his spirit to be denominated as vanity. Then, why do we waste time in this vain discussion? Why try to argue out the whole thing? This question is coming before the public for the first time, and is being handled in this matter of fact way for the first time, hence this lengthy discussion.

As for the first question, I think I have cleared that it is not vanity that has led me to atheism. My way of argument has proved to be convincing or not, that is to be judged by my readers, not me. I know in the present circumstances my faith in God would have made my life easier, my burden lighter, and my disbelief in Him has turned all the circumstances too dry, and the situation may assume too harsh a shape. A little bit of mysticism can make it poetical. But I do not want the help of any intoxication to meet my fate. I am a realist. I have been trying to overpower the instinct in me by the help of reason. I have not always been successful in achieving this end. But man's duty is to try and endeavour, success depends upon chance and environments.

As for the second question that if it was not vanity, then there ought to be some reason to disbelieve the old and still prevailing faith of the existence of God. Yes, I come to that now. Reason there is. According to me, any man who has got some reasoning power at his command always tries to reason out his environments. Where direct proofs are lacking philosophy occupies the important place. As I have already stated, a certain revolutionary friend used to say that philosophy is the outcome of human weakness. When our ancestors had leisure enough to try to solve out the mystery of this world, its past, present and the future, its whys and wherefores, they having been terribly short of direct proofs, everybody tried to solve the problem in his own way. Hence we find the wide differences in the fundamentals of various religious creeds, which sometimes assume very antagonistic and conflicting shapes. Not only the Oriental and Occidental philosophies differ, there are differences even amongst various schools of thought in each hemisphere. Amongst Oriental religions, the Moslem faith is not at all compatible with Hindu faith. In India alone, Buddhism and Jainism are sometimes quite separate from Brahmanism, in which there are again conflicting faiths as Arya Samaj and Sanatan Dharma. Charwak is still another independent thinker of the past ages. He challenged the authority of God in the old times. All these creeds differ from each other on the fundamental question; and everybody considers himself to be on the right. There lies the misfortune. Instead of using the experiments and expressions of the ancient Savants and thinkers as a basis for our future struggle against ignorance and to try to find out a solution to this mysterious problem, we, lethargic as we have proved to be, raise the hue and cry of faith, unflinching and unwavering faith to their versions and thus are guilty of stagnation in human progress.

Any man who stands for progress has to criticize, disbelieve and challenge every item of the old faith. Item by item, he has to reason out every nook and corner of the prevailing faith. If after considerable reasoning one is led to believe in any theory or philosophy, his faith is welcomed. His reasoning can be mistaken, wrong, misled, and sometimes fallacious. But he is liable to correction because reason is the guiding star of his life. But mere faith and blind faith is dangerous: it dulls the brain and makes a man reactionary. A man who claims to be a realist has to challenge the whole of the ancient faith. If it does not stand the onslaught of reason it crumbles down. Then the first thing for him is to shatter the whole down and clear a space for the erection of a new philosophy. This is the negative side. After it begins the positive work in which sometimes some material of the old faith may be used for the purpose of reconstruction. As far as I am concerned, let me admit at the very outset that I have not been able to study much on this point. I had a great desire to study the Oriental philosophy but I could not get any chance or opportunity to do the same. But so far as the negative study is under discussion, I think I am convinced to the extent of questioning the soundness of the old faith. I have been convinced as to non-existence of a conscious supreme being who is guiding and directing the movements of nature. We believe in nature and the whole progressive movement aims at the domination of man over nature for his service. There is no conscious power behind it to direct. This is what our philosophy is.

As for the negative side, we ask a few questions from the 'believers'.

If, as you believe, there is an almighty, omnipresent, omniscient and omnipotent God, who created the earth or world, please let me know why did he create it? This world of woes and miseries, a veritable, eternal combination of numberless tragedies: Not a single soul being perfectly satisfied.

Pray, don't say that it is His Law. If he is bound by any law, he is not omnipotent. He is another slave like ourselves. Please don't say that it is his enjoyment. Nero burnt one Rome. He killed a very limited number of people. He created very few tragedies, all to his perfect enjoyment. And, what is his place in History? By what names do the historians mention him? All the venomous epithets are showered upon him. Pages are blackened with invective diatribes condemning Nero, the tyrant, the heartless, the wicked. One Changezkhan sacrificed a few thousand lives to seek pleasure in it and we hate the very name. Then, how are you going to justify your almighty, eternal Nero, who has been, and is still causing numberless tragedies every day, every hour and every minute? How do you think to support his misdoings which surpass those of Changez every single moment? I say why did he create this world – a veritable hell, a place of constant and bitter unrest? Why did the Almighty create man when he had the power not to do it? What is the justification for all this? Do you say, to award the innocent sufferers hereafter and to punish the wrongdoers as well? Well, well: How far shall you justify a man who may dare to inflict wounds upon your body to apply a very soft and soothing ointment upon it afterwards? How far the supporters and organizers of the Gladiator institution were justified in throwing men before the half-starved furious lions to be cared for, and well looked after if they could survive and could manage to escape death by the wild beasts? That is why I ask: Why did the conscious Supreme Being create this world and man in it? To seek pleasure? Where, then, is the difference between him and Nero?

You Mohammadans and Christians: Hindu philosophy shall still linger on to offer another argument. I ask you, what is your answer to the above-mentioned question? You don't believe in previous birth. Like Hindus, you cannot advance the argument of previous misdoings of the apparently quite innocent suffers. I ask you, why did the omnipotent labour for six days to create the world through word and each day to say that all was well? Call him today. Show him the past history. Make him study the present situation. Let us see if he dares to say: 'All is well'.

From the dungeons of prisons, from the stores of starvation consuming millions upon millions of human beings in slums and huts, from the exploited labourers, patiently or say apathetically watching the procedure of their blood being sucked by the capitalist vampires, and the wastage of human energy that will make a man with the least common sense shiver with horror, and from the preference of throwing the surplus of production in oceans rather than to distribute amongst the needy producers – to the palaces of kings built upon the foundation laid with human bones. . . . let him see all this and let him say: 'All is well'. Why and wherefore? That is my question. You are silent. Alright then, I proceed.

Well, you Hindus, you say all the present sufferers belong to the class of sinners of the previous births. Good. You say the present oppressors were saintly people in their previous births, hence they enjoy power. Let me admit that your ancestors were very shrewd people; they tried to find out theories strong enough to hammer down all the efforts of reason and disbelief. But let us analyze how far this argument can really stand.

From the point of view of the most famous jurists, punishment can be justified only from three or four ends, to meet which it is inflicted upon the wrongdoer. They are retributive, reformative and deterrent. The retributive theory is now being condemned by all the advanced thinkers. Deterrent theory is also following the same fate. Reformative theory is the only one which is essential and indispensable for human progress. It aims at returning the offender as a most competent and a peace-loving citizen to the society. But, what is the nature of punishment inflicted by God upon men, even if we suppose them to be offenders? You say he sends them to be born as a cow, a cat, a tree, a herb, or a beast. You enumerate these punishments to be 84 lakhs. I ask you: what is its reformative effect upon man? How many men have met you who say that they were born as a donkey in previous birth for having committed any sin? None. Don't quote your Puranas. I have no scope to touch your mythologies. Moreover, do you know that the greatest sin in this world is to be poor? Poverty is a sin, it is a punishment. I ask you how far would you appreciate a criminologist, a jurist or a legislator who proposes such measures of punishment which shall inevitably force men to commit more offences. Had not your God thought of this, or he also had to learn these things by experience, but at the cost of untold sufferings to be borne by humanity? What do you think shall be the fate of a man who has been born in a poor and illiterate family of, say, a *chamar* or a sweeper? He is poor; hence he cannot study. He is hated and shunned by his fellow human beings who think themselves to be his superiors, having been born in, say, a higher caste. His ignorance, his poverty and the treatment meted out to him shall harden his heart towards society. Suppose he commits a sin, who shall bear the consequences? God, he or the learned ones of the society? What about the punishment of those people who were deliberately kept ignorant by the haughty and egotist Brahmans, and who had to pay the penalty by bearing the stream of[2] lead in their ears for having heard a few sentences of your Sacred Books of learning – the Vedas? If they committed any offence, who was to be responsible for them and who was to bear the brunt? My dear friends, these theories are the inventions of the privileged ones; they justify their usurped power, riches and superiority by the help of these theories. Yes, it was perhaps Upton Sinclair that wrote at some place that just makes a man a believer in immortality and then rob him of all his riches and possessions. He shall help you even in that ungrudgingly. The coalition among the religious preachers and possessors of power brought forth jails, gallows, knouts and these theories.

I ask why your omnipotent God does not stop every man when he is committing any sin or offence. He can do it quite easily. Why did he not kill warlords or kill the fury of war in them and thus avoid the catastrophe hurled down on the head of humanity by the Great War? Why does he not just produce a certain sentiment in the mind of the British people to liberate India? Why does he not infuse the altruistic enthusiasm in the hearts of all capitalists to forego their rights of personal possessions of means of production

2 [molten].

and thus redeem the whole labouring community, nay, the whole human society, from the bondage of capitalism? You want to reason out the practicability of socialist theory; I leave it for your almighty to enforce it. People recognize the merits of socialism in as much as the general welfare is concerned. They oppose it under the pretext of its being impracticable. Let the Almighty step in and arrange everything in an orderly fashion. Now don't try to advance round about arguments, they are out of order. Let me tell you, British rule is here not because God wills it, but because they possess power, and we do not dare to oppose them. Not that it is with the help of God that they are keeping us under their subjection, but it is with the help of guns and rifles, bomb and bullets, police and militia, and our apathy, that they are successfully committing the most deplorable sin against society – the outrageous exploitation of one nation by another. Where is God? What is he doing? Is he enjoying all these woes of human race? A Nero, a Changez! Down with him!

Do you ask me how I explain the origin of this world and origin of man? Alright, I tell you, Charles Darwin has tried to throw some light on the subject. Study him. Read Soham Swami's *Common Sense*. It shall answer your question to some extent. This is a phenomenon of nature. The accidental mixture of different substances in the shape of nebulae produced this earth. When? Consult history. The same process produced animals and, in the long run, man. Read Darwin's *Origin of Species*. And all later progress is due to man's constant conflict with nature and his efforts to override it. This is the briefest possible explanation of the phenomenon.

Your other argument may be just to ask why a child is born blind or lame if not due to his deeds committed in the previous birth? This problem has been explained away by biologists as a mere biological phenomenon. According to them, the whole burden rests upon the shoulders of the parents, who may be conscious or ignorant of their own deeds, which led to mutilation of the child previous to its birth.

Naturally, you may ask another question, though it is quite childish in essence. If no god existed, how did the people come to believe in him? My answer is clear and brief. As they came to believe in ghosts and evil spirits; the only difference is that belief in God is almost universal and the philosophy well developed. Unlike certain of the radicals, I would not attribute its origin to the ingenuity of the exploiters who wanted to keep the people under their subjection by preaching the existence of a supreme being and then claiming an authority and sanction from him for their privileged positions, though I do not differ with them on the essential point that all faiths, religions, creeds and such other institutions became, in turn, the mere supporters of the tyrannical and exploiting institutions, men and classes. Rebellion against king is always a sin, according to every religion.

As regards the origin of God, my own idea is that having realized the limitation of man, his weaknesses and shortcoming having been taken into consideration, God was brought into imaginary existence to encourage man to face boldly all the trying circumstances, to meet all dangers manfully and to check and restrain his outbursts in prosperity and affluence. God, both with his private laws and parental generosity, was imagined and painted in greater details. He was to serve as a deterrent factor when his fury and private laws were discussed, so that man may not become a danger to society. He was to serve as a father, mother, sister and brother, friend and helper, when his parental qualifications were to be explained. So that when man be in great distress, having been betrayed and deserted by all friends, he may find consolation in the idea that an ever-true friend, was still there to help him, to support him and that he was almighty and could do anything. Really that was useful to the society in the primitive age. The idea of God is helpful to main in distress.

Society has to fight out this belief as well as was fought the idol worship and the narrow conception of religion. Similarly, when man tries to stand on his own legs and become a realist, he shall have to throw the faith aside, and to face manfully all the distress, trouble, in which the circumstances may throw him. That is exactly my state of affairs. It is not my vanity, my friends. It is my mode of thinking that has made me an atheist. I don't know whether, in my case, belief in God and offering of daily prayers, which I consider to be most selfish and degraded act on the part of man, whether these prayers can prove to be helpful or they shall make my case worse still. I have read of atheists facing all troubles quite boldly; so am I trying to stand like a man with an erect head to the last, even on the gallows.

Let us see how I carry on. One friend asked me to pray. When informed of my atheism, he said: 'During your last days you will begin to believe'. I said: 'No, dear Sir, it shall not be. I will think that to be an act of degradation and demoralization on my part. For selfish motives I am not going to pray'. Readers and friends: Is this 'vanity'? If it is, I stand for it.

To Young Political Workers

This essay is in two parts. The first, written in English in February 1931, the month before his execution, was published in parts soon after his death.[1] It ends with: 'LONG LIVE REVOLUTION 2nd February, 1931'. This is perhaps Bhagat Singh's most important political document. It stresses the difference between necessary compromises made by a revolutionary organization, that is, those made as a tactical decision, and compromises which are, in fact, a basic strategy. The latter were those of the Indian National Congress (INC) under Gandhi. We can see in modern-day India how that has turned out. Just as we can see, for example, how labour unions in the United States compromised with employers, the strategy of 'labour-management cooperation' has gravely weakened the labour movement by giving the advantage in the class struggle to employers.

Bhagat Singh argues here for the primacy of revolutionary principles, those that can never be compromised. This ideal makes this document relevant today everywhere in the world. In a sense, the politics of the INC is similar to that of social democratic parties worldwide. The adherents of social democracy claim that achieving certain social democratic ends, such as universal health insurance, paves the way for socialism. However, there is no case of this ever happening, with the Scandinavian welfare states proving the point.

The second part of the essay was uncovered later, which may also have been written in February 1931. Readers will

1 After Bhagat Singh's execution this document was published in a mutilated form. All references to Soviet Union, Marx, Lenin and the Communist Party were carefully deleted. Subsequently, the Government of India published it in one of its secret reports in 1936. A photostat copy of the full report is preserved in the library of the Martyrs' Memorial and Freedom Struggle Research Centre at Lucknow.

notice that this section is rougher in form than the first part as if written in haste as a sketch outlining specific features of a revolutionary organization and the duties of each. What is most interesting about it is that it begins to lay out the need for what we might call socio-political geography. It urges revolutionaries to read military manuals, both to learn the thinking of the enemy and to look for tactics that might be useful in revolutionary work. In addition, it asks that a revolutionary party construct a detailed description of the physical features of the country, such as roads, bridges, rivers, crops, grain transport, and the like. Along with this, a description of the people – their religions, languages, dress, and other important characteristics, such as caste and class.

It is important to note in this context that the Maoists in Nepal did precisely this, which was critical to their eventual seizing power. Much the same can be said of Mao and China. This kind of concrete analysis would be valuable in many situations. For example, it could be very useful in labour and peasant organizing, as well as in political organizing.

Dear Comrades,

Our movement is passing through a very important phase at present. After a year's fierce struggle some definite proposals regarding the constitutional reforms have been formulated by the Round Table Conference, and the Congress leaders have been invited to give this . . .[2] think it desirable in the present circumstances to call off their movement. Whether they decide in favour or against is a matter of little importance to us. The present movement is bound to end in some sort of compromise.

2 Missing text.

The compromise may be effected sooner or later. And compromise is not such ignoble and deplorable a thing as we generally think. It is rather an indispensable factor in the political strategy. Any nation that rises against the oppressors is bound to fail in the beginning, and to gain partial reforms during the medieval period of its struggle through compromises. And it is only at the last stage – having fully organised all the forces and resources of the nation – that it can possibly strike the final blow in which it might succeed to shatter the ruler's government. But even then, it might fail, which makes some sort of compromise inevitable. This can be best illustrated by the Russian example.

In 1905 a revolutionary movement broke out in Russia. All the leaders were very hopeful. Lenin had returned from the foreign countries where he had taken refuge. He was conducting the struggle. People came to tell him that a dozen landlords were killed and a score of their mansions were burnt. Lenin responded by telling them to return and to kill twelve hundred landlords and burn as many of their palaces. In his opinion that would have meant something if revolution failed. The Duma (an advisory assembly) was introduced (by Tsar Nicholas II). The same Lenin advocated the view of participating in the Duma. This is what happened in 1907. In 1906 he was opposed to the participation in this first Duma, which had granted more scope of work than this second one whose rights had been curtailed. This was due to the changed circumstances. Reaction was gaining the upper hand and Lenin wanted to use the floor of the Duma as a platform to discuss socialist ideas.

Again, after the 1917 revolution, when the Bolsheviks were forced to sign the Brest Litovsk Treaty, everyone except Lenin was opposed to it. But Lenin said: 'Peace'. 'Peace and again peace: peace at any cost-even at the cost of many of the Russian provinces to be yielded to the German War Lord'. When some anti-Bolshevik people condemned Lenin for this treaty, he declared frankly that the Bolsheviks were not in a position to face a German onslaught and they preferred the treaty to the complete annihilation of the Bolshevik Government.

The thing that I wanted to point out was that compromise is an essential weapon which has to be wielded every now and then as the struggle develops. But the thing that we must keep always before us is the idea of the movement. We must always maintain a clear notion as to the aim for the achievement of which we are fighting. That helps us to verify the success and failures of our movements and we can easily formulate the future program. Tilak's policy, quite apart from the ideal, that is, his strategy, was the best. You are fighting to get sixteen annas from your enemy, you get only one anna. Pocket it and fight for the rest. What we note in the moderates is of their ideal. They start to achieve one anna and they can't get it. The revolutionaries must always keep in mind that they are striving for a complete revolution. Complete mastery of power in their hands. Compromises are dreaded because the conservatives try to disband the revolutionary forces after the compromise from such pitfalls. We must be very careful at such junctures to avoid any sort of confusion of the real issues especially the goal. The British Labor leaders betrayed their real struggle and have been reduced to mere hypocrite imperialists. In my opinion the diehard conservatives are better to us than these polished imperialist Labor leaders. About the tactics and strategy, one should study life-work of Lenin. His definite views on the subject of compromise will be found in 'Left Wing' Communism.

I have said that the present movement, that is, the present struggle, is bound to end in some sort of compromise or complete failure.

I said that, because in my opinion, this time the real revolutionary forces have not been invited into the arena. This is a struggle dependent upon the middle-class shopkeepers and a few capitalists. Both these, and particularly the latter, can never dare to risk its property or possessions in any struggle. The real revolutionary armies are in the villages and in factories, the peasantry and the labourers. But our bourgeois leaders do not and cannot dare to tackle them. The sleeping lion once awakened from its slumber shall become irresistible even after the achievement of what our leaders aim at. After his first experience with the Ahmedabad labourers in 1920, Mahatma Gandhi declared: 'We must not tamper with the labourers. It is dangerous to make political use of the factory proletariat' (*The Times*, May 1921). Since then, they never dared to approach them. There remains the peasantry. The Bardoli resolution of 1922 clearly defines the horror the leaders felt when they saw the gigantic peasant class rising to shake off not only the domination of an alien nation but also the yoke of the landlords.

It is there that our leaders prefer a surrender to the British than to the peasantry. Other than by Pt. Jawahar Lal (Nehru), can you point out any effort to organize the peasants or the labourers? No, they will not run the risk. There they lack. That is why I say they never meant a complete revolution. Through economic and administrative pressure, they hoped to get a few more reforms, a few more concessions for the Indian capitalists. That is why I say that this movement is doomed to die, may be after some sort of compromise or even without. The young workers, who in all sincerity raise the cry 'Long Live Revolution', are not well organized and strong enough to carry the movement themselves. As a matter of fact, even our great leaders, with the exception of perhaps Pt. Motilal Nehru, do not dare to take any responsibility on their shoulders, that is why every now and then they surrender unconditionally before Gandhi. In spite of their differences, they never oppose him seriously and the resolutions have to be carried for the Mahatma

In these circumstances, let me warn the sincere young workers who seriously mean a revolution that harder times are coming. Let them beware lest they should get confused or disheartened. After the experience made through two struggles of the Great Gandhi, we are in a better position to form a clear idea of our present position and the future program.

Now allow me to state the case in the simplest manner. You cry 'Long Live Revolution'. Let me assume that you really mean it. According to our definition of the term, as stated in our statement in the Assembly Bomb Case, revolution means the complete overthrow of the existing social order and its replacement with the socialist order. For that purpose, our immediate aim is the achievement of power. As a matter of fact, the state, the government machinery is just a weapon in the hands of the ruling class to further and safeguard its interest. We want to snatch and handle it to utilize it for the consummation of our ideal, that is, social reconstruction on a new, that is, Marxist, basis. For this purpose, we are fighting to handle the government machinery. All along we have to educate the masses and to create a favourable atmosphere for our social program. In the struggles we can best train and educate them.

With these things clear before us, that is, our immediate and ultimate object having been clearly put, we can now proceed with the examination of the present situation. We must always be very candid and quite business-like while analyzing any situation.

We know that since a hue and cry was raised about the Indians' participation in and share in the responsibility of the Indian government, the Minto-Morley Reforms were introduced, which formed the Viceroy's council with consultation rights only. During the Great War, when Indian help was needed the most, promises about self-government were made and the existing reforms were introduced. Limited legislative powers have been entrusted to the Assembly but subject to the goodwill of the Viceroy. *Now is the third stage.*

Now reforms are being discussed and are to be introduced in the near future. How can our young men judge them? This is a question; I do not know by what standard the Congress leaders will judge them. But for us, the revolutionaries, we can have the following criteria:

1. Extent of responsibility transferred to the shoulders of the Indians.
2. Form of the Government institutions that are going to be introduced and the extent of the right of participation given to the masses.
3. Future prospects and the safeguards.

These might require a little further elucidation. In the first place, we can easily judge the extent of responsibility given to our people by the control our representatives will have on the executive. Up till now, the executive was never made responsible to the Legislative Assembly and the Viceroy had the veto power, which rendered all the efforts of the elected members futile. Thanks to the efforts of the Swaraj Party, the Viceroy was forced every now and then to use these extraordinary powers to shamelessly trample the solemn decisions of the national representatives under foot. It is already too well known to need further discussion.

Now in the first place we must see the method of the executive formation: Whether the executive is to be elected by the members of a popular assembly or is to be imposed from above as before, and further, whether it shall be responsible to the house or shall absolutely affront it as in the past?

As regards the second item, we can judge it through the scope of franchise. The property qualifications making a man eligible to vote should be altogether abolished and universal suffrage be introduced instead. Every adult, both male and female, should have the right to vote. At present we can simply see how far the franchise has been extended.

I may here make a mention about provincial autonomy. But from whatever I have heard, I can only say that the Governor imposed from above, equipped with extraordinary powers, higher and above the legislative, shall prove to be no less than a despot. Let us better call it the 'provincial tyranny' instead of 'autonomy'. This is a strange type of democratization of the state institutions.

The third item is quite clear. During the last two years the British politicians have been trying to undo Montague's promise for another dole of reforms to be bestowed every ten years till the British Treasury exhausts.

We can see what they have decided about the future.

Let me make it clear that we do not analyze these things to rejoice over the achievement, but to form a clear idea about our situation, so that we may enlighten the masses and prepare them for further struggle. For us, compromise never means surrender, but a step forward and some rest. That is all and nothing else.

* * *

Having discussed the present situation, let us proceed to discuss the future program and the line of action we ought to adopt.

As I have already stated, for any revolutionary party a definite program is very essential. For, you must know that revolution means action. It means a change brought about deliberately by an organized and systematic work, as opposed to sudden and unorganized or spontaneous change or breakdown. And for the formulation of a programme, one must necessarily study:

1. The goal.
2. The premises from where we're to start, that is, the existing conditions.
3. The course of action, that is, the means and methods.

Unless one has a clear notion about these three factors, one cannot discuss anything about programme.

We have discussed the present situation to some extent. The

goal also has been slightly touched. We want a socialist, revolution, the indispensable preliminary to which is the political revolution. That is what we want. The political revolution does not mean the transfer of state (or more crudely, the power) from the hands of the British to the Indians, but to those Indians who are at one with us as to the final goal, or to be more precise, the power to be transferred to the revolutionary party through popular support. After that, to proceed in right earnest is to organise the reconstruction of the whole society on the socialist basis. If you do not mean this revolution, then please have mercy. Stop shouting 'Long Live Revolution'. The term revolution is too sacred, at least to us, to be so lightly used or misused. But if you say you are for the national revolution and the aims of your struggle is an Indian republic of the type of the United States of America, then I ask you to please let me know on what forces you rely that will help you bring about that revolution. The only forces on which you can rely to bring about any revolution, whether national or the socialist, are the peasantry and the labour. Congress leaders do not dare to organize those forces. You have seen it in this movement. They know it better than anybody else that without these forces they are absolutely helpless. When they passed the resolution of complete independence – that really meant a revolution – they did not mean it. They had to do it under pressure of the younger element, and then they wanted to use it as a threat to achieve their hearts' desire – Dominion Status. You can easily judge it by studying the resolutions of the last three sessions of the Congress. I mean Madras, Calcutta and Lahore. At Calcutta, they passed a resolution asking for Dominion Status within twelve months, otherwise they would be forced to adopt complete independence as their object, and in all solemnity waited for some such gift till midnight after the 31st December, 1929. Then they found themselves 'honour bound' to adopt the Independence resolution, otherwise they did not mean it. But even then Mahatmaji made no secret of the fact that the door (for compromise) was open. That was the real spirit.

At the very outset they knew that their movement could not but end in some compromise. It is this half-heartedness that we hate, not the compromise at a particular stage in the struggle. Anyway, we were discussing the forces on which you can depend for a revolution. But if you say that you will approach the peasants and labourers to enlist their active support, let me tell you that they are not going to be fooled by any sentimental talk. They ask you quite candidly: what are they going to gain by your revolution for which you demand their sacrifices, what difference does it make to them whether Lord Reading is the head of the Indian government or Sir Purshotamdas Thakordas? What difference for a peasant if Sir Tej Bahadur Sapru replaces Lord Irwin! It is useless to appeal to his national sentiment. You can't 'use' him for your purpose; you shall have to mean seriously and to make him understand that the revolution is going to be his and for his good. The revolution of the proletariat and for the proletariat.

When you have formulated this clear-cut idea about your goals you can proceed in right earnest to organize your forces for such an action. Now there are two different phases through which you shall have to pass. First, the preparation; second, the action.

After the present movement ends, you will find disgust and some disappointment amongst the sincere revolutionary workers. But you need not worry. Leave sentimentalism aside. Be prepared to face the facts. Revolution is a very difficult task. It is beyond the power of any man to make a revolution. Neither can it be brought about on any appointed date. It is brought about by special environments, social and economic. The function of an organized party is to utilize any such opportunity offered by these circumstances. And to prepare the masses and organize the forces for the revolution is a very difficult task. And that requires a very great sacrifice on the part of the revolutionary workers. Let me make it clear that if you are a businessman or an established worldly or family man, please don't play with fire. As a leader you are of no use to the party. We have already very many such leaders who spare some evening hours for delivering speeches. They are useless. We require – to use the term so dear to Lenin – the 'professional revolutionaries'. The whole-time workers who have no other ambitions or life-work except the revolution. The greater the number of such workers organised into a party, the greater the chances of your success. To proceed systematically, what you need the most is a party with workers of the type discussed above with clear-cut ideas and keen perception and ability of initiative and quick decisions. The party shall have iron discipline and it need not necessarily be an underground party, rather the contrary. Though the policy of voluntarily going to jail should altogether be abandoned. That will create a number of workers who shall be forced to lead an underground life. They should carry on the work with the same zeal. And it is this group of workers that shall produce worthy leaders for the real opportunity

The party requires workers that can be recruited only through the youth movement. Hence we find the youth movement as the starting point of our program. The youth movement should organize study circles, class lectures and publication of leaflets, pamphlets, books and periodicals. This is the best recruiting and training ground for political workers.

Those young men who may have matured their ideas and may find themselves ready to devote their life to the cause, may be transferred to the party. The party workers shall always guide and control the work of the youth movement as well. The party should start with the work of mass propaganda. It is very essential. One of the fundamental causes of the failure of the efforts of the Ghadar Party (1914–15) was the ignorance, apathy and sometimes active opposition of the masses. And apart from that, it is essential for gaining the active sympathy of and organizing the peasants and workers. The name of party or rather . . .[3] a communist party. This party of political workers, bound by strict discipline, should

3 Missing text.

handle all other movements. It shall have to organise the peasants' and workers' parties, labour unions, and may even venture to capture the Congress and kindred political bodies. And in order to create political consciousness, not only of national politics but class politics as well, the party should organise a big publishing campaign. Subjects on all proletens (!)[4] enlightening the masses of the socialist theory shall be within easy reach and distributed widely. The writings should be simple and clear. There are certain people in the labour movement who enlist some absurd ideas about the economic liberty of the peasants and workers without political freedom. They are demagogues or muddle-headed people. Such ideas are unimaginable and preposterous. We mean the economic liberty of the masses, and for that very purpose we are striving to win the political power. No doubt in the beginning, we shall have to fight for little economic demands and privileges of these classes. But these struggles are the best means for educating them for a final struggle to conquer political power. Apart from these, there shall necessarily be organized a military department. This is very important. At times its need is felt very badly. But at that time you cannot start and formulate such a group with substantial means to act effectively. Perhaps this is the topic that needs a careful explanation. There is very great probability of my being misunderstood on this subject. Apparently I have acted like a terrorist. But I am not a terrorist. I am a revolutionary who has got such definite ideas of a lengthy programme as is being discussed here. My 'comrades in arms' might accuse me, like Ram Prasad Bismil, for having been subjected to certain sort of reaction in the condemned cell, which is not true. I have got the same ideas, same convictions, same zeal and same spirit as I used to have outside, perhaps – nay, decidedly – better. Hence I warn my readers to be careful while reading my words. They should not try to read anything between the lines. Let me announce with all the strength

---

4 Unclear. Probably some missing text.

at my command, that I am not a terrorist and I never was, except perhaps in the beginning of my revolutionary career. And I am convinced that we cannot gain anything through those methods. One can easily judge it from the history of the Hindustan Socialist Republican Association. All our activities were directed towards an aim, i.e., identifying ourselves with the great movement as its military wing. If anybody has misunderstood me, let him amend his ideas. I do not mean that bombs and pistols are useless, rather the contrary. But I mean to say that mere bomb-throwing is not only useless but sometimes harmful. The military department of the party should always keep ready all the war-material it can command for any emergency. It should back the political work of the party. It cannot and should not work independently

On these lines indicated above, the party should proceed with its work. Through periodical meetings and conferences, they should go on educating and enlightening their workers on all topics.

If you start the work on these lines, you shall have to be very sober. The program requires at least twenty years for its fulfilment. Cast aside the youthful dreams of a revolution within ten years of Gandhi's Utopian promises of Swaraj in One Year. It requires neither the emotion nor the death, but the life of constant struggle, suffering and sacrifice. Crush your individuality first. Shake off the dreams of personal comfort. Then start to work. Inch by inch you shall have to proceed. It needs courage, perseverance and very strong determination. No difficulties and no hardships shall discourage you. No failure and betrayals shall dishearten you. No troubles imposed upon you shall snuff out the revolutionary will in you. Through the ordeal of sufferings and sacrifice you shall come out victorious. And these individual victories shall be the valuable assets of the revolution.

LONG LIVE REVOLUTION
2nd February, 1931

OUR OPPORTUNITY

Indian freedom is not perhaps any longer a far distant dream; events are moving apace and it may become a reality sooner than we expect. British Imperialism is admittedly in a tight corner. Germany is about to topple down, France is tottering, even the United States is shaky. And their difficulty is our opportunity. Everything points to that long-prophesized eventuality–the ultimate and inevitable breakdown of the Capitalistic order of Society. Diplomats may agree to save themselves and Capitalistic conspiracy may yet keep the wolf of Revolution away from their doors. The British budget may be balanced, the moribund mark granted some hours of respite and King Dollar may retain his crown; but the trade depression if continued and continued it must be, we know the members of unemployed being multiplied daily as a result of the Capitalistic race in production and competition is bound to throw the Capitalistic system out of gear in the months to come. The Revolution is, therefore, no longer a prophecy and prospect but 'practical politics' for thoughtful planning and remorseless execution. Let there be no confusion of thought as to its aspect or as to its immediacy, its methods and its objective.

GANDHISM

We should not have any illusion about the possibilities, failures and achievements of the Congress movement, which should be, as it is today, be better stamped Gandhism. It does not stand for freedom avowedly; it is in favour of 'Parternership'–a strange interpretation of what 'complete independence' signifies. Its method is novel, and but for the helplessness of the people, Gandhism would gain no adherent for the Saint of Sabarmati. It has fulfilled and is fulfilling the role of an intermediate party of Liberal-Radical combination fighting shy of the reality of the situation and controlled mostly by men with stakes in the country, who prize their stakes with bourgeois tenacity, and it is bound to stagnate unless rescued from its own fate by an infusion of Revolutionary blood. It must be saved from its friends.

TERRORISM

Let us be clear on this thorny question of terrorism. The cult of the bomb is old as 1905 and it is a sad comment on Revolutionary India that they have not yet realized its use and misuse. Terrorism is a confession that the Revolutionary mentality has not penetrated down into the masses. It is thus a confession of our failure. In the initial stages it had its use; it shook the torpor out of the body politic, enkindled the imagination of young intelligentsia, fired their spirit of self-sacrifice and demonstrated before the world and before our enemies the truth and the strength of the movement. But by itself it is not enough. Its history is a history of failure in every land–France, in Russia, in Balkan countries, in Germany, in Spain, everywhere. It bears the germ of defeat within itself. The Imperialist knows that to rule 300 millions he must sacrifice 30 of his men annually. The pleasure of ruling may be bombed out or pistoled down, but the practical gain from exploitation will make him stick to his post. Even though arms were as readily available as we hope for, and were it pushed with a thoroughness unknown anywhere else, terrorism can at most force the Imperialist power to come to terms with the party. Such terms, a little more or less, must fall short of our objective–complete independence. Terrorism thus hopes to wring out what Gandhism bids fair to attain – compromise and an installment of reforms – a replacement of a white rule at Delhi by a brown rule. It is aloof from the life of the masses and once installed on the throne runs the risk of being petrified into a tyranny. The Irish parallel, I have to warn, does not apply in our case. In Ireland it was not sporadic terroristic activities she witnessed; it was a nationwide rising; the rank and file were bound by an intimate knowledge and sympathy with the gunmen. Arms they could have very easily, and the American-Irish poured out their money. Topography favored such a warfare, and Ireland after all had to be satisfied with an unaccomplished movement. It has lessened the bonds but not released the Irish proletariat from the shackles of the Capitalist, native and foreign. Ireland is a lesson to India and a warning–warning how nationalistic idealism devoid of Revolutionary social basis although with all other circumstances in its favor, may be lost itself in the shoals of a compromise with Imperialism. Should India, if she could, imitate Ireland still?

In a sense Gandhism with its counter-revolutionary creed of quietism makes a nearer approach to the revolutionary ideas. For it counts on mass action, though not for the masses alone. It has paved the way for the proletariat revolution by trying to harness it, however crudely and selfishly, to its political program. The Revolutionary must give to the angle of nonviolence his due.

The devil of terrorism needs, however, no compliments. The terrorist has done much, taught us much and has his use still, provided we do not make a confusion of our aims and means. At desperate moments we can make of terrorist outrages our best publicity works, but it is none the less fireworks and should be reserved for a chosen few. Let not the revolutionary be lashed round and round the vicious circle of aimless outrages and individual self-immolation. The inspiring ideal for all and sundry workers should not be that of dying for the cause but of living for the cause and living usefully and worthily.

Needless to point out, that we do not repudiate terrorist activities altogether. We want to assess its proper value from the standpoint of proletariat Revolution. The youth, who is found not to fit in with the cold and silent organization work, has another role to play–he is to be released from the dry work and allowed to fulfill his destiny. But the controlling body should always foresee the possible reaction of the deed on the party, the masses and on the enemy. It may divert the attention of the first two from militant mass action to the stirring sensational action, and it may supply the last with clues for striking at the root of the whole party. In either case it does not advance the cause.

Secret military organization is, however, not an anathema. Indeed, it is the front line, 'the firing line' of the Revolutionary party. It must be linked with the 'base' formed by a mobile and militant mass party. Collections of arms and finances for organization are therefore to be undertaken without any scruple.

REVOLUTION

What we mean by Revolution is quite plain. In this century it can mean only one thing–the capture of the political power by the masses for the masses. It is, in fact, The Revolution. Other risings attempt a mere change of your lordships, trying to perpetuate the rotting capitalistic order. No amount of profession of sympathy for the people and the popular cause can ultimately hoodwink the masses about the true nature and portent of such superficial replacement. In India too, we want nothing less than the regime of the Indian proletariat in the place of the Indian Imperialists and their native allies who are barricaded behind the same economic system of exploitation. We can suffer no black evil to replace the white evil. Both evils have a community of interest.

The proletariat revolution is the only weapon of India to dislodge the Imperialist. Nothing else can attain this object. Nationalists of all shades are agreed on the objective–Independence from the Imperialists. They must realize that rebelliousness of the masses is the motive force behind their agitation and militant mass action alone can push it to success. Having no recourse to it easily, they always delude themselves with the vision of the what they consider a temporary but quick and effective remedy, viz overthrowing the foreign rule by an armed opposition of a few hundreds of determined idealist nationalists and then reconstructing the State on Socialistic lines. They should see into the reality of the situation: arms are not plenty, and in the modern world the insurrection of an untrained body isolated from the militant masses stands no chance of success. The nationalists to be effective must harness the nation into action, into revolt. And the nation is not the loudspeakers of the Congress. It is the peasants and the laborers who form more than 95 per cent of India. The nation will stir itself to action only on assurance of nationalization, that is. Freedom from the slavery of the Imperialists–the capitalists.

What we need to keep in mind is that no revolution can succeed or is to be desired, but the proletariat revolution.

THE PROGRAM

The need of the hour is therefore for a clear, honest program for the revolution, and determined action for realization of the program.

In 1917 before the October Revolution had come off, Lenin, still in hiding in Moscow, wrote that for a successful revolution three condition are essential:

1. A political-economic situation
2. A rebellious mass mind, and
3. A party of revolutionaries, trained and determined to lead the masses when the hour of trial arrives

The first condition has been more than fulfilled in India; the second and third yet await completeness. To mobilize them is the work before all workers of freedom, and the program should be farmed with that end in view. We propose to discuss its outline in the following and our suggestion on each section are to be detailed in the Appendix A and Appendix B.

(1) The base work: The foremost duty before workers is to mobilize the masses for militant mass action. We need not play on his blind prejudices, sentiment, piety or passive idealism. Our promises to him are not mere sops or half a loaf. They are complete

and concrete, and we can be with him sincere and plain, and should never create in his mind any miasma of prejudices. The revolution is for him, for to name only the prominent heads:

1. Abolition of Landlordism.
2. Liquidation of the peasants' indebtedness.
3. Nationalization of land by the Revolutionary State with a view finally to lead to improved and collective farming.
4. Guarantee of housing security.
5. Abolition of all charges on the peasantry except a minimum unitary land tax.
6. Nationalization of the Industries and industrialization of the country.
7. Universal education.
8. Reduction of the hours of work to the minimum necessary.

The masses are bound to respond to such a program. We have only to reach them. It is the supreme task. Enforced ignorance on their part, and apathy of the intelligent classes on the other, have created an artificial barrier between the educated revolutionary and his less fortunate comrade of the sickle and the hammer. That must be demolished by the revolutionary and for that purpose:

1.The Congress platform is to be availed of.
2. The Trade Unions are to be captured and new Unions and bodies shaped and modelled on aggressive lines.
3. Every social and philanthropic organization (even the cooperative societies) that offers an opportunity to approach the masses should be secretly entered into and its activities controlled so as to further the real objective.
4. The Unions are Committees of artisan workers as well as intellectual workers and are to be set up everywhere.

These are the lines of approach for the educated and trained revolutionary to reach the masses. And once they are reached, they can be moved easily by training, at first in aggressive assertion of their rights, and later on, by militant offensives like strikes combined with sabotage.

THE REVOLUTIONARY PARTY

It is on the active group of Revolutionaries that the main task of reaching the masses as well as preparing them for the action rests. They are the mobile, determined mind which will energize the nation into a militant life. As circumstances arise, they come and will also come for some time longer from the ranks of the revolutionary intelligentsia, who have broken away from their bourgeois or petty bourgeois traditions. The revolutionary party will be composed of these souls, and they will gather around them the more and more active recruits from the labor, peasant or small artisan classes. It will be mainly a body of revolutionary-intellectuals, men and women, and on them will devolve the duty of planning and executing, publicity and propaganda, initiating and organizing, or coordinating the activities and linking up the different unions into an offensive, of seducing the army and the police and forming the army of revolution with themselves and these forces, of offering combined and organized armed resistance in the shape of raids and risings, of mobilizing forces for mass insurrection and fearlessly guiding them when that hour comes. In fact, they are the brains of the movement. Hence what they will require is character, that is, capacity for initiative and revolutionary leadership, and above all, it should be disciplined and strengthened by an intensive study of politics, economic problems, of history and social tendencies, and current diplomatic relations, of the progressive sciences and the science and art of modern warfare. Revolution is the creation of hard thinkers and hard workers. Unfortunately, the intellectual equipment of the Indian Revolutionaries is often neglected, but this has made them lose sight of the essential of revolution as well as the proper bearing of their actions. So a revolutionary must make of his studies a holy duty.

The party, it is clear, can in certain matters act openly and publicly. It should not be secret in so far as it can help it. This will disarm suspicion and will bestow on it prestige and power. The Party will have to shoulder high responsibilities, so it will be convenient to divide it into certain committees for every area with special tasks allocated to each of them. The division should be flexible, and according to the needs of the hour, or, on the study of the possibilities of a member, he should be assigned duties under any such local committee. The local committees are subordinate to the Provincial Boards, and they in their turn to the Supreme Council. The work of liaison, linking within the province, should be the concern of the Provincial Boards, and inter-provincial liaison is to be maintained by the Supreme Council All sporadic actions or disintegrating Factors are to be checked, but over centralization is not feasible, and hence better to not be attempted yet.

All the local committees should work in close cooperation, having on each one a representative of the other committees. The Committee should be small, composite and efficient, never allowed to degenerate into discussion clubs.

The local Revolutionary Party in each area should have:

(a) General Committee: Recruitment, propaganda amongst military, general policy, organization. Coordination of the popular Unions (See App. A).
(b) Committee of Finance: This Committee may be composed with a majority of Women members. On it rests the most difficult of all takes and hence it should have ungrudging help from the others. The source of Finance are Voluntary contribution, Forced contribution (Govt. money). Foreign capitalist and Banking houses, native ones in order of precedence, outrages on private personal wealth (however

repugnant to our policy reacts against the party and should not be encouraged), Contraband sources (embezzlement).

(c) Committee of action: A secret body for sabotage, collection of arms, training for insurrection.

Groups (1) Younger: Espionage, local military survey (2) Experts: collection of arms, military training, etc.

(d) Committee of Women: Though no artificial barrier is recognized between men and women, yet for the sake of convenience and safety of the party there should be for the time being such a body entirely responsible for its own members. They may be put in entire charge of the (b) Finance Committee and of the considerable activities of the (a) General Committee. Their scope on (c) is very limited. Their primary duties will be to revolutionize the women folk and select from them active members for direct service.

It might be concluded from the program outlined that there is no short cut to Revolution or freedom. It cannot 'dawn on us one fine morning'; that would, were it possible, be a sad day. Without the base work, without the militant masses and the party ready in every way, it would be a failure. So we have to stir ourselves. And we have to remember all the time that the capitalistic order is drifting ahead for a disaster–the catastrophe will come off perhaps in the course of two or three years. And if we still dissipate our energies or do not mobilize the revolutionary forces, the crisis will come and find us wanting. Let us be warned and accept a two- and three-year plan of Revolution.

APPENDIX A.

Duties of the General Committee.

Recruiting groups: A countrywide youth league chain, which is almost complete. It has to be linked together and most closely cooperate with the other Schools, Colleges, Gymnasiums, Clubs, Libraries, Study circles, Welfare Association, and even Ashrams- every inch of it are to be nabbed by the Youth Movement

Propaganda

The Press is the best medium, but in rural areas the platform is to be utilized. Nothing is so helpful for workers and the masses as cheap, plainly written periodicals, books or leaflets. A warning is to be given against the present supply-the stuff we consume. It is not an easy art to say what one has to say and make others hear him. A special duty of seducing the military should be assigned to tried workers; for example, 27 percent of the army, comprised of Punjabi Muslims, are to be recruited by their Punjabi kinsmen. The Gurkhas are a problem, but the Sikhs, Marhattas and Rajputs are not so.

General policy

Substitution of the bureaucratic authority by that of the masses. The Union of laborers, ryots [peasant cultivators], artisans, in their aggressive struggle to enforce their own right must be trained for the revolutionary offensive for the capture of the political power.

Coordination

Calling for representatives of the local union, from the local general Committees, calling for representatives to form the central committee of the party, and for delegates from time to time to meet in conferences for deciding on policy or program.

Organization

Besides the foregoing, the selection of the personnel and members of other committees.

APPENDIX B.

Duties of the Committee of Action.

Two classes of members (i) Junior and Women (ii) Senior. It is to be in charge of underground work.

(1) Composition: Its membership is bound to be not large but efficient. It should insist on a rigorous discipline. It will supply the leaders for the Revolutionary 'Red Army', hence, extreme care and caution should be taken in its composition, and its existence and activities are to be kept secret from the ordinary members of the party.

Duty of the Junior and Women

(1) Espionage and intelligence supply (2) Collection of Arms, and to the present method should be added the method of direct acquisition through international sources; (3) Members should be sent to Western Countries for the purpose of learning the use of arms, for example, Lewis and Vickers guns, preparation of hand grenades, etc; (4) Action–Survey of the locality. (The Government maps are to be spotted showing routes, canals, and possible shelters for members.) The model is indicated below from 'Field notes, Afghanistan, 1914' [by British Intelligence]:

I. Physical Features, General Boundary, Rivers, Flood seasons, Bridges, Forts and Ferries, Navigability.

II. Populations, Religion, Language, Tribes, Castes , Distinctive dress and character.

III. Supply, such as Fodder, Firewood, Grain Transport, Ponies, Mules, Bullocks, Donkeys, Horses, Camels, Motors and Buses.

IV. Forces, such as Police, Military Police, Military, along with their strength, their activities if tempered, Outpost stations, cantonments. Distribution of Police, of the military police, of the infantry, cavalry or artillery, of arms and magazines, guns, pistols, rifles, small arms and big arms. Possible fighting men from the locality–hostile and friendly.

V. Roads: Description and a chart as follows:

1. From ....to .... Miles

2. Stages: ....stop .... Miles

3. Nature: Metalled [made wit small pieces of stone], Motorable, Kutcha [unfinished, in a rough state, etc.

4. Obstacles; Difficult in rains, etc

5. Water supply, fuel, fodder connection, with remarks.

Training In volunteer corps, such as University corps, etc. A Thorough study of the military's 'Field Service Regulation, Vol. I and Vol. II' is bound to be profitable. This knowledge is essential. Study of more military Literature and acquaintance with wherever possible, Soldiers in barracks and cantons to be encouraged.

Duty of the Seniors

Action of Finance: To be undertaken at the request of the Finance Committee and the General Committee. To be limited to public money and Foreign capitalistic gains, for the present. The effect on popularity and unpopularity should be final test for such action.

Sabotage: On behalf of the Unions at the direction of the General Committee

Collection of Arms: See above.

Terrorism: Against individual only in very extreme cases when his offence is against the public, not against mere groups or individuals. Generally to be discouraged unless there are forced circumstances.

Insurrections: When the Supreme Council directs. Group rising essential. Raids for arms.

The First Anti-Colonial Unrest in Punjab

Bhagat Singh was an ardent student of both Indian and world history. His knowledge of history and current events across nations was remarkable for someone so young and limited in his material resources.

In this essay, first serialized in Urdu in the weekly *Bande Mataram*, he looks at the political history of the part of India he hailed from – Punjab. A region of considerable geographical, religious, ethnic, and cultural diversity, it has seen many conquests and in- and out-migrations over centuries. It was late to develop a script for the Punjabi language, which no doubt retarded somewhat the development of popular political understanding and action.

However, Bhagat Singh tells us in this essay that matters changed dramatically in the early part of the twentieth century. He also shows the inadequacy of any politics that compromises with the ruling class – in this case, the British imperialists and their domestic retainers – is bound to fail. Revolutionary politics must awaken the understanding of workers and peasants of their exploitation and expropriation at the hands of their rulers. Given that the British were quick to oppress, those who wanted radical change must take advantage of at least the most egregious forms of repression to lead and enlighten the masses.

This essay was first translated from the original Urdu, which has been lost, to Hindi and then into English by the co-editor Chaman Lal.

In his book, the erstwhile Governor of Punjab, Sir Michael O'Dwyer, has revealed a very unpalatable but extremely significant truth. He has said that Punjab is the most backward region in political upheaval. Those who have even the slightest knowledge of Punjab's political struggle can appreciate the truth of this statement.

Look at the history until now. This state has made the maximum number of sacrifices for the freedom of the country. For this, terrible calamities have been endured by the people of this state. In political, religious, and other social agitations, Punjab has been ahead of other regions of India and has given the country the largest number of sacrifices of life and property. Still, even so, we have to accept with bowed heads that Punjab is the most backward in the political sphere.

This is because political agitation has not become an essential part and parcel of the personal lives of the public here. Even in the field of literature, this region has not achieved its true place. Until O'Dwyer's book came out, for the educated class, the question of the country's slavery had not become the most immediate and important one, so it is generally held that this region was very backward. Many other regions in India are far more backward than Punjab, but, unfortunately, this ill-fated region remained backward despite such allegations.

Punjab has no language specific of its own. Due to the lack of a language, it has not been able to progress in creating literature. That is why the educated class had to remain dependent upon western literature. The unfortunate consequence was that the educated class remained aloof from the political turmoil. That is why politics have not been able to become a part of Punjab's literature and field of culture. That is why only a handful of people have devoted their entire lives to politics. It is on this basis that such allegations are made against this state. This essay intends to draw the attention of the local leaders and the society to this drawback.

From the Kuka Revolt under the leadership of Guru Ram Singh to all the agitations that have taken place in Punjab till now and the way political consciousness rose among the public, the people became prepared to sacrifice all they had at the altar of freedom. How these people laid down their lives, their biographies and history would give courage to every man and woman so that they can manage even future movements better in light of their studies and experiences. It is certainly not my aim in penning down this history that those revolts would succeed only in the future. I aim only for the public to be inspired by the sacrifices of these martyrs and their lifelong service to the country and be able to follow them. The activists may decide how they would work when the time comes, keeping in mind the prevailing conditions.

HOW DID POLITICAL AGITATIONS BEGIN IN PUNJAB?

In 1907 there was complete quiet in eastern Punjab. After the Kuka Revolt, no political agitation was unleashed that could shatter the slumber of the rulers. In 1908, a Congress Session took place in Punjab for the first time, but at that point, the basis of the activities of Congress was to express loyalty towards the rulers, so it did not have much effect in the political arena. The powerful agitation that had arisen following the partition of Bengal in 1905-06, the propaganda of Swadeshi and the shunning of all foreign things greatly influenced Punjab's industrial life and the common man. In those days, the question of making objects indigenously was alive even in Punjab, especially the question of preparing sugar, and soon a couple of mills were opened. Although it did not impact the political life of the region much, yet the government tried to destroy this industry by raising the tax on the harvest of sugarcane three times. Earlier, the tax for approximately 2000 square yards of land was only Rs. 2.50/, but now they had to shell out Rs. 7.50/. So, suddenly a colossal burden came upon the farmers, and they were paralyzed.

NEW COLONY ACT

On another front, the government had dug several new canals in Lyallpur and other places. They lured many people residing in Jalandhar, Amritsar, and Hoshiarpur by promising them a great many facilities. These people gave up their old lands and property and spent their sweat and blood to make this jungle arable. But they had not even been able to breathe a sigh of relief when the New Colony Act was thrust upon them. This Act was a ploy to destroy the very existence of peasants. According to this Act, only the eldest son of a person could inherit the property. The younger sons were given no share in it. Upon the eldest son's death, that piece of land or property would not go to the younger sons and would revert to the government.

No man could fell the trees standing upon his land. He couldn't even break off a twig to brush his teeth with. They had got those lands, but they could only farm on that land. They could not build any kind of house or hutment, so much so, that even troughs to put animal fodder in could not be made. The slightest infringement of the laws could lead to a 24-hour notice being issued and then lands could be confiscated. It is said that the government wanted the entire land to come into the hands of a few foreigners through this law, keeping the Indian tenant farmers dependent on them forever. Apart from this, the government also wanted that, as in other regions, there should only be a small number of big landowners, and the rest should be extremely poor tenant farmers. In this manner, the people should be divided into two classes.

The rich would never, under any circumstances whatsoever, be ready to support the opponents of the government, and the poor farmers, who would not be able to fill their bellies even after hard labour, would not get an opportunity to do so. In this manner, the government could do whatever it wished.

SEEDS OF UNREST

In those days, the condition of Uttar Pradesh, Bihar, and other regions was similar, but the people of Punjab prepared themselves more quickly. They started a powerful agitation against this policy of the government. This new state of affairs had only recently been accomplished in the Rawalpindi region, and the tax raised. Thus at the beginning of 1907 itself, conditions were ripe for unrest. Even the Governor of Punjab, Sir Denzil Ibbetson, had said at the beginning of this year that though there was apparent peace at that time, agitation in the minds of the people was growing.

These days, a kind of quiet was spread all over the country. The people were in a state of 'wait and watch'. This was the lull before the storm. All the causes of unrest were present, especially in Punjab. Conditions were ripe and necessary for unrest.

THE CONGRESS OF 1906

In 1906, the annual Congress convention was held in Calcutta. Dadabhai Nauroji was the President. For the first time, he uttered the word '*Swarajya*' (Home Rule) in his speech at this convention. Based on their experience, the members of the British Parliament had told Dadabhai that if we wanted to achieve anything, we would first have to acquire inner strength. We would have to stand on the power of our own two feet; it was not enough to stare ahead with a stony glance.

LALA LAJPAT RAI

Exactly this thing was said by *Punjab Kesri* Lala Lajpat Rai, one year previously in the Banaras Congress Convention[1]. The revered Lalaji had been sent with the Congress President, the late

1 *Punjab Kesri*: The Lion of Punjab.

Gokhale, as part of a deputation to England. He had delivered a
stinging speech after his return from there.

LOKMANYA TILAK

Lokmanya Tilak was very popular in the Congress Convention
of 1906; the youth became devoted to him due to his honest and
frank talk. His fearlessness, his desire to do something, and his
being prepared every moment to endure the greatest of hardships
attracted the youth towards him. Apart from speaking during the
Congress Convention, Lokmanya Tilak delivered several speeches
outside the ambit of the Congress convention at this time.

SARDAR KISHAN SINGH AND SARDAR AJIT SINGH

A few Punjabi youths among the men were especially drawn
towards the Lokmanya. Two such Punjabi youths were Kishan
Singh and my respected uncle, Sardar Ajit Singh ji.

THE PERIODICAL BHARAT MATA AND MEHTA NAND KISHORE

Sardar Kishan Singh and Sardar Ajit Singh returned to Lahore
and started publishing a monthly magazine called *Bharat Mata*.
They began to disseminate their views by taking the respected
Mehta Nand Kishore along. They had neither any money nor any
contacts among the wealthy. They were not even the leaders or
priests of any community, so they had to muster all the resources
for dissemination themselves. One day in the bazar, they attracted
some people by ringing the bell and delivered a speech on how
the foreigners had destroyed Indian industry and trade. They
also announced that the following Sunday, an important meeting
would take place near the office of *Bharat Mata*, which was situated
midway between the Lahori and the Shalimar gateways.

The first meeting was held in the Papad Mandi, and the second in the Lahori Mandi.[2] Before the speeches in the third meeting, a Punjabi youth read a touching poem steeped in patriotism and received much praise from the people. Now this young man also joined this group. This young man was a popular poet of Punjab, Lala Lalchand 'Falak', who had been rousing the country with his inspirational poetry. Several others like Lala Pindi Das ji and Dr Ishwari Prasad ji joined the group the same week. With all these people joining the group, an institution by the name of *Anjuman-e-Muhbban-e-watan* was established, which later became famous under the name of Bharat Mata Society.[3]

Another public meeting was to be held the following Sunday as well. The same day, Mrs Annie Besant was to speak in Lahore. Some friends suggested that the Bharat Mata Society be dissolved that day, but this suggestion was not accepted, nor was it considered appropriate to postpone the meeting. Finally, when the meeting took place, there was adequate attendance. It was declared that a meeting would be held every Sunday. Sardar Ajit Singh was elected as the President, and Mehta Nand Kishore as its Secretary.

THE JAT SABHA

This propaganda continued to be disseminated for a month or so. One day the Jat peasants of the Lahore and Amritsar region decided to hold a meeting to protest the rise in the tax. This meeting was organized in the Ratan Chand Sarai outside the Ajmeri gateway, but when the Jats mustered there, the Deputy Commissioner summoned Ratan Chand's son and threatened to confiscate his property. So Ratan Chand's son threw out all the Jats from the inn. In such a situation, the peasants established contact with the influential members of the society of that city, but they

---

2 Mandi means market in Hindustani.
3 *Anjuman-e-Muhbban-e-watan* in Persian means the love of nation or country, it was organization formed by Ajit Singh and also the title a small book penned by him in Urdu.

only received a cold response. Meeting with disappointment on all sides, the peasants finally went to sit in the Municipal Garden. In the meantime, the members of the Bharat Mata Society received this information, and took these people to their place. Apart from a room, the Bharat Mata Society had a large ground. Durries were spread on the ground, a large tent was erected, and arrangements were made to provide food to these peasants. This energized the peasants, and then, for an entire week, daily meetings were held there, and fearless speeches were made. The enthusiasm of the peasants in these meetings also emboldened the members of the Bharat Mata Society.

Then a schedule was drawn to make trips to the rural areas so that they could prepare the peasants to shun taxes. There was so much zeal among the people that they were willing to sacrifice everything in this struggle. This was a battle cry against the government.

SUFI AMBA PRASAD

Right then, a great patriot, statesman and writer joined the Bharat Mata Society. He was Shri Sufi Amba Prasad. Sufi ji was born in 1858 in Moradabad. He was an influential Urdu writer, a strong supporter of Hindu-Muslim unity, and a fearless champion of freedom. He published a weekly and, after a year, was sentenced to two and a quarter years of jail for treason. Within a year of completing this sentence, another case was lodged against him, and he was sentenced for six years this time. In those days, the people convicted of treason were considered dangerous criminals and mistreated in jail.

He was released from jail in 1906, and, finding a new political awareness in Punjab, he came here. Here he became the co-editor of the weekly *Hindustan*. His stinging articles and his name on the editorials gave sleepless nights to the newspaper owners. So he had to resign from the job. He had then participated in the meeting of the Jats, and stayed on, becoming so close to Sardar Ajit Singh that it was impossible to separate the two.

A huge rally was to be held in Lyallpur during these days. This was popularly known as *Mandi Maveshiyan*.[4] People used to gather in large numbers to buy and sell animals. This year the owner of the daily, *Zamindar*, Mian Siraj-ud-din, and a few other gentlemen decided to hold a meeting on the occasion.[5] They were going to pass a resolution against the New Colony Act. Lalaji was a special invitee to deliver a lecture at the meeting. The members of the Bharat Mata Society also decided to hold a meeting. The Bharat Mata Society was very over-zealous, so the gentlemen who thought of running an agitation according to constitutional means were a little uncomfortable with it. The Bharat Mata Society sent two workers in advance to prepare the ground first so that after a day or two, Sardar Ajit Singh and his comrades could reach there and disseminate their ideas more successfully.

The workers of the Bharat Mata Society were able to deliver some lectures in the tents that had been put up by the Zimindar Sabha and garner considerable public sympathy. And when Lalaji set off from Lahore, Sardar Ajit Singh also set off the same day. Lala ji got someone to ask Sardar Ajit Singh what his projected program was. He also gave information about his program, saying he would thank the government for the minor alteration they had made in the Colony Act and request the government repeal the law.

Sardar ji replied that their program was that they would try and prepare the people to resist the payment of the tax. Moreover, they could give no space to thank the government in their program.

Both Lalaji and Sardar ji arrived in Lyallpur. A huge procession was taken out for Lala ji, so Lala ji could reach the venue only after two hours. But some people did not participate in the procession, reached the dais directly, and began to deliver speeches. After a couple of short speeches, it was Sardar Ajit Singh's turn to speak.

4 *Mandi Maveshiyan* is animal fair.
5 Maulana Sirajuddin Ahmed founder of the daily, *Zamindar*.

He was a powerful orator. The people became enamoured of his fearless oration, and the public also became enthusiastic. By the time the organizers of the procession reached the dais, the public was fully with the Bharat Mata Society. A couple of moderate leaders tried to prevent Sardar Ajit Singh's speech, but the public rebuked them so much that they could do nothing. This emboldened the crowd further. One peasant got up and announced that he had 10 squares of land, which he was bestowing upon the struggle, and he was ready, along with his wife, to serve his country.

Lala Lajpat Rai rose to deliver his speech after Sardar Ajit Singh. Lala ji was an incomparable orator of Punjab, but the fearlessness, magnificence, and determination with which he spoke that day was something out of the ordinary. Every line of Lala ji's speech fetched applause, and slogans of 'Jai' rent the air.[6] After the meeting, a large number of people declared their desire to serve their country.

The Deputy Commissioner of Lyallpur was also present there. The activities of the meeting made him conclude that the entire organization was a conspiracy. Lala Lajpat Rai was their leader, and the young man, Sardar Ajit Singh, was his pupil. The government carried this impression for a long time. This was probably the reason for the house arrest of Lala ji and Ajit Singh.

After Lala ji's speech, Shri Banke Dyal read a compelling poem, which became very popular later on. This was 'Pagri sambhaal O Jatta'.[7]

Lala Banke Dyal was a Sub-Inspector of Police, and he resigned from his job and joined the agitation. That day when he came down from the dais after reciting his poem, the worker of the Bharat Mata Society embraced him.

After the riots in Lahore, the Municipal Board passed a resolution that the Principals of all the colleges in the city ask to stop the students from participating in political agitations and not

6 Jai is victory.
7 Protect your turban, O peasant!

be allowed to leave their hostels. The students who did not follow orders would be given the severest punishment.

Lokmanya Tilak had written a sharp essay regarding this resolution in his Marathi paper, *Kesri*. Lokmanya wondered who would not be sad and regret the riots. 'Who says that young men should not act with more patience? But what did the resolution of the Municipal Board mean? Today, after fifty years, the youth of this country have shown some awareness. Why should there be a proposal to destroy that because of normal turbulence? Today if the youth are being filled with feelings of patriotism and are impatient for freedom, they should be dealt with affectionately and told that they must not waste their energies like this'.

When the public does something in the heat of the moment, then this is the policy of the radical group. The leaders of the radical groups know that when awareness is spread among the people then enthusiasm and impatience are a normal part of it. They also knew that those over-cautious people who weigh every step before taking it do not stay long in the freedom struggle. The builders of the nation are always the youth. Someone has said truly, 'It is not the old who can bring about improvement because they are very wise and intelligent. Improvement is brought about by the labour, courage, sacrifice and selflessness of the youth who don't know the meaning of fear and who think less and do more'.

It seems that at that time, the youth of this region were influenced by such emotions and jumped into the freedom struggle. Whereas three years ago there was complete silence, now the Swadeshi and Swarajya agitation was so powerful, that the bureaucracy took fright. On the other hand, agitation against the New Colony Act in Lyallpur districts and others was raging. The railway workers also went on strike in sympathy for the peasant struggle and funds began to be collected to help them. The result was that at the end of April the Punjab government became afraid. The Governor at that time, apprising the Indian government of the entire situation in a letter said, 'The new ideas are limited to only the educated class, and especially the lawyer and student groups in the northern districts of the region, but as we proceed towards the middle of the region it is evident that dissatisfaction and unrest are spreading rapidly'.

Further in the letter he noted, 'These people (the leaders of the agitation) have got special success in Amritsar and Ferozepur. They have been able to spread disaffection even in Rawalpindi and Lyallpur. And the situation in Lahore is for all to see'. At the end of the letter, he writes, 'Some leaders are making plans to compel the English to leave the country. They want to do it either forcibly or by creating an atmosphere of non-cooperation between the public and the government and create hatred and ill will against the English in an irresponsible manner. The present situation is very delicate and we must do something to deal with it as soon as possible'.

Shri Kartar Singh Sarabha

During his short life, Bhagat Singh wrote numerous biographical sketches of those who fought for Indian independence and socialist revolution. Not only are these historical and political documents, but they are also important in terms of keeping the memory alive. These admirable men and women serve as role models for future revolutionaries, their words and deeds worth contemplating and emulating, as well as providing invaluable lessons as to strategy and tactics in the struggle.

Again, note Bhagat Singh's belief that youth must form the militant and activist wing of revolutionary struggle. This essay was originally published in the April and May 1927 issues of the Punjabi monthly *Kirti* from Amritsar. Note that the word '*Shri*' (a general honorific) and the word '*Bhai*' (brother), both terms of respectful address, are used to describe Kartar Singh. The essay is signed by one of Bhagat Singh's pseudonyms, Balwant, which means 'powerful, strong, of immense strength'.

This heroic devotee of the deity of battle – the rebel Kartar Singh Sarabha – was not even 20 years old when he sacrificed his life on the altar of freedom. He appeared from nowhere like a whirlwind, lighted a flame and tried to rouse the deity of battle from slumber. He conducted the *yajna* of revolution and finally offered himself to its flames.[1] We were unable to fathom what he was, from which world he suddenly appeared and where he disappeared.

It is astonishing to see how much he accomplished at the mere

---

1 In Hinduism *Yajna* refers to any ritual obaltions to the sacred fire, often with mantras.

age of 19 years. Such courage, such self-confidence, such a spirit of sacrifice, and such devotion are extremely rare to find. Very few people have been born in India who can be called revolutionaries in the true sense of the word, but Kartar Singh Sarabha's name would feature at the top among these few. The spirit of revolution suffused every pore of his body. There was only one ambition, one desire, and only one hope – revolution – this is what he was born for, and this is for what he ultimately laid down his life.

He was born in 1896 in the village of Sarabha in Ludhiana district. He was the only son of his parents. His father passed away while he was still very young. However, his paternal grandfather took great pains to bring him up well. His father's name was Mangal Singh; one of his uncles was a police sub-inspector in the United Province, and another uncle was a high official in the forest department of Orissa. After his initial education at a village school, he took admission in Khalsa High School Ludhiana. Academically he was an average student, too mischievous. He would play pranks on others and was termed Aflatoon/Plato by his classmates.[2] He was loved by all, had a separate group in school, was a sportsman, and had all qualities of a genuine leader. After doing 9th class at Ludhiana, he went to his father's younger brother in Orissa. After clearing his matriculation there, he took admission in a college. This was in 1910-1911. Here he got an opportunity to read a number of books beyond the narrow boundaries of school and college syllabi. This was the age of revolutionary movements, and his patriotism was fostered in this environment.

Kartar Singh expressed a desire to go to America after his college. His family did not raise any opposition to it. He was sent to America. He reached the San Francisco coast in the year 1912. He was subjected to rigorous questioning by immigration authorities. He told immigration authorities that he had come here for studies.

2 *Aflatoon* is the Arabic form of the name of the philosopher Plato (from the Greek Platon) and has also popularly come to mean an eccentric person or a maverick in Hindustani (Hindi-Urdu).

When asked why he did not study in India, Sarabha said that he had come for higher studies and intended to join California University. Being asked about being denied admission, Sarabha instantly responded, 'that will be a grave injustice. If hurdles are created in the path of students, the progress of the world will stop. Who knows, the education here might empower me to achieve some great deed for the betterment of the world. In case I am not allowed to land here, won't the world suffer due to the lack of that great deed?' Officers were impressed, and he was allowed to land.

After stepping on that free soil, the humiliation faced at every stage began to hammer upon his tender heart. He would go mad with anger upon hearing 'Damn Hindu' and 'Black Man', etc., on the lips of the whites. He began increasingly to feel that the honour and respect of his country were in danger. Whenever he felt homesick, the vision of a helpless country in shackles would swim before his eyes. His tender heart began to harden gradually, and his resolve to sacrifice his life for the freedom of his country began to deepen. How can we understand what went on in his heart at that time!

It was impossible for him to remain unaffected by the events around him. He was constantly tormented by the question of how the country would attain freedom if the path of non-violence failed. Then, without further ado, he began to organize Indian workers together. He was able to inculcate a spirit of independence in them. He would spend hours talking to each worker to impress upon him that death was a thousand times preferable to a life of humiliation and slavery. Once he had begun, other people too joined in. They held a special meeting in May 1912, in which some nine Indians took part. They decided to sacrifice everything they had – wealth, mind and life for the freedom of their country. During this time, the exiled patriot Bhagwan Singh also reached there. There was a flurry of meetings, processions, and lectures. The need for a newspaper was felt, so *Ghadar* was published. The first issue of the paper was published in November 1913. Kartar Singh Sarabha was on the editorial board. There was infinite enthusiasm in his pen. The printing of the paper was manually done on a hand press by the editorial board. Kartar Singh would hum songs to keep him going when he got tired during his work.

Seva desh di jindadiye badi aukhi
Gallan karnian dher sukhllian ne
Jinhan is seva vich pair paya
Uhnan lakh musibtan jhallian ne
Service to the nation is very difficult, O, life!
It is easy to converse.
One who serves the nation
Faces a million hardships.

Kartar Singh's zeal inspired the others who saw him work so hard. One doesn't know whether others had thought about how to free India, or whether to keep their work a secret or not, but Kartar Singh was deeply involved in this issue. In the meantime, he took employment with an aircraft company in New York and began to learn the ropes wholeheartedly.

In September 1914, the Kamagatamaru ship had to return without completing its mission after undergoing untold suffering at the hands of the white imperialists. Then our Kartar Singh came to Japan along with Gupta, who advocated revolutions, and an American revolutionary. They met Baba Gurdit Singh in Kobe to discuss these issues. *Ghadar, Ghadar di Goonj* and several books were published in the Yugantar Ashram Printing Press in San Francisco. The net of their propaganda spread wider. Their enthusiasm grew. In February 1914, the flag of freedom was unfurled in a public meeting in Stockton, and pledges were made in the name of equality and freedom. Kartar Singh was among the chief speakers at this meeting. All of them declared that they would lay down their lives in the struggle for freedom of the country. Time passed. Suddenly they received news of the outbreak of the

First World War. They were delighted. All of them began to sing,

> Come; let us go to fight for our country,
> This is our last oath and decree.

Kartar Singh exhorted people to return to their motherland. He himself boarded a ship and reached Colombo in Sri Lanka. In those days, those who returned to Punjab from America often found themselves arrested under the Defence of India Rules (D.I.R.). Very few would reach home safe and sound. Kartar Singh was among those who did. He launched his plans with fervour. There was a problem of organization, but that was somehow sorted out. The Maratha youth Vishnu Ganesh Pingle, also joined him in December 1914. They made efforts to ensure that Shri Sachindra Nath Sanyal and Ras Behari came to Punjab. Kartar Singh would manage to attend all the meetings everywhere. Today there is a secret meeting in Moga, and he's here. Tomorrow there is a lecture for students there, and Kartar Singh is in the first row. The next day, the soldiers in the Ferozepur Cantonment are being organized. Then he is leaving for Calcutta to procure weapons. When they faced a problem of insufficient funds, he suggested *dacoity*[3] as an answer. Most people were stunned at the suggestion, but he said that there was nothing to fear, and even said that Bhai Parmanand, too, was in favour of this idea. Kartar Singh was asked to get approval from him. The next day he reported, though without meeting Bhai Parmanand, 'I've asked; he's agreeable'. He could not bear the thought that they should delay the revolution merely due to a paucity of funds.

One day he went to a village to commit a dacoity. Kartar Singh was the leader of the gang. The house was being looted. There was an extremely beautiful girl in the house. One of the Ghadarite cast an evil eye upon the girl. He grabbed the girl's hand. The girl raised

---

3 Armed robbery.

an alarm. Kartar Singh rushed to her rescue, aimed a revolver at the man's temple and disarmed him. Then he roared, 'Sinner! You have committed a heinous crime. You deserve a death sentence, but you are pardoned due to the exigencies of the situation. Fall at the girl's feet immediately and beg forgiveness. Say, 'Sister! Forgive me'. Then touch her mother's feet and say, 'Mataji, I am sorry for this lapse'. If she forgives you, your life will be spared; otherwise, you'll be shot dead'. The man did as he was told. Kartar managed to save the situation before it deteriorated too far. Both mother and daughter were very touched. The mother said affectionately to Kartar Singh, 'Son! How did a saintly and well-mannered youth like you get involved in something like this?' Kartar Singh's heart, too, overflowed with emotion and he said, 'Ma ji! We aren't doing this because of greed. We've put everything at stake to commit this robbery. We need money to buy weapons. Where can we get it from? Ma ji, it is only for this noble work that we are forced to do such jobs'. This was a very poignant scene. The mother said again, 'We have to marry this girl off. We'd be grateful if you could leave something for her'. Kartar placed all that they had gathered in front of the mother and said, 'Take whatever you want'. The mother took a little money and gave the rest to Kartar Singh with a blessing, 'Go, son! May you achieve success!' How sensitive, pure and large-hearted Kartar Singh was, even when involved in something like dacoity, is clear from this incident.

Before contacting a Bengal group, Sarabha had already planned the attack on the magazine of the Lahore cantonment. Once, he met with an army soldier in charge of the magazine in a train, he promised to give him the keys. On November 25th, Sarabha went there with some daring comrades, however, the soldier was transferred to some other place a day earlier. The whole plan collapsed, yet disheartenment or anxiety was not in the genes of such revolutionaries.

Preparations for a revolution were complete in February 1915. A week before the appointed date, Kartar Singh, Pingle, and a few other comrades went to Agra, Kanpur, Allahabad, Lucknow, Meerut and several other places to discuss the details of the revolution with people at large. Finally, the much-awaited day drew near, the 21st of February, 1915, had been decided as the day of revolution in India. Preparations for making it a success were underway. But at that very time, a rat was gnawing at the roots of the tree of their hopes. Four or five days before the day, they got suspicious of Kirpal Singh and feared his treachery would ruin all their plans. Due to this suspicion, Kartar Singh and Ras Behari Bose suggested advancing the date from the 21st to the 19th of February. But Kirpal Singh also managed to get information regarding this change of date. The presence of a traitor in this group of revolutionaries proved to have fatal consequences. Ras Behari and Kartar Singh were also unable to hide their identity due to a lack of preparedness. What could this result in but misfortune for India?

Kartar Singh reached Ferozepur with about fifty-sixty people as per the original plan. He met a comrade, an army *havildar* and discussed the revolution with him. But Kirpal Singh had already ruined everything. The Indian soldiers had, by now, been disarmed. A frantic round of arrests took place. The Havildar refused to help. Kartar Singh's attempt failed. Disappointed, he returned to Lahore. A round of arrests was made all over Punjab. People began to succumb to pressure.

Disappointed with this situation, Ras Behari Bose was lying on a bed in a house in Lahore. Kartar Singh also came there and lay down on another *charpoy* with his face turned towards the other side. They did not utter a word but understood the state of each other's hearts. We can gauge their condition, too.

Our fate is to bang our head on Lady Fortune's door
But the means to test our fate slipped from our hands.

They decided to leave Punjab by crossing the western border.

The three who crossed the border were Sarabha, Jagat Singh and Harnam Singh Tunda. After crossing a desert mountain, they reached a picturesque spot. A beautiful stream was flowing; they sat at its bank and started eating roasted gram. Then Kartar Singh began to sing,

Why should the lions run in the face of dire straits?

Poet Kartar wrote this poem in the United States. He repeatedly sang this in melodious voice and suddenly stopped to ask his companion, Jagat Singh, if this poem was written for others? Should we not be responsive to our comrades in dire straits? They looked at each other and decided to return to India, knowing well that death awaited them.

Kartar Singh's only desire was for a revolutionary war to attain freedom so that he could lay down his life for his country. Then he came to Chak No. 5 near Sargodha. Again he began to preach revolution. He was arrested there and shackled. The fearless revolutionary Kartar Singh was brought to the Lahore Railway Station. He said to the Police Officer, 'Mr Tomkin, please bring us some food'. How carefree he was! Friend and foe alike would be glad to meet this charismatic personality. He was happy even when he was arrested. He would often say, 'Bestow the title of "Rebel" upon me after I die a brave and courageous death. If anyone remembers me, let it be as "Kartar Singh, the Rebel"'.

Sarabha's restless soul was not pacified even behind bars. One day he managed to get some tools to cut through the bar and contacted 60-70 prisoners; they planned to escape by jailbreak and attack the Lahore cantonment to snatch weapons and revolt again. In times of dejection and failure, this hope was just a mirage. One prisoner got wind, which made all to be searched and shackled. Tools were recovered, and all efforts to break jail came to nought!

His case was brought to trial. Kartar Singh was merely 18½

years old at that time. He was the youngest among the accused, but
the judge wrote about him:

> He is among the most dangerous criminals amongst the
> accused. There is not a single part during his journey from
> America and the conspiracy in India in which he has not
> played a pivotal role.

When it was his turn to record his statement, he accepted all
the charges. He continued to speak the language of revolution.
With his pen between his teeth, the judge watched him and
didn't write a single word. Later he said, 'Kartar Singh, we have
not recorded your statement yet. Think about what you want to
say. Do you know what consequences your statement can have?'
Those who witnessed the trial say that upon hearing these words,
Kartar Singh answered cheerfully, 'At the most, you can give me
the hangman's noose. What else? I am not afraid of that!'

The proceedings of the court were adjourned till the next
day. The next day again began with Kartar Singh's statement.
The previous day the judges had been under the impression that
Kartar Singh had given the statement under the influence of Bhai
Parmanand, but they could not plumb the depths of the heart
of the revolutionary Kartar Singh. Kartar Singh's statement was
even more hard-hitting, passionate, and radical in spirit than
the previous day. He admitted to all the charges as he had on the
first day. He concluded his statement, saying, 'I'll get either life
imprisonment or death for this. But I shall prefer death, so that
I can be reborn till Hindustan is liberated, and go to the gallows
again and again. This is my last wish . . .'

The judge was highly impressed with Kartar Singh's courage,
but unlike a large-hearted enemy who would have called this
courage, he labelled it shamelessness. Kartar Singh was not only
awarded abuses but a death sentence. He thanked them smilingly.

While Kartar Singh was locked up in the cell awaiting his death, his paternal grandfather visited him and asked,

'Kartar Singh, you are dying for the sake of those who abuse you. One can't even fathom how your nation will benefit from your death.'

Kartar Singh asked in a soft voice, 'Dadaji, where is that relative of ours, Mr. So-and-so?'

'He died in the plague', grandfather responded.

'And he?', Kartar mentioned another relative.

'He died of cholera', replied the grandfather.

'So do you want that Kartar Singh should be bedridden in illness for months and die a painful death? Is this death not a thousand times better?', responded Kartar.

Dadaji had nothing more to say.

Even today this question is relevant: What benefit did his death have? Who did he die for? The answer is absolutely clear. He died for the country. His idea was to die in the service of his nation. He wanted nothing more than that. He was content to die unknown and unsung.

Only he labours in the garden of love,
Who values labour for the sake of labour.
One does not arrange flowers on display,
One strews pearls in the garden in the dark night.

The case continued for a year and a half. It was 16th of November, 1915 when he was hanged to death. He was as happy as ever on that day. His weight increased by ten pounds. With *Bharat Mata ki Jai*, on his lips, he embraced the noose.[4]

Balwant

---

4 *Bharat Mata ki Jai*: Hail Mother India!

Two Posters After Saunder's Murder

British police officer John Saunders was shot and killed on 17 December 1928. The following notices were posted on walls in Lahore on 18 and 23 December, respectively. Both were in English.

NOTICE - I

By Hindustan Socialist Republic Army.
'Bureaucracy Beware'
With the death of J.P. Saunders the assassination of Lala Lajpat Rai has been avenged.

It is a matter of great regret that a respected leader of 30 crores of people was attacked by an ordinary police officer like J.P. Saunders and met with his death at his mean hands. This national insult was a challenge to young men.

Today the world has seen that the people of India are not lifeless; their blood has not become cold. They can lay down their lives for the country's honour. The proof of this has been given by the youth who are ridiculed and insulted by the leaders of their own country.

'Tyrant Government Beware'

Do not hurt the feelings of the oppressed and suffering people of this country. Stop your devilish ways. Despite all your laws preventing us from keeping arms and despite all your watchfulness, people of this country would continue to get pistols and revolvers. Even if these arms are not adequate in numbers for an armed revolution, they would be sufficient for avenging the insult to the country's honour. Even if our own people condemn us and ridicule us and if foreign government subjects us to any amount of repression, we shall be ever ready to teach a lesson to foreign tyrants who insult our national honour. Despite all opposition and repression, we shall carry forward the call for revolution and even we go to the scaffold for being hanged, we shall continue to shout:

'Long Live Revolution!'

We are sorry to have killed a man. But this man was a part of cruel, despicable and unjust system and killing him was a necessity. This man has been killed as an employee of the British government. This Government is the most oppressive government in the world.

We are sorry for shedding human blood but it becomes necessary to bathe the alter of Revolution with blood. Our aim is to bring about a revolution which would end all exploitation of man by man.

'Long live Revolution!'

Sd/- BALRAJ

18th December, 1928. Commander-in-Chief, HSRA

NOTICE - II

The Hindustan Socialist Republican Army
Notice
No more secrets No more Special Guess
About
The incident of 17th December
J.P. Saunders is dead!
Lala Lajpat Rai is avenged!!

Under the rules and regulations of the H.S.R.A. (Rule 10th B.R.C) it is hereby notified that it was retaliatory action of none but a direct political nature. The most dastardly attack made on the great old man of India Lala Lajpat Rai that caused his death was greatest insult hurled down on the head of nationhood. And hereby is it avenged!

Further on everybody is hereby requested to abstain from offering any sort of assistance to our enemy the police in finding out our clues. Anybody acting contrary will be severely dealt with.

Long Live the Revolution

Balraj

Commander-in-chief

Dated 23rd December 1928

Leaflet Thrown in the Central Assembly

This is the text of the typed leaflet thrown in the Central Assembly by Bhagat Singh and B.K. Dutta after they exploded the bombs. Shiv Verma, Bhagat Singh's comrade and editor of Selected Writings of Shaheed Bhagat Singh, recalls that this was written by Bhagat Singh in their Sitaram Bazar den. He also typed about 30 to 40 copies of it on the party letterhead. Jaidev Kapoor helped make arrangements for the typing. A full-size block of the leaflet was published in The Hindustan Times in its special evening edition the same day, 8 April 1929. It became a turning point in the Indian Freedom Struggle. The leaflet was written in English

'It takes a loud voice to make the deaf hear', with these immortal words uttered on a similar occasion by Valliant, a French anarchist martyr, do we strongly justify this action of ours.

Without repeating the humiliating history of the past ten years of the working of the reforms[1] and without mentioning the insults hurled at the Indian nation through this House, the so-called Indian Parliament – we want to point out that, while the people are expecting some more crumbs of reforms from the Simon Commission, and are ever quarrelling over the distribution of the expected bones, the Government is thrusting upon us new repressive measures like the Public Safety and the Trade Disputes Bill, while reserving the Press Sedition Bill for the next session. The indiscriminate arrests of labour leaders working in the open field clearly indicate whither the wind blows.

In these extremely provocative circumstances, the Hindustan

1 Montague-Chelmsford Reforms.

Socialist Republican Association, in all seriousness, realizing their full responsibility, had decided and ordered its army to do this particular action, so that a stop be put to this humiliating farce and to let the alien bureaucratic exploiters do what they wish, but they must be made to come before the public eye in their naked form.

Let the representatives of the people return to their constituencies and prepare the masses for the coming revolution, and let the Government know that while protesting against the Public Safety and Trade Disputes Bills and the callous murder of Lala Lajpat Rai. On behalf of the helpless Indian masses, we want to emphasize the lesson often repeated by history, that it is easy to kill individuals, but you cannot kill the ideas. Great empires crumbled while the ideas survived. Bourbons and Czars fell while the revolution marched ahead triumphantly.

We are sorry to admit that we who attach so great a sanctity to human life, we who dream of a glorious future, when man will be enjoying perfect peace and full liberty, have been forced to shun human blood. But the sacrifice to individuals at the altar of the great revolution that will bring freedom to all, rendering the exploitation of man by man impossible, is inevitable.

Long Live the Revolution
Sd/-BALRAJ
Commander-in Chief

Message to the Punjab Students' Conference

The Second Punjab Students' Conference was held at Lahore on 19 October 1929, under the presidentship of Subhash Chandra Bose, and this message was read in the open session. Bhagat Singh signed this message jointly with B.K. Dutta. Shiv Verma recalls that the message was received with 'a thunderous applause' and 'slogans of Bhagat Singh Zindabad!' It once again illustrates the primary role of youth in India's revolutionary independence efforts.

Comrades,

Today, we cannot ask the youth to take to pistols and bombs. Today, students are confronted with a far more important assignment. In the coming Lahore Session, the Congress is to give call for a fierce fight for the independence of the country. The youth will have to bear a great burden in this difficult time in the history of the nation. It is true that students have faced death at the forward positions of the struggle for independence. Will they hesitate this time in proving their same staunchness and self-confidence? The youth will have to spread this revolutionary message to the far corner of the country. They have to awaken crores of slum-dwellers of the industrial areas and villagers living in worn-out cottages, so that we will be independent and the exploitation of man by man will become an impossibility. Punjab is considered politically backward even otherwise. This is also the responsibility of the youth. Taking inspiration from the martyr Yatindra Nath Das and with boundless reverence for the country, they must prove that they can fight with steadfast resolve in this struggle for independence.

Statement to the Delhi Sessions Court

This statement was made on 6 June 1929 by Bhagat Singh and B.K. Dutt and read in court by lawyer Asaf Ali on their behalf. It was written before they were convicted for throwing bombs into the Central Assembly in Delhi in April 1929. It compares favourably to Fidel Castro's famous speech, 'History Will Absolve Me' ('*La Historia Me Absolverá*'), during his trial for the raid on the Moncada Barracks in Cuba in 1953.

The significance of this statement cannot be overemphasized, especially considering the fate that awaited these Indian revolutionaries. The profound argument that Indian independence, which simply substituted Indian rule for that of the British, was no independence is even relevant today. True independence requires the liberation of the masses of peasants and workers from the exploitation and expropriation that has been their fate. Today, we speak of the trappings of democracy as if these made us free while we still labour for others and have our bodies and our lands taken from us. This is surely not real freedom.[1]

Crown versus Bhagat Singh & B.K. Dutta.
Charge. S.S. 307 I.P.C. & 3 & 4 Explosive Substances Act.

1 Large portions of the Statement were expunged from the record on 9 June 1929, because they were deemed 'irrelevant'. These portions have been enclosed within square brackets here. The text of the Statement published here is the same as the original statement signed by Bhagat Singh and Batu Keshwar Dutta preserved in the National Archives of India, New Delhi (accession no. 246, Crown vs Bhagat Singh and B.K. Dutta). Many of the previously published versions of the Statement differ from this text. Why these variations have come into being is unclear.

The written statement of accused Bhagat Singh & B.K. Dutta.

1. We stand charged with certain serious offences, and at this stage, it is but right that we must explain our conduct.

In this connection, the following questions arise:

(1) Were the bombs thrown into Chamber, and if so, why?

(2) Is the charge, as framed by the Lower Court, correct or otherwise?

2. To the first half of first question, our reply is in the affirmative, but since some of the so-called 'eye witnesses' have perjured themselves and since we are not denying our liability to that extent, let our statement about them be judged for what it is worth. By way of an illustration, we may point out that the evidence of Sergeant Terry regarding the seizure of the pistol from one of us is a deliberate falsehood, for neither of us had the pistol at the time we gave ourselves up. Other witnesses, too, who have deposed to having seen bombs being thrown by us, have not scrupled to tell lies. This fact had its own moral for those who aim at judicial purity and fair play.

At the same time, we acknowledge the fairness of the Public Prosecutor and the judicial attitude of the Court so far.

3. In our reply to the next half of the first question we are constrained to go into some detail to offer a full and frank explanation of our motive and the circumstances leading up to what has now become an historic event. When we are told by some of the Police Officers who visited us in jail that Lord Irwin in his address to the joint session of the two houses after the event in question described it as an attack directed against no individual but against the institution itself, we readily recognized that the true significance of the incident had been correctly appreciated. We are next to none in our love for humanity. Far from having any malice against any individual, we hold human life sacred beyond words. We are neither perpetrators of dastardly outrages,

nor, therefore, a disgrace to the country, [as the pseudo-socialist, Diwan Chaman Lal is reported to have described us,] nor are we 'lunatics' [as *The Tribune* of Lahore and some others would have it believed.] We humbly claim to be no more than serious students of the history and conditions of our country and her aspirations. We despise hypocrisy, [our practical protest was against the institution, which since its birth, has eminently helped to display not only its worthlessness but its far-reaching power for mischief. They more than we have been convinced that it exists only to demonstrate to the world Indian's humiliation and helplessness, and it symbolizes the overriding domination of an irresponsible and autocratic rule. Time and again the national demand has been pressed by the people's representatives only to find the wastepaper basket as its final destination. Solemn resolutions passed by the House have been contemptuously trampled underfoot on the floor of the so-called Indian Parliament. Resolution regarding the repeal of the repressive and arbitrary measures has been treated with sublime contempt, and the government measures and proposals, rejected as unacceptable by the elected members of the legislatures, have been restored by mere stroke of the pen. In short, we have utterly failed to find any justification for the existence of an institution which, despite all its pomp and splendour, organized with the hard-earned money of the sweating millions of India, is only a hollow show and a mischievous make-believe. Alike, have we failed to comprehend the mentality of the public leaders who help the Government to squander public time and money on such a manifestly stage-managed exhibition of Indian's helpless subjection.] We have been ruminating upon all these matters, as also upon the wholesale arrests of the leaders of the labour movement. When the introduction of the Trade Disputes Bill brought us into the Assembly to watch its progress, [and the course of the debate only served to confirm our conviction that the labouring millions of India had nothing to expect from an institution that stood as a menacing monument to the strangling of the exploiters and the serfdom of the helpless labourers.

Finally, the insult of what we consider, an inhuman and barbarous measure was hurled on the devoted head of the representatives of the entire country, and the starving and struggling millions were deprived of their primary right and the sole means of improving their economic welfare. None who has felt like us for the dumb driven drudges of labourers could possibly witness this spectacle with equanimity. None whose heart bleeds for them, who have given their life-blood in silence to the building up of the economic structure, could repress the cry which this ruthless blow had wrung out of our hearts.] Consequently, [bearing in mind the words of the late Mr. S.R. Das, once Law Member of the Governor General's Executive Council, which appeared in the famous letter he had addressed to his son, to the effect that the 'Bomb was necessary to awaken England from her dreams,'] we dropped the bomb on the floor of the Assembly Chamber to register our protest on behalf of those who had no other means left to give expression to their heart-rending agony. Our sole purpose was 'to make the deaf hear' and to give the heedless a timely warning. [Others have as keenly felt as we have done, and from under the seeming stillness of the sea of Indian humanity, a veritable storm is about to break out.] We have only hoisted the 'danger-signal' to warn those who are speeding along without heeding the grave dangers ahead.

[We have only marked the end of an era of Utopian non-violence, of whose futility the rising generation has been convinced beyond the shadow of doubt. Out of our sincerest good-will to and love of humanity have we adopted this method of warning to prevent the untold suffering which we like millions of others clearly foresee.

4. We have used the expression Utopian non-violence, in the foregoing paragraph which requires some explanation.] Force when aggressively applied is 'violence' and is, therefore, morally unjustifiable, but when it is used in the furtherance of a legitimate

cause, it has its moral justification. [The elimination of force at all costs in Utopian, and the new movement which has arisen in the country, and of that dawn we have given a warning, is inspired by the ideal which guided Guru Gobind Singh and Shivaji, Kamal Pasha and Riza Khan, Washington and Garibaldi, Lafayette and Lenin.

As both the alien Government and the Indian public leaders appeared to have shut their eyes to the existence and voice of this movement,] we felt it as our duty to sound a warning where it could not go unheard.

5. We have so far dealt with the motive behind the incident in question, and now we must define the extent of our intention. We bore no personal grudge or malice against anyone of those who received slight injuries or against any other person in the Assembly. On the contrary, we repeat that we hold human life sacred beyond words, and would sooner lay down our own lives in the service of humanity than injure anyone else. [Unlike the mercenary soldiers of the imperialist armies who are disciplined to kill without compunction,] we respect, and, in so far as it lies in our power, we attempt to save human life. And still we admit having deliberately thrown the bombs into the Assembly Chamber. Facts however, speak for themselves and our intention would be judged from the result of the action without bringing in Utopian hypothetical circumstances and presumptions. Despite the evidence of the Government Expert, the bombs that were thrown in the Assembly Chamber resulted in slight damage to an empty bench and some slight abrasions in less than half a dozen cases, while Government scientists and experts have ascribed this result to a miracle, we see nothing but a precisely scientific process in all this incident. Firstly, the two bombs exploded in vacant spaces within the wooden barriers of the desks and benches, secondly, even those who were within 2 feet of the explosion, for instance, Mr. P. Rau, Mr. Shanker Rao and Sir George Schuster were either not hurt or only slightly

scratched. Bombs of the capacity deposed to by the Government Expert (though his estimate, being imaginary is exaggerated), loaded with an effective charge of potassium chlorate and sensitive (explosive) picrate would have smashed the barriers and laid many low within some yards of the explosion.

Again, had they been loaded with some other high explosive, with a charge of destructive pellets or darts, they would have sufficed to wipe out a majority of the Members of the Legislative Assembly. Still again we could have flung them into the official box which was occupied by some notable persons. And finally we could have ambushed Sir John Simon whose luckless Commission was loathed by all responsible people and who was sitting in the President's gallery at the time. All these things, however, were beyond our intention and bombs did no more than they were designed to do, and the miracle consisted in no more than the deliberate aim which landed them in safe places.

6. We then deliberately offered ourselves to bear the penalty for what we had done [and to let the imperialist exploiters know that by crushing individuals, they cannot kill ideas. By crushing two insignificant units, a nation cannot be crushed. We wanted to emphasize the historical lesson that *lettres de cachets* and *Bastilles* could not crush the revolutionary movement in France. Gallows and the Siberian mines could not extinguish the Russian Revolution. Bloody Sunday, and Black and Tans failed to strangle the movement of Irish freedom. Can ordinances and Safety Bills snuff out the flames of freedom in India? Conspiracy cases, trumped up or discovered and the incarceration of all young men, who cherish the vision of a great ideal, cannot check the march of revolution. But a timely warning, if not unheeded, can help to prevent loss of life and general] sufferings. We took it upon ourselves to provide this warning and our duty is done.

[7. I, Bhagat Singh was asked in the lower court what he meant by word 'Revolution'. In answer to that question, I said]: In answer to the question, I would say that Revolution does not necessarily involve sanguinary strife, nor is there any place in it for individual vendetta. It is not the cult of the bomb and the pistol. By 'Revolution', we mean that the present order of things, which is based on manifest injustice, must change. Producers or labourers in spite of being the most necessary element of society are robbed by their exploiters of the fruits of their labour and deprived of their elementary rights. On the one hand the peasant who grows corn for all starves with his family; the weaver who supplies the world market with textile fabrics cannot find enough to cover his own and his children's bodies; the masons, the smiths and the carpenters who rear magnificent palaces live and perish in slums; and on the other hand the capitalist exploiters, the parasites of Society squander millions on their whims. These terrible inequalities, and forced disparity of chances are heading towards chaos. This state of affairs cannot last long; and it is obvious that the present order of Society is merry-making is on the brink of a volcano and the innocent children of the Exploiters no less than millions of the exploited are walking on the edge of a dangerous precipice. The whole edifice of this civilization, if not saved in time, shall crumble. A radical change, therefore, is necessary; and it is the duty of those who realize this to reorganize Society on the Socialistic basis. Unless this thing is done and the exploitation of man by man and nations by nations, which goes masquerading as Imperialism, is brought to an end, the sufferings and carnage with which humanity is threatened today cannot be prevented and all talks of ending war and ushering in an era of universal peace is undisguised hypocrisy. By 'Revolution' we mean the ultimate establishment of an order of society which may not be threatened by such a break-down, and in which the sovereignty of the proletariat should be recognized, and as the result of which a world-federation should redeem humanity from the bondage of capitalism and the misery of imperial wars.

8. This is our ideal, and with this ideology as our inspiration, we have given a fair and loud enough warning.

If, however, it goes unheeded and the present system of

Government continues to be an impediment in the way of the natural forces that are swelling up, a grim struggle will ensue involving the overthrow of all obstacles, and the establishment of the dictatorship of the proletariat to pave the way for the consummation of the ideal of revolution. Revolution is an inalienable right of mankind. Freedom is an imperishable birth right of all. Labour is the real sustainers of society, the sovereignty of the ultimate destiny of the workers.

For these ideals, and for this faith, we shall welcome any suffering to which we may be condemned. At the altar of this revolution we have brought our youth as incense, for no sacrifice is too great for so magnificent a cause. We are content; we await the advent of Revolution.

'Long Live Revolution'.

Bhagat Singh

Batu Keshwar Dutta

Statement in High Court Bench of Delhi

Written in English and stated before the High Court in January 1930, this is an appeal against conviction. Not only did it carry forward further their ideas about the Indian revolution, but it also brilliantly demolished the basis of the Sessions Court judgment and emphasized the importance of motive. Bhagat Singh argued that the motive behind the action should be the primary consideration in judging the offence of an accused.

My Lords,

We are neither lawyers nor masters of English language, nor holders of degrees. Therefore, please do not expect any oratorial speech from us. We therefore pray that instead of going into the language mistakes of our statement Your Lordships will try to understand the real sense of it.

Leaving other points to our lawyers, I will confine myself to one point only. The point is very important in this case. The point is as to what were our intentions and to what extent we are guilty. This is a very complicated question, and no one will be able to express before you that height to mental elevation which inspired us to think and act in a particular manner. We want that this should be kept in mind while assessing our intentions, our offence. According to the famous jurist Solomon, one should not be punished for his criminal offence if his aim is not against law.

We had submitted a written statement in the Sessions Court. That statement explains our aim and, as such, explains our intentions also. But the learned judge dismissed it with one stroke of pen, saying that 'generally the operation of law is not affected by how or why one committed the offence. In this country the aim of the offence is very rarely mentioned in legal commentaries.'

My Lords, our contention is that under the circumstances the learned judge ought to have judged us either by the result of our action or on the basis of the psychological part of our statement. But he did not take any of these factors into consideration.

The point to be considered is that the two bombs we threw in the Assembly did not harm anybody physically or economically. As such the punishment awarded to us is not only very harsh but revengeful also. Moreover, the motive of the offense of an accused can not be found out without knowing his psychology and no one can do justice to anybody without taking his motive into consideration. If we ignore the motive, the biggest general of the world will appear like ordinary murderers; revenue officers will look like thieves and cheats. Even judges will be accused of murder. This way the entire social system and the civilization will be reduced to murders, thefts and cheating. If we ignore the motive, the government will have no right to expect sacrifice from its people and its officials. Ignore the motive and every religious preacher will be dubbed as a preacher of falsehoods, and every prophet will be charged of misguiding crores of simple and ignorant people.

If we set aside the motive, then Jesus Christ will appear to be a man responsible for creating disturbances, breaking peace and preaching revolt, and will be considered to be a 'dangerous personality' in the language of the law. But we worship him. He commands great respect in our hearts and his image creates vibrations of spiritualism amongst us. Why, because the inspiration behind his actions was that of a high ideal. The rulers of that age could not recognize that high idealism. They only saw his outward actions. Nineteen centuries have passed since then. Have we not progressed during this period? Shall we repeat that mistake again? It that be so, then we shall have to admit that all the sacrifices of the mankind and all the efforts of the great martyrs were useless and it would appear as if we are still at the same place where we stood twenty centuries back.

From the legal point of view also, the question of motive is of special importance. Take the example of General Dyer. He resorted to firing and killed hundreds of innocent and unarmed people. But the military court did not order him to be shot. It gave him lakhs of rupees as award. Take another example. Shri Kharag Bahadur Singh, a young Gurkha, killed a Marwari in Calcutta. If the motive be set aside, then Kharag Bahadur Singh ought to have been hanged. But he was awarded a mild sentence of a few years only. He was even released much before the expiry of his sentence. Was there any loophole in the law that he escaped capital punishment? Or, was the charge of murder not proved against him? Like us, he also accepted the full responsibility of his action, but he escaped death. He is free today. I ask, Your Lordship, why was he not awarded capital punishment? His action was well calculated and well planned. From the motive end, his action was more serious and fatal than ours. He was awarded a mild punishment because his intentions were good. He saved the society from a dirty leach who had sucked the life-blood of so many pretty young girls. Kharag Singh was given a mild punishment just to uphold the formalities of the law.

This principle[1] is quite absurd. This is against the basic principles of the law which declares that 'the law is for man and not man for the law'. As such, why the same norms are not being applied to us also? It is quite clear that while convicting Kharag Singh his motive was kept in mind, otherwise a murderer can never escape the hangman's noose. Are we being deprived of the ordinary advantage of the law because our offence is against the government, or because our action has a political importance?

My Lords, under these circumstances, please permit us to assert that a government which seeks shelter behind such mean

---

1 That the law does not take motive into consideration.

methods has no right to exist. If it exists, it is for the time being only, and that too with the blood of thousands of people on its head. If the law does not see the motive there can be no justice, nor there can be stable peace.

Mixing of arsenic (poison) in the flour will not be considered to be a crime, provided its purpose is to kill rats. But if the purpose is to kill a man, it becomes a crime of murder. Therefore, such laws which do not stand the test of reason and which are against the principle of justice should be abolished. Because of such unjust laws, many great intellectuals had to adopt the path of revolt.

The facts regarding our case are very simple. We threw two bombs in the legislative Assembly on April 8, 1929. As a result of the explosion, a few persons received minor scratches. There was pandemonium in the chamber, hundreds of visitors and members of the Assembly ran out. Only my friend B.K. Dutt and myself remained seated in the visitor's gallery and offered ourselves for arrest. We were tried for attempt to murder, and convicted for life. As mentioned above, as a result of the bomb explosion, only four or five persons were slightly injured and one bench got damaged. We offered ourselves for arrest without any resistance. The Sessions Judge admitted that we could have very easily escaped, had we had any intention like that. We accepted our offence and gave a statement explaining our position. We are not afraid of punishment. But we do not want that we should be wrongly understood. The judge removed a few paragraphs from our statement. This we consider to be harmful for our real position.

A proper study of the full text of our statement will make it clear that, according to us, our country is passing through a delicate phase. We saw the coming catastrophe and thought it proper to give a timely warning with a loud voice, and we gave the warning in the manner we thought proper. We may be wrong. Our line of thinking and that of the learned judge may be different, but that does not mean that we be deprived of the permission to express our ideas, and wrong things be propagated in our name.

In our statement we explained in detail what we mean by 'Long Live Revolution' and 'Down with Imperialism'. That formed the crux of our ideas. That portion was removed from our statement. Generally a wrong meaning is attributed to the word revolution. That is not our understanding. *Bombs and pistols do not make revolution. The sword of revolution is sharpened on the whetting-stone of ideas.* This is what we wanted to emphasize. By revolution we mean the end of the miseries of capitalist wars. It was not proper to pronounce judgment without understanding our aims and objects and the process of achieving them. To associate wrong ideas with our names is out and out injustice.

It was very necessary to give the timely warning that the unrest of the people is increasing and that the malady may take a serious turn, if not treated in time and properly. If our warning is not heeded, no human power will be able to stop it. We took this step to give proper direction to the storm. We are serious students of history. We believe that, had the ruling powers acted correctly at the proper time, there would have been no bloody revolutions in France and Russia. Several big power of the world tried to check the storm of ideas and were sunk in the atmosphere of bloodshed. The ruling people cannot change the flow of the current. We wanted to give the first warning. Had we aimed at killing some important personalities, we would have failed in the attainment of our aim.

My Lords, this was the aim and the spirit behind our action, and the result of the action corroborates our statement. There is one more point which needs elucidation, and that is regarding the strength of the bombs. Had we had no idea of the strength of the bombs, there would have been no question of our throwing them in the presence of our respected national leader like Pandit Motilal Nehru, Shri Kelkar, Shri Jayaker and Shri Jinnah. How could we have risked the lives of our leaders? After all we are not mad and, had we been so, we would have certainly been sent to the lunatic asylum, instead of being put in jail. We had full knowledge about the strength of the bombs, and that is why we acted with so much confidence. It was very easy to have thrown the bombs on the occupied benches, but it was difficult to have thrown them on unoccupied seats. Had we not been of saner mind or had we been mentally unbalanced, the bombs would have fallen on occupied benches and not in empty places. Therefore I would say that we should be rewarded for the courage we showed in carefully selecting the empty places. Under these conditions, My Lords, we think we have not been understood properly. We have not come before you to get our sentences reduced. We have come here to clarify our position. We want that we should not be given any unjust treatment, nor should any unjust opinion be pronounced about us. The question of punishment is of secondary importance before us.

Notice to the Indian Government

Bhagat Singh wrote this notice to the Government of India on behalf of his comrades to begin their second hunger strike, as the demands met in the first hunger strike were not implemented after four months. This letter, titled 'Lahore Conspiracy Case Prisoners Threaten Hunger-strike' was published in *The Tribune* of Lahore on 20 January 1930. While they gave a week's notice for beginning the hunger strike, they began the second hunger strike in the first week of February 1930, which continued for more than two weeks, after which the notification for accepting their demands was issued.

This letter could not be included in earlier editions of the writings of Bhagat Singh. It is a profoundly political document that cuts at the heart of the legitimacy of the British authority. At the same time, what is said in it would apply to any unjust government.

Lahore Conspiracy Case Prisoners Threaten Hunger-strike
Sir,
With reference to our telegram, dated the 20th June, 1930, reading as follows, we have not been favoured with the reply:

'Home Member, India Government, Delhi-Under-trial, Lahore Conspiracy Case and the other political prisoners suspended hunger-strike on the assurance that the Indian Government was considering the Provincial Jail Committee's Reports. All-India Jail officials' Conference is over. No action yet taken. As vindictive treatment to political prisoners still continues we request we be informed within a week final Government decision–Lahore Conspiracy under-trials.'

As briefly stated in the above telegram we beg to bring to your kind notice that the Lahore Conspiracy Case under-trial and several other political prisoners, confined in the Punjab Jails suspended Hunger-strike on the assurance given by the members of the Punjab Jail Enquiry Committee that the question of the treatment of the political prisoners was going to be finally settled to our satisfaction within a very short period. Further, after the death of our great martyr Jitendra Nath Das, the matter was taken up in the Legislative Assembly, and the same assurance was given publicly by Sir James Crerar. It was then pronounced that there had been a change of heart, and the question of the treatment of the political prisoners was receiving the utmost sympathy of the Government. Such political prisoners who were still on hunger-strike in jails of the different parts of the country then suspended their hunger-strike on the request being made to this effect in an A.I.C.C. (All India Congress Committee) resolution passed in view of the said assurance and the critical condition of some of these prisoners.

Since then, all the local Governments have submitted their reports, a meeting of the I.G. Prisons of different provinces has been held at Lucknow, and the deliberations of the All-India Jail officials' Conference have been concluded at Delhi. The All-India Conference was held in the month of December last. Over one month has passed by, and still, the Government of India has not carried into effect any final recommendations. By such dilatory attitude of the Government, we, no less than the general public, have begun to fear that perhaps the question has been shelved. Our apprehension has been strengthened by the vindictive treatment meted out to the hunger-strikers and other political prisoners during the last four months. It is very difficult for us to know the details of the hardships and sufferings to which the political prisoners are being subjected. Still, the little information that has trickled out of the four walls of the Jails is sufficient to furnish us with glaring instances. We give below a few such instances which, we cannot but feel, are not in conformity with the Government assurances.

1. Sh. B.K. Banerji undergoing five years' imprisonment in connection with the Dakshiveshwar Bomb case in the Lahore Central Jail, joined the general hunger-strike last year. Now as a punishment for the same, for each day of his period of hunger-strike two days of remission, so far earned by him, had been forfeited. Under usual circumstances, his release was due in December last, but now it will be delayed by full 4 months. In the same Jail, similar punishment has been awarded to Baba Sohan Singh, an old man of about 70, now undergoing his sentence of life transportation in connection with the Lahore Conspiracy Case. Besides, among others, S. Kabul Singh and S. Gopal Singh confined in the Mianwali Jail, Master Mota Singh, in the Rawalpindi Jail, have also been awarded vindictive punishment for joining the general hunger-strike. In most of these cases the period of imprisonment has been enhanced while some of them have been even removed from special class.

2. For the same offence, i.e., joining the general hunger-strike, Messrs Sachindra Nath Sanyal, Ram Kishan Khatri and Suresh Chandra Bhattacharya confined in Agra Central Jail, Rajkumar Sinha, Manmatha Nath Gupta, Sachindra Nath Bakshi and several other Kakori Conspiracy Case prisoners have been severely punished. It is reliably learnt that Mr. Sanyal was given bar-fetters and solitary cell confinement, and as a consequence, there has been a breakdown in his health. His weight has gone down by 18 pounds. Mr. Bhattacharya is reported to be suffering from tuberculosis. The three Bareilly Jail prisoners have also been punished. It is learnt that all their privileges were withdrawn. Even their usual rights of interviewing relatives and communicating with them were forfeited. They have all been considerably reduced in their weight. Two press statements were issued in this connection in Sept., 1929 and January 1930 by Pt. Jawaharlal Nehru.

3. After the passing of the A.I.C.C. resolution regarding

hunger-strike, copies of the same, which were wired to different political prisoners, were withheld by the Jail authorities. Further, the Govt. even refused Congress deputation to meet the prisoners in this connection.

The Conspiracy Case under-trials were assaulted brutally on the 23rd and 24th October, 1929. Full details have appeared in the Press. The copy of the statement of one of us, as recorded by the Special Magistrate Pt. Sri Krishna, has been duly forwarded to in a communication dated 16th December 1929.

Neither the Punjab Government nor the Government of India felt it necessary to reply or acknowledge receipt of our communication, praying for enquiry. While on the other hand, the local Government has felt the imperative necessity of prosecuting us in connection with the same incident for offering non-violent resistance.

In the last week of December 1929 Sh. Kiron Chandra Das and 8 others, confined in the Lahore Borstal Jail, while produced in the Magistrate's Court, were found handcuffed and chained together in flagrant breach of the unanimous recommendations of the Punjab Jail Enquiry Committee and also of the Inspector-General Prisons Punjab. It is further noteworthy that these prisoners were undertrials charged with a bailable offence. A long statement issued by Doctor Mohd. Alam, L. Duni Chand of Lahore and L. Duni Chand of Ambala in this connection was published in *The Tribune*.

While we learnt of these and other sufferings of the political prisoners, we refrained from resuming hunger-strike though we were much grieved, as we thought the matter was going to be finally settled at an early date. But in the light of the above instance, are we now believe that all the untold sufferings of the hunger-strikers and the supreme sacrifice made by Jitendra Nath Das have all been in vain? Are we to understand that the Government gave its assurance only to check the growing tide of public agitation and to avert a crisis? We hope you will agree with us when we say that we have waited patiently for a sufficiently reasonable period of time. But we cannot wait indefinitely. The Government by its dilatory attitude and continuation of vindictive treatment of political prisoners, have left us no other option but to resume the struggle. We realize that to go on hunger-strike and to carry it on is no easy task. But let us at the same time point out that the revolutionaries can produce many more Jatins and Wazias, Ram Rakhas and Bhan Singhs.[1]

Enough has been said by us and the members of the public in justification of a better treatment of political prisoners and it is unnecessary here to repeat the same. We would, however, like to say a few words as regards the inclusion of motive as the basis and the most important factor in the matter of classification. Great fuss has been created on the question of criteria of classification.

We find that motive has altogether been excluded so far from the criteria suggested by different Provincial Governments. This is really a strange attitude. It is through motive alone that the real value of any action can be decided.

Are we to understand that the Government is unable to distinguish between a robber who robs and kills his victim and a Kharak Bahadur, who killed a villain and saves the honour of a young lady and redeems the society of a most licentious parasite? Are both to be treated as two men belonging to the same category? Is there no difference between two men who commit the same offence, one guided by the selfish motive and the other by a selfless one?

Similarly, is there no difference between a common murderer and a political worker, even if the latter resorts to violence? Does not his selflessness elevate his place amongst those of the ordinary criminals? In these circumstances, we think that motive should be

---

1 The last two, Ram Rakha and Bhan Singh, laid down their lives in the Andaman prison in 1917. Ram Rakha breathed his last after 92 days of hunger strike, while Bhan Singh died the death of a great hero after silently undergoing hardships for a full six months.

held as the most important factor in the criteria for classification.

Last year at the beginning of our hunger-strike, when public leaders, including Doctor Gopichand and L. Duni Chand of Ambala – the last named being one of the signatories to the Punjab Jail Enquiry Committee Report approached us to discuss the same thing and when they told us that the Government considered it impossible to treat the political prisoners convicted of offences of violent nature as special class prisoners, then by way of compromise we agreed to the proposal to the extent of excluding those actually charged with murder. But later on, the discussion took a different turn. And the communique containing the terms of reference for the Punjab Jail Enquiry Committee was so worded that the question of motive seemed to be altogether excluded, and the whole classification was based on the two things:

1. Nature of offence.
2. The social status of the offenders.

This criterion, instead of solving the problem, made it all the more complicated. We could understand two classes among the political prisoners – those charged with non-violent offences and those charged with violent ones. But then there creeps in the question of social status in the report of the Punjab Jail Enquiry Committee. As Choudhary Afzal Haq has pointed out, and rightly too, in his note of dissent to this report, what would be the fate of those political workers who have been reduced to pauperism due to their honorary services in the cause of freedom? Are they to be left at the mercy of a Magistrate who will always try to approve the bona fide of his loyalty by classifying everyone as an ordinary convict? Or is it expected that a non-co-operator will stretch his hand before the people against whom he is fighting as an opponent, begging for better treatment in the jail? Are these the reforms that are demanded of the nature of luxury? Are they satisfying them? It might be argued that people living in poverty outside the jails should not expect luxuries inside the Jail where they are detained for the purpose of punishment. But are the reforms that are demanded of nature of luxury? Are they not the bare necessities of life? In spite of all the facilities that can possibly be demanded, jails will ever remain a jail. The prison in itself does not contain and can never contain any magnetic power to attract the people from outside. Nobody will commit to come to jail.

Moreover, may we venture to say that it is very poor argument on the part of the Government to say that its citizens have been driven to such extreme destitution that their standard of living has fallen even lower than of that of their Jails? Does not such an argument cut at the very root of that Government's right of existence? Anyhow, we are not concerned with that at present. What we want to say is that the best way to remove the prevailing dissatisfaction would be to classify political prisoners as such into a separate class which may further be sub-divided, if need be, into two classes, one for those convicted of non-violent offences and the other for persons whose offences include violence. In that case, motive will become one of the deciding factors. To say that motive cannot be ascertained in political cases is not correct. What is it that today leads the Jail authorities to deprive the 'politicals' even of the ordinary privileges? What is it that deprives them of the special grades or numberdaries, etc? What makes the authorities keep them aloof and separated from all other convicts? The same things can help in the classification also.

As for the specific demands, we have already stated them in full in our memorandum to the Punjab Jail Enquiry Committee. We would, however, particularly emphasize that no political prisoner, whatever his offence may be, should be given any hard and undignified labour for which he may not have aptitude. All of them confined in any one jail should be kept together in the same ward. At least one standard daily newspaper in vernacular or English should be given to them. Full and proper facilities for study should be granted. Lastly, they should be allowed to supplement their allowance for diet and clothing from their private sources. We still hope that the Government will carry into effect, without further delay, its promise made to us and to the public, so that there may not be another occasion for resuming the hunger-strike. Unless and until we find a definite move on the part of the Government to redeem its promise, in the course of the next 7 days, we shall be forced to resume hunger-strike.

The Magistrate has forwarded the letter to the executive authorities.

Letter to His Father

When the case was in its final stage, Bhagat Singh's father, Sardar Kishan Singh, in a written appeal to the Tribunal, claimed that his son was innocent and had nothing to do with Saunders' murder. He said his son was not in Lahore when Saunders was assassinated. He also requested that Bhagat Singh be given an opportunity to prove his innocence.

This letter records Bhagat Singh's response to his father. It was widely published in Indian newspapers on 7 October 1930, before the verdict was reached. The response shows the great integrity and independence of the mind of Bhagat Singh. The original letter was written in Urdu.

Oct. 4, 1930

My Dear Father,

I was astounded to learn that you had submitted a petition to the members of the Special Tribunal in connection with my defence. This intelligence proved to be too severe a blow to be borne with equanimity. It has upset the whole equilibrium of my mind. I have not been able to understand how you could think it proper to submit such a petition at this stage and in these circumstances. In spite of all the sentiments and feelings of a father, I don't think you were at all entitled to make such a move on my behalf without even consulting me. You know that in the political field, my views have always differed with those of yours. I have always been acting independently without having cared for your approval or disapproval.

I hope you can recall to yourself that since the very beginning you have been trying to convince me to fight my case very seriously and to defend myself properly. But you also know that I was always opposed to it. I never had any desire to defend myself and never did I seriously think about it. Whether it was a mere vague ideology or that I had certain arguments to justify my position, is a different question and that cannot be discussed here.

You know that we have been pursuing a definite policy in this trial. Every action of mine ought to have been consistent with that policy, my principle and my program. At present the circumstances are altogether different, but had the situation been otherwise, even then I would have been the last man to offer defence. I had only one idea before me throughout the trial, i.e. to show complete indifference towards the trial in spite of the serious nature of the charges against us. I have always been of opinion that all the political workers should be indifferent and should never bother about the legal fight in the law courts and should boldly bear the heaviest possible sentences inflicted upon them. They may defend themselves but always from purely political considerations and never from a personal point of view. Our policy in this trial has always been consistent with this principle; whether we were successful in that or not is not for me to judge. We have always been doing our duty quite disinterestedly.

In the statement accompanying the text of Lahore Conspiracy Case Ordinance the Viceroy had stated that the accused in this case were trying to bring both law and justice into contempt. The situation afforded us an opportunity to show to the public whether we were trying to bring law into contempt or whether others were doing so. People might disagree with us on this point. You might be one of them. But that never meant that such moves should be made on my behalf without my consent or even my knowledge. My life is not so precious, at least to me, as you may probably think it to be. It is not at all worth buying at the cost of my principles. There are other comrades of mine whose case is as serious as that of mine. We had adopted a common policy and we shall stand to the last, no matter how dearly we have to pay individually for it.

Father, I am quite perplexed. I fear I might overlook the ordinary principle of etiquette and my language may become a little bit harsh while criticizing or rather censoring this move on your part. Let me be candid. I feel as though I have been stabbed at the back. Had any other person done it, I would have considered it to be nothing short of treachery. But in your case, let me say that it has been a weakness – a weakness of the worst type.

This was the time where everybody's mettle was being tested. Let me say, father, you have failed. I know you are as sincere a patriot as one can be. I know you have devoted your life to the cause of Indian independence, but why, at this moment, have you displayed such a weakness? I cannot understand.

In the end, I would like to inform you and my other friends and all the people interested in my case that I have not approved of your move. I am still not at all in favour of offering any defence. Even if the court had accepted that petition submitted by some of my co-accused regarding defence, etc., I would have not defended myself. My applications submitted to the Tribunal regarding my interview during the hunger strike, were misinterpreted and it was published in the press that I was going to offer defence, though in reality I was never willing to offer any defence. I still hold the same opinion as before. My friends in the Borstal Jail will be taking it as a treachery and betrayal on my part. I shall not even get an opportunity to clear my position before them.

I want that public should know all the details about this complication, and, therefore, I request you to publish this letter.

Your loving son,
Bhagat Singh

Regarding Suicide: Last Letter to Sukhdev

Shiv Verma, Bhagat Singh's comrade, annotates this letter as follows: 'Hearing of the case was over. Judgement was expected any day. Sukhdev expected life transportation for him. To him, the idea of remaining in jail for 20 years was repulsive. He wrote to Bhagat Singh that in case he (Sukhdev) is convicted for life he will commit suicide. He stood for release or death; no middle course. Bhagat Singh's reaction to Sukhdev's letter was very sharp. Serve, suffer and live to struggle for the cause – that was his stand. 'Escaping from hardships is cowardice', he said. This letter provides one more window to peep into the martyr's mind'.

Sukhdev, though, redeemed himself by not seeking a pardon, becoming a bigger victim of the British justice system. He received a death sentence, despite not being part of Saunders murder. Translated from Hindi.

Dear brother,

I have gone through your letter attentively and many times. I realise that the changed situation has affected us differently. The things you hated outside have now become essential to you. In the same way, the things I used to support strongly are of no significance to me any more. For example, I believed in personal love, but now this feeling has ceased to occupy any particular position in my heart and mind. While outside, you were strongly opposed to it but now a drastic change and radicalisation is apparent in your ideas about it. You experience it as an extremely essential part of human existence and you have found a particular kind of happiness in the experience.

You may still recollect that one day I had discussed suicide with you. That time I told you that in some situations suicide may be justifiable, but you contested my point. I vividly remember the time and place of our conversation. We talked about this in the Shahanshahi Kutia one evening. You said in jest that such a cowardly act can never be justified. You said that acts of this kind were horrible and heinous, but I see that you have now made an about-turn on this subject. Now you find it not only proper in certain situations but also necessary, even essential. My opinion is what you had held earlier, that suicide is a heinous crime. It is an act of complete cowardice. Leave alone revolutionaries, no individual can ever justify such an act.

You say you fail to understand how suffering alone can serve the country. Such a question from a person like you is really perplexing, because how much thoughtfully we loved the motto of the Naujawan Bharat Sabha – 'to suffer and sacrifice through service'. I believe that you served as much as was possible. Now is the time when you should suffer for what you did. Another point is that this is exactly the moment when you have to lead the entire people.

Man acts only when he is sure of the justness of his action, as we threw the bomb in the Legislative Assembly. After the action, it is the time for bearing the consequences of that act. Do you think that had we tried to avoid the punishment by pleading for mercy, we would have been more justified? No, this would have had an adverse effect on the masses. We are now quite successful in our endeavour.

At the time of our imprisonment, the condition for the political prisoners of our party were very miserable. We tried to improve that. I tell you quite seriously that we believed we would die very shortly. Neither we were aware of the technique of forced feeding nor did we ever think of it. We were ready to die. Do you mean to say that we were intending to commit suicide? No. Striving and sacrificing one's life for a superior ideal can never be called suicide.

We are envious of the death of our Comrade Yatindra Nath Das. Will you call it suicide? Ultimately, our sufferings bore fruit. A big movement started in the whole of the country. We were successful in our aim. Death in the struggles of this kind is an ideal death.

Apart from this, the comrades among us, who believe that they will be awarded death, should await that day patiently when the sentence will be announced and they will be hanged. This death will also be beautiful, but committing suicide – to cut short the life just to avoid some pain – is cowardice. I want to tell you that obstacles make a man perfect. Neither you nor I, rather none of us, have suffered any pain so far. That part of our life has started only now.

You will recollect that we have talked several times about realism in the Russian literature, which is nowhere visible in our own. We highly appreciate the situations of pain in their stories, but we do not feel that spirit of suffering within ourselves. We also admire their passion and the extraordinary height of their characters, but we never bother to find out the reason. I will say that only the reference to their resolve to bear pain has produced the intensity, the suffering of pain, and this has given great depth and height to their characters and literature. We become pitiable and ridiculous when we imbibe an unreasoned mysticism in our life without any natural or substantial basis. People like us, who are proud to be revolutionary in every sense, should always be prepared to bear all the difficulties, anxieties, pain and suffering which we invite upon ourselves by the struggles initiated by us and for which we call ourselves revolutionary.

I want to tell you that in jail, and in jail alone, can a person get an occasion to study empirically the great social subjects of crime and sin. I have read some literature on this and only the jail is the proper place for the self-study on all these topics. The best parts of the self-study for one is to suffer oneself.

You know it that the suffering of political prisoners in the jails of Russia caused, in the main, the revolution in the prison-administration after the overthrow of Czardom. Is India not in need of such persons who are fully aware of this problem and have personal experience of these things? It will not suffice to say that 'someone else would do it, or that many other people are there to do it. Thus, men who find it quite dishonourable and hateful to leave the revolutionary responsibilities to others should start their struggle against the existing system with total devotion. They should violate these rules but they should also keep in mind the propriety, because unnecessary and improper attempts can never be considered just. Such agitations will shorten the process of revolution. All the arguments which you gave to keep yourself aloof from all such movements, are incomprehensible to me. Some of our friends are either fools or ignorant. They find your behaviour quite strange and incomprehensible. (They themselves say they cannot comprehend it because you are above and very far from their understanding.)

In fact, if you feel that jail life is really humiliating, why don't you try to improve it by agitating? Perhaps, you will say that this struggle would be futile, but this is precisely the argument which is usually used as a cover by weak people to avoid participation in every movement. This is the reply which we kept on hearing outside the jail from the people who were anxious to escape from getting entangled in revolutionary movements. Shall I now hear the same argument from you? What could our party of a handful of people do in comparison to the vastness of its aims and ideals? Shall we infer from this that we erred gravely in starting our work altogether? No, inferences of this kind will be improper. This only shows the inner weakness of the man who thinks like this.

You write further that it cannot be expected of a man that he will have the same thinking after going through 14 long years of suffering in the prison, which he had before, because the jail life will crush all his ideas. May I ask you whether the situation outside the jail was any bit more favourable to our ideas? Even then, could we have left it because of our failures? Do you mean to imply that had we not entered the field, no revolutionary work would have taken place at all? If this be your contention, then you are mistaken, though it is right that we also proved helpful to an extent in changing the environment. But, then, we are only a product of the need of our times.

I shall even say that Marx – the father of communism – did not actually originate this idea. The Industrial Revolution of Europe itself produced men of this kind. Marx was one among them. Of course, Marx was also instrumental to an extent in gearing up the wheels of his time in a particular way.

I (and you too) did not give birth to the ideas of socialism and communism in this country; this is the consequence of the effects of our time and situations upon ourselves. Of course, we did a bit to propagate these ideas, and therefore I say that since we have already taken a tough task upon ourselves, we should continue to advance it. The people will not be guided by our committing suicides to escape the difficulties; on the contrary, this will be quite a reactionary step.

We continued our work despite the testing environment of disappointments, pressures and violence ordained by the Jail rules. While we worked, we were made target of many kinds of difficulties. Even men who were proud to proclaim themselves to be great revolutionaries, deserted us. Were these conditions not testing in the extreme? Then, what was the reason and the logic of continuing our agitation and efforts?

Does this simple argument not by itself give added strength to our ideas? And, don't we have instances of our revolutionary comrades who suffered for their convictions in jails and are still working on return from jails? Had Bakunin argued like you he would have committed suicide right in the beginning. Today, you find many revolutionaries occupying responsible posts in the Russian state who had passed the greater part of their lives in prison, completing their sentences. Man must try hard to stick to his beliefs. No one can say what future has in store.

Do you remember that when we were discussing that some concentrated and effective poison should also be kept in our bomb factories, you opposed it very vehemently. The very idea was repugnant to you. You had no faith in it. So, what has happened now? Here, even the difficult and complex condition's do not obtain. I feel revulsion even in discussing this question. You hated even that attitude of mind which permits suicide. You will kindly excuse me for saying that had you acted according to this belief right at the time of your imprisonment (that is, you had committed suicide by taking poison), you would have served the revolutionary cause, but at this moment, even the thought of such an act is harmful to our cause.

There is just one more point which I will like to draw your attention to. We do not believe in God, hell and heaven, punishment and rewards, that is in any Godly accounting of human life. Therefore, we must think of life and death on materialist lines. When I was brought here from Delhi for the purpose of identification, some intelligence officers talked to me on this topic, in the presence of my father. They said that since I did not try to save my life by divulging secrets, it proved the presence of an acute agony in my life. They argued that a death of this kind will be something like suicide. But I had replied that a man with beliefs and ideals like mine, could never think of dying uselessly. We want to get the maximum value for our lives. We want to serve humanity as much as possible. Particularly a man like me, whose life is nowhere sad or worried, can never think of suicide even, leave alone attempting it. The same thing I want to tell you now.

I hope you will permit me to tell you what I think about myself. I am certain of capital punishment for me. I do not expect even a bit of moderation or amnesty. Even if there is amnesty, it will not be for all, and even that amnesty will be for others only, not for us; it will be extremely restricted and burdened with various conditions. For us, neither there can be any amnesty nor it will ever happen. Even then, I wish that release calls for us should be made collectively and globally. Along with that, I also wish that when the movement reaches its climax, we should be hanged. It is my wish that if at any time any honourable and fair compromise is possible, issues like our case may never obstruct it. When the fate of the country is being decided, the fate of individuals should be forgotten. As revolutionaries, we are fully aware of all the past experiences. Therefore, we do not believe that there can be any sudden change in the attitude of our rulers, particularly in the British race. Such a surprising change is impossible without revolution. A revolution can be achieved only through sustained striving, sufferings and sacrifices. And it shall be achieved. As far as my attitude is concerned, I can welcome facilities and amnesty for all only when its effect is permanent and some indelible impressions are made on the hearts of the people of the country through our hanging. Only this much and nothing more.

Last Letter to Comrades: Written to the Second Lahore Conspiracy Case Convicts

This letter was written on 22 March 1931 the day before Bhagat Singh's execution.

This is Bhagat Singh's last letter, written a day before his execution.

Shiv Verma's annotation: 'On March 22, the Second Lahore Conspiracy Case convicts, who were locked up in Ward Number 14 (near condemned cells), sent a slip to Bhagat Singh asking if would like to live. This letter was in reply to that slip'.

While his comrades thought he still might be saved, he concluded that his death was more important than his life in terms of the liberation of India from British rule and the building of a socialist country. The letter was written in Urdu.

Comrades!

It is natural that the desire to live should be in me as well, I don't want to hide it. But I can stay alive on one condition that I don't wish to live in imprisonment or with any binding.

My name has become a symbol of Hindustani revolution, and the ideals and sacrifices of the revolutionary party have lifted me very high – so high that I can certainly not be higher in the condition of being alive.

Today my weaknesses are not visible to the people. If I escape the noose, they will become evident and the symbol of revolution will be tarnished, or possibly be obliterated. But to go to the gallows with courage will make Hindustani mothers aspire to have children who are like Bhagat Singh and the number of those who

229

will sacrifice their lives for the country will go up so much that it will not be possible for imperialistic powers or all the demoniac powers to contain the revolution.

And yes, one thought occurs to me even today – that I have not been able to fulfil even one thousandth parts of the aspirations that were in my heart to do something for my country and humanity. If I could have stayed alive and free, then I may have got the opportunity to accomplish those and I would have fulfilled my desires. Apart from this, no temptation to escape the noose has ever come to me.

Who can be more fortunate than me? These days, I feel very proud of myself. Now I await the final test with great eagerness. I pray that it should draw closer.

Your comrade

Bhagat Singh

'No Hanging, Please Shoot Us':
Last letter to British Government in India

This letter, addressed by Bhagat Singh, Rajguru, and Sukhdev to the Punjab Governor on 20 March 1931, three days before their hanging, demanded that, since they were prisoners of war, they should be shot and not 'executed'. They make clear the nature of their actions, that they were at war with the British government, in a battle to secure the revolutionary independence of India. Given the undeniability of this fact, there could be no question of their status as combatants who were due the rights ordinarily accorded such persons.

To
The Punjab Governor
Sir,

With due respect we beg to bring to your kind notice the following:

That we were sentenced to death on 7th October 1930 by a British Court, L.C.C Tribunal, constituted under the Special Lahore Conspiracy Case Ordinance, promulgated by the H.E. The Viceroy, the Head of the British Government of India, and that the main charge against us was that of having waged war against H.M. King George, the King of England.

The above-mentioned finding of the Court pre-supposed two things:

Firstly, that there exists a state of war between the British Nation and the Indian Nation and, secondly, that we had actually participated in that war and were, therefore, war prisoners.

The second presupposition seems to be a little bit flattering, but nevertheless it is too tempting to resist the design acquiescing in it.

As regards the first, we are constrained to go into some detail. Apparently there seems to be no such war as the phrase indicates. Nevertheless, please allow us to accept the validity of the pre-supposition, taking it at its face value. But in order to be correctly understood we must explain it further. Let us declare that the state of war does exist and shall exist so long as the Indian toiling masses and the natural resources are being exploited by a handful of parasites. They may be purely British Capitalist or mixed British and Indian, or even purely Indian. They may be carrying on their insidious exploitation through mixed or even on purely Indian bureaucratic apparatus. All these things make no difference. No matter, if your Government tries and succeeds in winning over the leaders of the upper strata of the Indian Society through petty concessions and compromises and thereby cause a temporary demoralization in the main body of the forces. No matter, if once again the vanguard of the Indian movement, the Revolutionary Party, finds itself deserted in the thick of the war. No matter if the leaders to whom personally we are much indebted for the sympathy and feelings they expressed for us, but nevertheless we cannot overlook the fact that they did become so callous as to ignore and not to make a mention in the peace negotiation of even the homeless, friendless and penniless of female workers who are alleged to be belonging to the vanguard and whom the leaders consider to be enemies of their utopian non-violent cult which has already become a thing of the past; the heroines who had ungrudgingly sacrificed or offered for sacrifice their husbands, brothers, and all that were nearest and dearest to them, including themselves, whom your government has declared to be outlaws.

No matter if your agents stoop so low as to fabricate baseless calumnies against their spotless characters to damage their and their party's reputation. The war shall continue.

It may assume different shapes at different times. It may

become now open, now hidden, now purely agitational, now fierce life and death struggle. The choice of the course, whether bloody or comparatively peaceful, which it should adopt rests with you. Choose whichever you like. But that war shall be incessantly waged without taking into consideration the petty . . .[1] and the meaningless ethical ideologies. It shall be waged ever with new vigour, greater audacity and unflinching determination till the Socialist Republic is established and the present social order is completely replaced by a new social order, based on social prosperity, and thus every sort of exploitation is put an end to and the humanity is ushered into the era of genuine and permanent peace. In the very near future the final battle shall be fought and final settlement arrived at.

The days of capitalist and imperialist exploitation are numbered. The war neither began with us nor is it going to end with our lives. It is the inevitable consequence of the historic events and the existing environments. Our humble sacrifices shall be only a link in the chain that has very accurately been beautified by the unparalleled sacrifice of Mr. Das and most tragic but noblest sacrifice of Comrade Bhagawati Charan and the glorious death of our dear warrior Azad.

As to the question of our fates, please allow us to say that when you have decided to put us to death, you will certainly do it. You have got the power in your hands and the power is the greatest justification in this world. We know that the maxim 'might is right' serves as your guiding motto. The whole of our trial was just a proof of that.

We wanted to point out that according to the verdict of your court we had waged war and were therefore war prisoners. And we claim to be treated as such, i.e., we claim to be shot dead instead of to be hanged. It rests with you to prove that you really meant what your court has said.

1 Illegible words.

We request and hope that you will very kindly order the military department to send its detachment to perform our execution.

Yours,

Bhagat Singh Rajguru Sukhdev

Protest Letter from the British Communist Party

We note here that anger at the imprisonment and death sentence of Bhagat Singh drove people into the streets not only throughout India but resonated outside the country. Here is the statement of the Communist Party of Great Britain.

THE COMMUNIST PARTY OF GREAT BRITAIN,
16, King Street,
Covent Garden, London. 1.0.2.
5th March, 1931.
Dear Comrades,
Enclosed you will find a statement drawing your attention to the facts in regard to the LAHORE CONSPIRACY TRIAL.

Some of the comrades concerned stand in danger of execution and we are asking that you should organise meetings and demonstrations of protest to demand that Comrade Bhagat Singh should not be executed by the Labour Government. We believe that the facts that are given to you will provide you with the necessary material upon which to wage the campaign.

With Communist Greetings,
Yours fraternally,
The SECRETARIAT.

Excerpts on Law and the State from the Jail Notebooks of Bhagat Singh

The jail notebooks of Bhagat Singh are a remarkable document. While in prison, before his death, he undertook several long hunger strikes, significantly weakening him. He was also severely beaten. Despite these physically debilitating traumas, which might have defeated most people, he continued to read widely and to write.

His notebooks are both a bibliography of what he read and a diary of his thoughts on various subjects. He had an insatiable desire to learn, understand the underlying forces at work in India's subjugation by the British, and grasp the basic principles of global capitalist development and the class struggle countering it.

Two critical aspects of capitalism that he wanted to examine and analyze were the interrelated supporting mechanisms of law and state. In pre-capitalist class societies, there were customary laws, personal-political power tied intimately to economic control of enslavers and feudal lords, and primary reliance upon violence to enforce political-economic dominance.

Capitalism replaced these with formal laws, a separation between economic and political institutions, and more subtle control mechanisms reliant upon an impersonal market. All of this meant that it became necessary to study law and state carefully to ascertain their connections to each other and to the dominance of the capitalist class.

We find that law and state are necessary for unimpeded capital accumulation. The latter is the central feature of capitalism, and it must have exploitable labour and peasant classes to continue. Thus, law and state are inherent features of capitalism. And the corollary of this is that both must be abolished if humanity is to liberate itself from the alienation that is capitalism's calling card. The state and its laws must be forced, by the collective struggles of workers, peasants, and their allies, to, as Marx put, *wither away*, so that direct democracy and egalitarian relationships in all spheres of life can prevail.

In his book, *The Bhagat Singh Reader*, co-editor Chaman Lal describes the tortured history of the eventual publication of the jail notebooks. It was first serialized in the monthly journal, 'Indian Book Chronicle', in 1992. The first full edition was published in 1994; many other editions have been published since then. We include two excerpts here, the first on Law and the second on the State.

They offer glimpses into Bhagat Singh's growing political sophistication, much as Marx's notebooks, which contain commentaries and passages from what he was reading. The tragedy is that Marx had an adult lifetime to make notebooks, while Bhagat Singh had only a year. As you read these extracts, mainly quotes from his readings, remember that the subtext is always his desire to make a revolution that brought independence to India and built India into a socialist society.

LAW

We are continually exhorted to obey the law. Most of us take this for granted. Yet, what exactly is the law? Great Britain and the United States have a body of law known as the common law. It is essentially judge-made law, which over time, as one judge follows the precedent set by a predecessor judge, gains the force of laws encoded in statutes.

Jeremy Bentham, the philosopher who inspired the building of the infamous Circular Jail, quipped that the common law was like 'dog law', which a master arbitrarily sets for his pets – such laws changes according to the preferences of judges. But if we ask who these justices are, we quickly learn that they are selected from society's elites, carrying all the biases of those at the top of society.

The same can surely be said for the laws enacted by legislatures, all the more so when these legislators are foreign conquerors, as in India. Even when some of the legislators are natives of the subjugated land, they serve at the whim of the imperial occupiers.

Here we see with great clarity that laws are not independent entities, deriving from universal truths and thus obviously right. While laws, courts, and judges might have a certain autonomy at certain times, even this is circumscribed by the logic of the production and distribution systems.

That is, laws come from the structure of society, which has been a class structure for at least 10,000 years. The excerpts from the jail notebooks show Bhagat Singh coming to grasp this reality. They must be seen in the light of the horrendously contrived, unfair, and brutal trials of Bhagat Singh and his fellow political

PAGE 13

'The English people love liberty for themselves. They hate all acts of injustice, except

those which they themselves commit. They are such liberty-loving people that they interfere in the Congo and cry, 'Shame' to the Belgians. But they forget their heels are on the neck of India.'

An Irish Author

PAGE 45

Sir Henry Maine has said:[1]

1 Perhaps Sir Henry James Sumner Maine (1822–88), English historian and comparative jurist. Also legal member of Council in India from 1863 to 1869 and Vice-Chancellor, Calcutta University.

'That most of the land of England has passed to its present owners by the Mistake of lawyers – mistakes that in lesser criminals were punished by Hanging.'

'The law convicts the man or woman
Who steals the goose from of the Common?
But lets the greater felon loose
Who steals the Common from the goose.'

PAGE 46

Democracy is theoretically a system of political and legal equality. But in concrete and practical operation it is false, for there can be no equality, not even in politics and before the law, so long as there is glaring inequality in economic power. So long as the ruling class owns the workers' jobs and the press and the schools of the country and all organs for the molding and expression of public opinion; so long as it monopolize(s) all trained public functionaries and disposes of unlimited funds to influence elections, so long as the laws are made by the ruling class and the courts are presided over by members of the class; so long as lawyers are private practitioners who sell their skill to the highest bidder, and litigation is technical and costly, so long will the nominal equality before the law be a hollow mockery.

In a capitalist regime, the whole machinery of democracy operates to keep the ruling class minority in power through the suffrage of the working-class majority, and when the bourgeois govt. feels itself endangered by democratic institutions, such institutions are often crushed without compunction.

From Marx to Lenin, p. 58
(by Morris Hillquit[2])

---

2 Morris Hillquit (1869–1933), socialist lawyer from New York.

The Revd. E.D., Simon, Doctor of Divinity, a professor in Methodist College of Virginia wrote:

'Extracts from Holy Writ unequivocally assert the right of property in slaves, together with the usual incidents to that right. The right to buy and sell is clearly stated. Upon the whole, then, whether we consult the Jewish policy instituted by God Himself, or the uniform opinion and practice of mankind in all ages, or the injunctions of the New Testament and the moral law, we are brought to the conclusion that slavery is not immoral. Having established the point that the first African slaves were legally bought into bondage, the right to detain their children in bondage follows as an indispensable consequence. Thus we see that the slavery that exists in America was founded in right.'

Kautsky had written a booklet with the title 'Proletariat Dictatorship' and had deplored the act of Bolsheviks in depriving the bourgeoisie people from the right of vote.[3] Lenin writes in his 'Proletarian Revolution' (pp. 77–78):

'Arbitrariness! Only think what a depth of meanest subserviency to the bourgeoisie, and of the most idiotic pedantry, is contained in such a reproach. When thoroughly bourgeois and, for the most part, even reactionary jurists of capitalist countries, have in the course of, we may almost say, centuries, been drawing up rules and regulations and writing up hundreds of volumes of various codes and laws, and of interpretations of them to oppress the workers, to bind hand and foot the poor men, and to place a hundred and one hindrances and obstacles in the way of the simple and toiling mass of the people–when this is done, the bourgeois Liberals and Mr. Kautsky can see no 'arbitrariness'! It is all Law and Order! It has all been thought out and written down, how the poor man is

---

3 Karl Kautsky (1854–1938), leading social democratic theoretician. Author of numerous works, among which *The Dictatorship of the Proletariat* (1918) is the most pertinent in the context of Bhagat Singh's readings of Lenin.

to be kept down and squeezed. There are thousands and thousands of bourgeois lawyers and officials able to interpret the laws that the worker and average peasant can never break through their barbed wire entanglements. This, of course, is not any arbitrariness. This, of course, is not a dictatorship of the filthy or profit-seeking exploiters who are drinking the blood of the people. Oh, it is nothing of the kind! It is 'pure democracy,' which is becoming purer and purer every day. But when the toiling and exploited masses, for the first time in history, separated by Imperialist War from their brothers across the frontier, have constructed their Soviets, have summoned to the workers of political construction, the classes which the bourgeois used to oppress and to stupefy, and begun themselves to build up a new proletarian State, begun, in the midst of raging battles, in the fire of Civil War, to lay down the fundamental principles of 'a State without exploiters,' then all the scoundrels of the bourgeoisie, the entire band of blood suckers, with Kautsky, singing 'obliger to,' scream about arbitrariness!'

((Lenin) pp. 77–78)

PAGE 65[4]

'Law, morality, religion are to him (the working man) so many bourgeois prejudices, behind which lurk in ambush just as many bourgeois interests.

Karl Marx, Manifesto[5]

PAGE 101

'Society, however, does not rest upon law. This is a legal fiction. Rather the law must rest on society. It must be the expression of

4 The upper half of this page is blank, except the (slanting) signature of B.K. Dutta with the date 12.7.30 written twice. The quotation from Karl Marx is given below the signature.
5 From *The Communist Manifesto* by Karl Marx and Friedrich Engels, 1848. The subsequent quotations are also from this work.

The Political Writings of Bhagat Singh

the interest and needs of society which result from the social and invariably material method of production as against the arbitrariness of the industrial. As for Napoleon Code, which I have in my hand, that has not engendered modern civil society.

The society which arose in the 18th century and developed in the 19th finds in the Code only a legal expression. As soon as that no longer corresponds to social conditions, it is merely so much waste paper. . . The law necessarily changed with the changing conditions of life. The maintaining of the old law against the new needs and demands of the social development is at bottom nothing but a hypocritical assertion (in accord with the spirit of the age) of special interest against the common interest.'

Karl Marx, Marx (Before the Court of Jury of Cologne)[6]

PAGE 105[7]

Jurisprudence
Law:
1. Legal exposition } as it exists.
2. Legal History } as it developed.
3. Science of Legislation } as it ought to be.
    1. Theoretical } (i) Philosophy. Supplying foundation for the science
    2. General }Jurisprudence

6 'The Trial of the Rhenish District Committee of Democrats,' 1849. The trial of the Rhenish District Committee of Democrats took place on 8 February 1849. Karl Marx, Karl Schapper and the lawyer Schneider II were summoned to the Cologne jury court, accused of incitement to revolt in connection with the Committee's appeal of 18 November 1848, on the refusal to pay taxes. They were acquitted. The backdrop to these happenings was the revolutionary ferment in Europe in 1848

7 About midway through the jail notebooks, we see that Bhagat Singh wanted to study the law systematically. Below is an outline he made to guide his thinking. He goes on to give descriptions of various kinds of laws, the concept of justice, and punishments, with their respective justifications, for those who violate the law.

1. Analytical }
2. Historical }Jurisprudence
3. Ethical }

1. Analytical jurisprudence explains the first principles of Law. It deals with:

(a) Conception of Civil Law

(b) Relation between Civil and other Laws

(c) Various constituent ideas that constitute the idea of Law viz. State, Sovereignty and administration of justice.

(d) Legal sources of Law and Theory of Legislation etc.

(e) Scientific arrangements of Law

(f) Legal rights

(g) Theory of Legal (civil and criminal) liability

(h) Other legal conceptions.

PAGE 114

Retributive Punishment: The most horrible theory! People thinking in these terms are really maintaining the barbaric faculties of ancient and pre-civilization times.

It gratifies the instinct of revenge or retaliation, which exists not merely in the individual wronged, but also by way of sympathetic extension in society at large.

According to this view, it is right and proper that evil should be returned for evil. An eye for an eye and a tooth for a tooth is deemed a plain and self-sufficient rule of natural justice. *Punishment becomes an end in itself.*

PAGE 115

'That you be taken back to the prison whence you came, to a long dungeon into which no light can enter; then you be laid on your back on the bare floor, with a cloth round your loins, but elsewhere naked, that there be set upon your body a weight of iron as great as you can bear, and greater; that you have no substance save, on the first day, the morsels of the coarsest bread; on the second day, three draughts of stagnant water from the pool nearest to the prison door; on the third day again three morsels of bread as before, and such bread and such water alternately from day to day until you die.'[8]

PAGE 118

'. . . With readymade opinions one cannot judge of crime. Its philosophy is a little more complicated than people think. It is acknowledged that neither convict prisons, nor the hulks; nor any system of hard labor ever cured a criminal. These forms of chastisement only punish him and reassure society against the offences he might commit. Confinement, regulation, and excessive work have no effect but to develop with these men profound hatred, a thirst for forbidden enjoyment and frightful recalcitrations. On the other hand, I am convinced that the celebrated cellular system gives results, which are specious and deceitful. It deprives a criminal of his force of his energy, energates his soul by weakening and frightening it, at last exhibits a dried up memory as a model of repentance and amendment.'

The House of the Dead p. 17 Fedore Dostoivsky[9]

THE STATE

While the law and the State are intimately connected in that the state is effectively the lawgiver, they are not the same. The State is much more than its laws. It serves as a guarantor of the power of

---

8 Bhagat Singh give an example of retributive punishment, somewhat reminiscent of his own treatment in prison. The excerpt following this one is from Dostoevsky's *The House of the Dead*.

9 Fyodor Mikhailovich Dostoevsky (1821–81) was among the greatest Russian novelists. *The House of the Dead* is a novel published in 1862, and is based on his own experience of spending four years in a Siberian prison.

the ruling class, whether they are slave, feudal, capitalist, or (so far) most actually existing post-capitalist states.

Around 6,000 years ago, they have their origins in the needs of those beginning to accumulate wealth by expropriation and exploitation. The modern state comprises vast civil and military (including police) bureaucracies, legislators, executives, and judges.

They spend enormous sums of money, most to maintain their structures but also to build the infrastructure necessary for the functioning of markets and the accumulation of capital, with some allocated for social needs such as education and healthcare. The state can sometimes be a terrain of class struggle and can be bent, partially and only through massive popular power, to the will of workers and peasants. Bhagat Singh had limited resources available in prison. Yet, his quoted excerpts and commentary show that he was on track to develop a clear understanding, analysis, and critique of the state. It is a great pity that he did not live to write a book theorizing the state. When India became radically independent, a worker-peasant state could come into being and then, as society moved toward full communism, this state would 'wither away'. This would likely have been a possibility given what Bhagat Singh wrote about anarchism.

PAGE 11

'The State presupposes a public power of coercion separated from the aggregate body of its members.'
(Engels) pp. 116

'Only one thing was missing [given the growing exploitation of one class by another]: an institution that not only secured the newly acquired property of private individuals against the communistic tradition of the gens, that not only declared as sacred the formerly so despised private property and represented the protection of this sacred property as the highest purpose of human society, but that also stamped the gradually developing new forms of acquiring property of constantly increasing wealth with the universal sanction of the society. An institution

PAGE 12

that lent the character of perpetuity not only to the newly rising division into classes, but also to the right of the possessing classes to exploit and rule the nonpossessing classes. And this institution was found. The State arose.'

pp. 129-130 [10]

PAGE 15

'It was not against Louis XVI but against despotic principles of government that the Nation revolted. The principles had not their origin in him, but in the original establishment, many centuries back, and they were become too deeply rooted to be removed, and the Augean stable of parasites and plunderers too abominably filthy to be cleaned by anything short of a complete revolution.'
(pp. 19)[11]

'Not a grave for the murder'd for freedom,
but grows seed for freedom, in its turn to bear seed.
Which the winds carry afar and re-sow, and the
rains and the snows nourish.
Not a disembodied spirit can the weapons of
tyrant let loose
But it stalks invincibly over the earth, whispering,
counselling, cautioning.'

---

10 Friedrich Engels, *The Origin of the Family, Private Property and the State* (1884).
11 From Thomas Paine, *The Rights of Man* (1791). Source not indicated in the notebook, however. Thomas Paine, English author and publicist (1737–1809) known for his significant contributions to the American War of Independence and the French Revolution.

p. 268 Walt Whitman[12, 13]

PAGE 21

'Away with the State! I will take part in that revolution. Undermine the whole conception of a state, declare free choice and spiritual kinship to be the only all important conditions of any union, and you will have the commencement of a liberty that is worth something.'

Henrik Ibsen, letter to Georg Brandes[14]

PAGE 34

'Under the Socialist movement there is coming a time, and the time may be even now at hand, when improved conditions or adjusted wages will no longer be thought to be an answer to the cry of labor; yes when these will be but an insult to the common intelligence. It is not for better wages, improved capitalist conditions or a share of capitalist profits that the Socialist movement is in the world; it is here for the abolition of wages and profits, and for the end of capitalism and the private capitalist. Reformed political institutions, boards of arbitration between capital and labor,

12 An excerpt from Walt Whitman's 'Liberty is Never Defeated'. Walt Whitman (1819–92) had a humble start with little education and worked his way through to win recognition late in life. Now acknowledged as a great and popular poet. From his masterpiece, *Leaves of Grass*.

13 It is not difficult to imagine Bhagat Singh seeing himself and his comrades when he read this poem by Walt Whitman. When the freedom being fought for is from a brutal foreign power, it must indeed have struck Indian radicals that the state that would succeed after the exodus of Great Britain from the country would be little different if Indian leaders replaced the British rulers, but not much else changed. This is why they sought revolutionary change, hitting the root of the country's miseries: the private, capitalist ownership of productive property. No doubt, grasping this reality would have significantly aided Bhagat Singh in theorizing the state as a general social category.

14 Henrik Johan Ibsen (1828–1906), Norwegian playwright acknowledged as a founder of modern prose drama

philanthropies and privileges that are but the capitalists' gifts–none of these can much longer answer the question that is making the temples, thrones and Parliaments of the nation tremble.

There can be no peace between the man who is down and the man who builds on his back. There can be no reconciliation between classes; there can only be an end of classes. It is idle to talk of goodwill until there is first justice, and idle to talk of justice until the man who makes the world possesses the work of his own hands. The cry of the world's workers can be answered with nothing save the whole product of their work.'

George D. Herron[15]

PAGE 43

'Whether it be true or not that man was born in equity and conceived in sin, it is certainly true that Government was born of aggression and by aggression.'

Herbert Spencer[16]

'Good people, things will never go well in England, so long as goods be not in common, and so long as there be villains and gentlemen. By what right are they, whom we call lords, greater folk then we? On what grounds have they deserved it? Why do they hold us in serfage? If we all come of the same father and mother, Adam and Eve, how can they say or prove that they are greater or are better than we? If it be not that they make us gain for them by our toil what they spend in their pride. They are clothed in velvet and are warm in their furs and ermines, while we are covered with rags. They have wine and spices and their bread; and we oatcake,

---

15 'From Revolution to Revolution: An Address in Memory of the Paris Commune of 1871'. In all likelihood, this is George D. Herron (1862–1925), who was at one time a Christian Socialist minister, a founder of the Rand School of Social Science, and member of the Socialist Party (USA).

16 Herbert Spencer (1820–1903), English philosopher who applied evolutionary theory to philosophy. Works include *The Principles of Psychology* (1855) and *First Principles* (1862).

and straw, and water to drink! They have leisure and fine houses; we have pain and labour, rain and wind in the fields, and yet it is of our toil that these men hold their state.' . . .[17]

Friar of Wat Taylor's Rebel[18, 19]

'Since the state is only a temporary institution which is to be made use of in revolution, in order forcibly to suppress the opponents, it is perfectly absurd to talk of about a free popular state; so long as the proletariat still needs the state, it needs it not in the interest of freedom, but in order to suppress its opponents, and when it becomes possible to speak of freedom, the state, as such, ceases to exist.'

Engels in his letter to Babel March 28th 1875[20]

PAGE 111

The State is not really an end in itself and man is not here for the sake of Law or the State, but that these rather exist for man.[21]

17 This excerpt illustrates well the sham that democracy is without equality. That is, capitalism is incompatible with democracy.
18 A few words are not clear. Source torn out except the words: Friar of Wat Taylor's Rebel.
19 The following excerpt, from a friar in the English peasant revolt of 1381, led by Wat Tyler, reveals what Bhagat Singh believed himself. That a world of substantive equality must be the goal of socialism, something incompatible with any contemporary notion of the state. A revolutionary government must be one that institutes as much substantive equality as possible while at the same time empowering the people to rule themselves. Bhagat Singh would have admired Venezuela's Hugo Chavez and the formation of the communes he championed. The early Bolshevik Soviets are another excellent example.
20 As István Mészáros tells us in *Beyond Leviathan*, the only reason to study the state is to determine the conditions under which it can be abolished.
21 These may be Bhagat Singh's words. Unclear if this is a quote.

Ancient Polity; Rome and Sparta; Aristotle and Plato:

Subordination of the individual to the state was the dominant feature of these ancient polities, Sparta and Rome. In Hellas or in Rome, the citizen had but a few personal rights; his conduct was largely subject to public censorship, and his religion was imposed by State authority. The only true citizens and member of the Sovereign body being an aristocratic caste of freemen, whose manual work is performed by slaves possessing no civil rights.

Socrates:[23]

Socrates is represented as contending that whoever, after reaching man's estate, voluntarily remains in a city, should submit to the Govt. even when he deems its laws unjust; accordingly, on the ground that he would break his covenant with the State by escaping from prison into exile, he determines to await the execution of an unjust sentence.

Plato (Social Contract):[24]

He traces the origin of society and the State to mutual need, for men as isolated beings are incapable of satisfying their manifold wants. He, while depicting a kind of idealised Sparta says, 'In an ideal State, philosophers should rule; and to this aristocracy or government of the best, the body of citizens would owe implicit obedience.' He emphasises on the careful training and education

22 No source or reference has been indicated for this section. These appear to be Bhagat Singh's notes, rather than quotations. It appears to be his summary of what philosophers have thought about the state. Notice that for class society, it is assumed that the people will submit to the will of the state, the idea being that there has been made a covenant between the people and those who hold the levers of state power. And in the ancient world, slavery is taken as a given, with slaves obviously having no rights.

23 Socrates (c. 470–399BC), Greek philosopher, tried and condemned for 'corrupting' the youth. Writings of Plato, Xenophon and Aristotle have preserved his ideas.

24 Plato (c. 427–347 BC), Greek philosopher, disciple of Socrates. Author of numerous works, and founder of the Assembly in Athens (387 BC) where Aristotle was a student.

of citizens.

Aristotle:[25]

He was the first to disentangle politics from ethics, though he was careful not to sever them. 'The majority of men,' he argued, 'are ruled by their passions rather than by reason, and the State must therefore, train them to virtue by a life-long course of discipline, as in Sparta. Until political society is instituted, there is no administration of justice. . . . (but) it is necessary to enquire into the best constitution, and best system of legislation . . .'

PAGE 166

'The State is much more than an alliance which individuals can join or leave without effect, for the independent or cityless man is unscrupulous and savage, something different from a citizen.'

PAGE 168[26]

Though the Roman jurists did not postulate a contract as the origin of Civil Society, but there is a tendency to deduce recognized rights and obligations *from a supposed, but non-existent contract.*

With regard to sovereignty, the citizens assembled in the Comitia Tributa exercised the supreme power during the golden days of the Republic.

Under the Empire, the sovereign authority was vested in the Emperor, and according to the later juris consults, the people, by the Lex Regia, delegated the supreme command to each Emperor at the beginning of his reign, thus conferring on him all their rights to govern and legislate.

---

25 Aristotle (384–322 BC), Greek philosopher, pupil of Plato and tutor of Alexander the Great. Works include *Metaphysics*, *Nicomachean Ethics*, *Politics* and *Poetics*.
26 Bhagat Singh goes on to comment on Rome and the Middle Ages.

PAGE169

Middle Ages

Thomas Aquinas:[27] (1226–1274) is said to be the chief representative of the middle ages political Theory.

He following Roman jurists, recognized a natural law, the principles of which have been divinely implanted in human reason, together with positive laws that vary in different States.

He held that the legislative power, the essential attribute of sovereignty, should be directed to the common good, and that, for the attainment of this end, it should belong to the multitude or to their representative, the prince. A mixed government of monarch, nobles, and people, with the Pope as final authority, seemed to him the best.

PAGE 169[28]

In Renaissance, all departments of knowledge were vitalized and the circumscribed philosophy – having served as a hand-maid of theology for a thousand years, rapidly gave place to a new philosophy of *Nature and man*, more, liberal, more profound, and more comprehensive.

PAGE 170

After Reformation, the Papal authority having been shaken off, a wave of freedom swept minds of both the rulers and the people. But there was confusion.

27 St. Thomas Aquinas (1225–1274) philosopher and theologian, whose major work was *Summa Theologiae* (1267–73). Bhagat Singh's date incorrect.

28 Bhagat Singh continues his historical reading with some notes on Renaissance and Reformation, when the individual begins to come to the fore. The ground he covered in so short a time and the breadth of his reading are astonishing.

To settle new situation, great many thinkers began to meditate over the question of State. Different schools grew up.

Machiavelli–the famous Italian political thinker thought the Republican form of Government to be the best one, but doubting the stability of such a form of government, he inculcated maxims of securing a strong princely rule and hence he wrote 'The Prince'.[29]

His advocacy of *centralized government* had greatly affected political theory and practice in Europe.

Machiavelli was perhaps the first writer who treated 'Politics' from a purely secular point of view.

Other Thinkers

Pact and Contract

Majority of others favored the theory of pact or contract. [In Roman Law, a *pact* was the product of an agreement among individuals and fell short of a *contract*, which was a *pact* plus an obligation].

There were two different sects of these thinkers. The first one expounded the theory based on the Hebrew idea of covenant between God and man supplemented by the Roman idea of contract. It postulated a tacit contract between the government and the people.

The second or modern form, relates to the institution of Political Society by means of a compact among individuals. Prominent thinkers of this school were Hooker,[30] Hobbes,[31]

---

29 Niccolò di Bernardo dei Machiavelli (1467–1527), political philosopher, musician, poet, and romantic comedic playwright. A key figure of the Italian Renaissance, most widely known for his treatises on political theory (*The Prince*) and republicanism (*Discourses on Livy*).

30 Richard Hooker (1554–1600), English theologian who codified principles of Anglicanism in *Of the Lawes of Ecclesiastical Politie*.

31 Thomas Hobbes (1588–1679) English philosopher, author of the celebrated *Leviathan* (1651; on the social contract theory) and several other works.

Locke[32] and Rousseau.[33, 34]

PAGE 176

Rousseau[35]

Equality

No one should be rich enough to buy another nor poor enough to be forced to sell himself. Great inequalities pave the way for tyranny.

Property and Civil Society

The first man who, having enclosed a piece of land, thought of saying 'this is mine,' and found people simple enough, to believe him, was the true founder of Civil Society. What wars, crimes, and horrors would have been spared to the race, if someone had exposed this imposture, and declared that the *earth belonged to no one, & its fruits to all.*

PAGE 177

'The man who meditates is a depraved animal'

Civil Law

32 John Locke (1632–1704), English philosopher, leading empiricist, social contract theorist and author of several influential works, including *Two Treatises on Government* (1689) and *An Essay Concerning Human Understanding* (1690).

33 Jean Jacques Rousseau (1712–1778), a French philosopher regarded as the founder of Romanticism. His book on political theory, *The Social Contract* (1762), described an ideal state in which sovereignty was vested with the people as a whole and individuals would retain freedom by submitting to the 'general will'. His novel *Emile* (1762) dealt with the theme of education. He also wrote his autobiography *Confessions* in several volumes. He did not live to see it, but he was much idolized during the French Revolution. In the last years of his life, he was not fully sane.

34 Bhagat Singh sees that more modern thinkers begin to argue that sovereign power derives or should derive from the will of the people. He seems especially taken, and for good reasons, with Rousseau. He took notes on Rousseau's *Social Contract*.

35 The following are Bhagat Singh's notes from Rousseau's *Social Contract*.

Pointing to the oppression of the weak and the insecurity of all, the rich craftily devised rules of justice and peace, by which all should be guaranteed their possessions, and established a Supreme ruler to enforce the Laws.

This must have been the origin of Society and of the Laws, which gave new chains to the weak and new strength to the rich, finally destroyed natural liberty, and, for the profit of a few ambitious men, fixed forever the law of property and of inequality, *converted a clever usurpation into an irrevocable right,* and subjected the whole human race hence-forward to labor, servitude and misery.

Re: Inequalities

But it is manifestly opposed to natural law that a handful of people should gorge superfluities while the famished multitude lack the necessities of life.

PAGE 178

Fate of his Writings

Emile and *Social Contract,* both published in 1762, the former burnt in Paris, Rousseau narrowly escaping arrest, then both being publicly burnt in Genoa, his native place whence he expected greater response.

Sovereignty of Monarch to that of the People

Rousseau retains the French ideas of unity and centralization; but while in the seventeenth century, the State (or sovereignty) was confounded with the monarchy. Rousseau's influence caused it in the 18th Century to be identified with the people.

Pact

By pact men exchange natural liberty for civil liberty and moral liberty.

Right of First Occupancy

Right of Property:

Its justification depends on these conditions: (a) that the land is uninhabited; (b) that a man occupies only the area required for his subsistence; (c) that he takes possession of it not by an empty ceremonial, but by labor and cultivation.

PAGE 179

Religion

Rousseau places even religion under the tyranny of the sovereign.

Introductory Note

'I wish to enquire whether, taking men as they are and laws as they can be made, it is possible to establish some just and certain rule of administration in civil affairs . . .

. . . I shall be asked whether I am a prince or a legislator that I write on politics. I reply that I am not. If I were one, I should not waste time in saying what ought to be done; I should do it or remain silent.'

Man is born free, and everywhere he is in chains.

Shaking off the Yoke of Slavery by Force

I should say that so long as a people is compelled to obey and does obey, it does well; but that, so soon as it can shake off the yoke and does shake it off, it does better; for, if men recover their freedom by virtue of the same right (i.e. force) by which it was taken away, either they are justified in resuming it, or there was no justification for depriving them of it.

PAGE 180

Force

'Power which is acquired by violence is only a usurpation, and lasts only so long as the force of him who commands prevails over that of those who obey; so that if the latter become the strongest in their turn and shake off the yoke, they do so with as much right and justice as the other who had imposed it on them. The same law (of force) which has made the authority then unmakes it; it is the law of the strongest.'

Diderot, Encyclopedia[36]

'Authority'

Slaves lose everything in their bonds, even the desire to escape from them;[37]

Right of Slavery[38]

'Do subjects, then, give up their persons on condition that their property also shall be taken? I do not see what is left for them?'

'It will be said that the despot secures to his subjects civil peace. Be it so; but what do they gain by that, if the wars which his ambitions bring upon them, together with his insatiable greed and the vexations of his administration, harass them more than their own dissensions would?'

PAGE 181

'To say that a man gives himself for nothing is to say what is absurd and inconceivable.'

Whether addressed by a man to a man, or by man to a nation, such a speech as this will always be equally foolish: 'I make an agreement with you wholly at your expense and wholly for my benefit, and I shall observe it as long as I please, while you also shall observe it as long as I please.'

Equality

'If then you wish to give stability to the State, bring the two extremes as near together as possible; tolerate neither rich nor beggars. These two conditions, naturally inseparable, are equally fatal to the general welfare; from the one class spring tyrants, from

---

36 Denis Diderot (1713–84), French philosopher and Chief Editor of *Encyclopedie*. He also wrote the first French 'bourgeois' drama, *Le Neveu de Rameau*. He was anti-clerical and was imprisoned because of his works like *Lettres sur les Aveugeles* (1749).

37 Rousseau, *Social Contract*, chapter 2, 'The First Societies'.

38 Rousseau, *Social Contract*, chapter 4, 'Slavery'.

the other, the supporters of tyranny; it is always between these that the traffic in public liberty is carried on; the one buys the other sells.'

PAGE 182

'Hail lays waste a few cantons, but it rarely causes scarcity. Riots and civil wars greatly startle the chief men; but they do not produce the real misfortunes of nations, which may be abated, while it is being disputed who shall tyrannize over them. It is from their permanent conditions that their real prosperity or calamities spring; when all is left crushed under the yoke, it is then that everything perishes; it is then that the chief men, destroying them at their leisure, 'Where they make a solitude, they call it peace.'

pp. 176

PAGE 190

'From each according to his ability, to each according to his need.'[39]

Karl Marx

page 277

'How many of the Western educated Indians who have thrown themselves into political agitation against the tyranny of the British bureaucracy have ever raised a finger to free their own fellow countrymen from the tyranny of those social evils? How many of them are entirely free from it themselves, or, if free, have the courage to act up to their opinion?'

India Old & New[40]

---

39 After some comments on the French Revolution and some excerpts from Thomas Paine's *The Rights of Man*, Bhagat Singh gets to the heart of the matter, freedom for Great Britain and freedom from want for the Indian masses.

40 Valentine Chirol, *Indian Unrest*. This book is referred to again and again by Bhagat Singh, from page 273/130 onwards.

page 279[41]

'No one but the voice of the Mother herself will and can determine when once she comes to herself and stands free what constitution shall be adopted by Her for the guidance of Her life after the revolution is over . . . Without going into detail we may mention this much, that whether the head of the Imperial Government of the Indian Nation be a President or a King depends upon how the revolution develops itself . . . The mother must be free, must be one and united, must make her will supreme. Then it may be that she gives out this: Her will either wearing a kingly crown on her head or a Republican mantle round her sacred form.

Forget not, O Princes! that a strict account will be asked of your doings and non-doings, and a people newly born will not fail to pay in the coin you paid. Everyone who shall have actively betrayed the trust of the people, disowned his fathers, and debases his blood by arraying himself against the Mother–he shall be crushed to dust and ashes . . . Do you doubt our grim earnestness? If so, hear the name of Dhingra [a young revolutionary hanged for killing a British official] and be dumb. In the name of that martyr, O Indian princes, we ask you to think solemnly and deeply upon these words. Choose as you will and you will reap what you sow. Choose whether you shall be the first of the nation's fathers or the last of nation's tyrants.'

p. 196 Indian Unrest

From the pamphlet, 'Choose O Princes.'

page 191

'Philosophers,' said Marx, 'have merely interpreted the world in many ways; the really important thing is to change it.'

Karl Marx

---

41 From a leaflet then in circulation – 'Choose, O Indian Princes' – a 'characteristic document' sent by the 'extremists' to the rulers of the Native States. One chief gave it to Chirol, who has given two extracts from it on pages 196–197 of his book, with his interlinking comments.

Chronology of Events of the Life of Bhagat Singh[1]

1907: Bhagat Singh born on 28 September, Saturday, about 9 am, at village Chak No. 105, Lyallpur Bange, Dist. Lyallpur, now named Faisalabad in Pakistan.

1911–1917: Primary schooling in District Board Primary School Chak No. 105.

1917–1921: Schooling in DAV High School Lahore up to ninth class.

1921: Joins National College Lahore for Graduation.

1923: Clears Intermediate examination, called F.A., joins Hindustan Republican Association (HRA) during college days.

1923: Leaves for Kanpur mid-year after being pressured to marry by his family; end of his academic career as a student of B.A. first year.

1923–26: Works for Ganesh Shankar Vidyarthi's Hindi journal *Pratap* at Kanpur, under the pseudonym 'Balwant'; works in flood relief in the Kanpur area; and servs as headmaster of National School in Shadipur village of Aligarh district of UP. Confirmed dates not available.

1926: Forms Naujawan Bharat Sabha (Young India Association) in March, becoming its General Secretary.

1927: First arrest on 29 May, in connection with the October 1926 Dussehra Bomb Case in Lahore. Kept in police custody for five weeks. Released on bail of Rs 60,000 on 4 July.

1927–28: Lives on and works at a dairy farm set up by his father,

---

1 Sources: Bhagat Singh's niece Virender Sandhu's book *Bhagat Singh Aur Unke Mritanjyu Purkhe* (Bhagat Singh and his Immortal Ancestors); *The Tribune, Abhyuodey,* and *Bhavishya* reports of the period.

Kishan Singh, in Khwasarian village near Lahore, during the bail bound-up period. During this period, he also works and writes for *Kirti* (in Punjabi/Urdu, Akali Punjabi), *Maharathi*, *Prabha*, and *Chand* (in Hindi).

8–9 September 1928: Historic meeting of revolutionaries in Ferozeshah Kotla grounds of Delhi. Hindustan Republican Association/Army (HRA) renamed Hindustan Socialist Republic Association (HSRA), with an armed wing, Hindustan Socialist Republican Army.

30 October 1928: On the insistence of Bhagat Singh and his comrades, Lala Lajpat Rai agrees to lead a procession against the Simon Commission in Lahore. Lala Lajpat Rai injured by the lathi blows struck by DSP Lahore, John Saunders, ordered by SSP Lahore, James Scott.

17 November 1928: Lala Lajpat Rai dies in Lahore.

17 December 1928: DSP John Saunders is shot dead in front of the SSP office in Lahore in broad daylight by revolutionaries to avenge the death of Lala Lajpat Rai.

1928: Bhagat Singh escapes from Lahore posing at a British officer, accompanied by Durga Bhabhi, posing as his wife. Bhagat Singh sports a haircut and wears a hat.

3–4 April 1929: The iconic hat-wearing photograph of Bhagat Singh with B.K. Dutt taken by photographer Ramnath of Kashmiri Gate, Delhi.

8 April 1929: Harmless bombs, 'to make the deaf hear,' thrown in Central Assembly Delhi, later the Indian Parliament, from the visitors' gallery by Bhagat Singh and B.K. Dutt, along with leaflets.

1929: Historic statement by Bhagat Singh and B.K. Dutt in Delhi session court of 6 June, read by advocate Asaf Ali on their behalf.

12 June 1929: Bhagat Singh and B.K. Dutt convicted in the Delhi bomb case and sentenced to transportation for life. Transferred from Delhi jail to Mianwali and Lahore jails.

1929: Beginning of historic hunger strike by Bhagat Singh and B.K. Dutt from 15 June for the status of political prisoners.

10 July 1929: Bhagat Singh brought to Lahore from Mianwali jail to face trial in the Lahore Conspiracy case relating to Saunders's murder. Trial is to be held at the court of Special Magistrate Rai Sahib Kishan Chand in Lahore. The hunger strike continues, and Bhagat Singh brought on a stretcher to court because he had been on hunger strike since 15 June.

1929: Hunger strike ends on 4 October after demands are partially conceded. Death of Jatindernath Das on 13 September after 63 days of hunger strike. Bhagat Singh and Dutt complete 110 days' record hunger strike, with two days break on 2 and 3 September on the assurance by Congress leaders that British authorities were meeting demands. Hunger strike resumed on 4 September as British authorities refused to accept demands.

1929: Bhagat Singh and his comrades badly beaten by police in court and jail, 21 to 23 October.

1930: Two week hunger strike from 4 February to attain the demands of October 1929.

1930: Viceroy Lord Irwin, from the summer capital Simla, issues an ordinance on 1 May setting up a Special Tribunal for conducting the trial of the Lahore Conspiracy case, a case transferred from Special Magistrate to Special Tribunal.

5 May 1930: Trial of Lahore Conspiracy case begins at Special Tribunal.

12 May 1930: Bhagat Singh and the other accused again badly beaten up in court. The only Indian judge on the three-member tribunal, Justice Agha Haider, disassociates from Tribunal President's order. Revolutionaries begin boycott of the tribunal.

21 June 1930: Special Tribunal reconstituted, but sympathetic Indian judge Agha Haider removed from the tribunal.

10 July 1930: Charges made against the accused by the tribunal.

1930: Three weeks' hunger strike by accused 28 July onwards.

7 October 1930: Tribunal pronounces judgement that Bhagat Singh, Rajguru, and Sukhdev be to executed after conviction.

1930: Date of execution fixed for 27 October 1930, with an appeal filed in the Privy Council on behalf of Bhagat Singh in the same month.

1931: Appeal heard and dismissed by Privy Council on 11 February.

1931: Appeals against Privy Council and the tribunal heard and dismissed. Punjab High Court sets execution date as 23 March by 3 pm.

23 March 1931: Execution of Bhagat Singh, Rajguru, and Sukhdev between 7 p.m to 7.33 p.m at Lahore Central Jail. Bodies cut and filled into half-burnt sacks at Gandiwand village near Hussainiwala in Ferozepur district.

24 March 1931: Remains of bodies brought back to Lahore and proper cremation of bodies in the evening at Ravi bank, Lahore, with thousands of people in attendance. Tributes paid at Minto Park.

Glossary

Ahmedabad Mill Strike of 1918: Ahmedabad is the largest city in the western Indian state of Gujarat. After a crop-destroying monsoon and a resultant plague epidemic, compounded by wartime inflation, in 1918, the textile mill employers offered bonuses to work during the plague. Later these were rescinded, leading to strife. Mahatma Gandhi then intervened in this dispute between Ahmedabad workers and millowners, using Satyagraha and hunger strike to resolve an industrial dispute. The workers eventually returned to work with a wage increase, though below what they had initially demanded.

Amritsar: Northern Indian city in the state of Punjab. Site of the Jallianwalla Bagh Massacre in 1919. Amritsar is considered the holiest city of the Sikh religion.

Anushilan Samiti: Translated to the 'bodybuilding society', was an Indian fitness club founded in 1902 in Bengal, which was used as an underground society for anti-British revolutionaries. It supported revolutionary violence as the means for ending British rule in India. From its foundation to its dissolution during the 1930s, the Samiti challenged British rule in India by engaging in militant nationalism, including bombings, assassinations, and politically motivated violence.

Babbar Akali Agitation: The Babbar Akali movement was a 1921 splinter group of militant Sikhs who broke away from the mainstream Akali movement over the latter's insistence on non-violence over gurdwara reforms. The group published an illegal newspaper describing British exploitation of India and began killing informers, government officials, and ex-officials. The British authorities violently suppressed it.

Bal Bharat Sabha: A subsidiary organization of the Naujawan Bharat Sabha for students between 12 and 16 years of age.

Bal Gangadhar Tilak (1856-1920): An early Indian nationalist and independence advocate. The British rulers called him 'the father of the Indian unrest'. He was the best-known leader of the independence movement before Gandhi. Through his newspaper, *Kesari*, he took up the cause of Indian independence. He also exposed British atrocities during the plague epidemic in Pune through his paper.

Bande Mataram: Bande/Vande Mataram (Hail the Motherland!) was a rallying cry for Indian nationalists before independence. In 1937 the Congress chose it as the national song but limited it to the first two stanzas, thereby implicitly accepting the other three as anti-Muslim. In recent times, right-wing Hindu nationalists have used it as yet another tool to persecute Muslims.

Bardoli Satyagraha: A civil disobedience campaign waged in 1928 by farmers in

Bardoli, a town in what is now the western Indian state of Gujarat, against a 30 per cent increase in taxes. The struggle was ultimately successful, and it served to help renew the fight for Indian independence.

Battle of Plassey: The 1757 battle in Bengal resulted in a decisive victory for the British East India Company, a British private corporation with its military that seized much of the Indian subcontinent. Tightly allied with the British state, it paved the way for British colonial rule in India. The Company was intimately involved in the slave trade, among other nefarious enterprises.

Bharat: An alternative name for India, deriving from ancient Indian literature.

Bharat Mata Society: Pagri Sambhal Movement was a successful farm agitation against the British government. To galvanize this unrest into a rebellion against the British government, Ajit Singh (Bhagat Singh's uncle), Kishan Singh (Bhagat Singh's father), and their revolutionary friend Ghasita Ram, formed the Bharat Mata Society in 1907.

Central Assembly Bombing Case: On 8 April 1929, Bhagat Singh and B.K. Dutt threw two homemade smoke bombs in the chamber of the Central Legislative Assembly, located in Delhi. This was in protest against two bills the Assembly was considering and to publicize the revolutionary wing of the independence movement. Both Singh and Dutt welcomed their arrests. Both were tried and sentenced to imprisonment in the Lahore Circular Jail. However, in the meantime, Bhagat Singh was connected to the killing of Deputy Superintendent of the Lahore police John Saunders, for which he was ultimately tried, convicted, and hanged.

Chapekar Brothers: In the wake of the horrendous treatment of Indians by the British during a Bubonic Plague epidemic in the city of Pune (Poona) in 1896-97, including the stripping and examining of women in public and the desecration of religious symbols, the three Chapekar brothers (Damodar, Balkrishna, and Vasudeo) shot and killed Special Plague Committee commissioner, Walter Charles Rand, and his military escort, Lt. Ayerst. The killing took place on 22 June 1897, the day of the Diamond Jubilee of the coronation of Queen Victoria. The brothers were arrested, convicted, and hanged in 1899. The brothers' actions served both to help Indians regain their dignity and as an inspiration for mass efforts to expel the British from the country.

Charpoy: A bed frame strung with tape or light rope.

Chauri Chaura: The town in Uttar Pradesh where on 4 February 1922, police fired upon protesters taking part in the Gandhi-led Non-Cooperation Movement. In retaliation, the crowd set fire to the police station, killing all the occupants. In response, Gandhi halted the movement. However, not everyone, even in the Indian National Congress, agreed with Gandhi's decision. And the harsh penalties imposed by the British on the protesters, including multiple hangings, pushed many Indian nationalists to the Left.

Chittagong Uprising: The uprising began on 18 April 1930 with raids on two armouries in Chittagong, then in Bengal, but now in Bangladesh. The raids and ensuing battles with police were undertaken by left-wing rebels inspired by the 1916 Easter Rebellion in Ireland and led by Master Surya Sen. Sen was eventually captured, tortured, and killed by the British.

Cellular Jail: The British prison in the Andaman and Nicobar Islands, far off the eastern coast of India in the Bay of Bengal. Many independence fighters were imprisoned there. The jail was built according to the principles of English philosopher Jeremy Bentham. Bentham urged that society be organized so that everyone would be subject to surveillance at any time. He thought this would ensure universal good behaviour since people would not know if they were being watched by the authorities and would therefore refrain from doing wrong. This is called the principle of the panopticon – the total observation from a central point.

Communist University of the Toilers of the East: Established by the Soviet government in 1921, four years after the Bolshevik Revolution. In operation until the late 1930s, it provided training for revolutionaries worldwide.

Crore: Indian numerical measure, equal to ten million.

Dalit: Translated to broken or scattered, also previously known as 'untouchable', they are the most oppressed stratum of the castes in India. Dalits were excluded from the four-fold varna system of Hinduism. Dalits now profess various religious beliefs, including Hinduism, Buddhism, Sikhism, Christianity, and Islam. Scheduled Castes is the official term for Dalits as per the Constitution of India.

Dussehra Festival Bomb Case: In October 1926, a bomb exploded in Lahore at the Dussehra Fair celebration, an important Hindu festival. Bhagat Singh was arrested in connection with the bombing and eventually released on a large bond. The case was eventually dropped. It's possible Lahore police set up the bomb to falsely implicate the revolutionaries.

Feroze Shah Kotla: The Delhi Fortress was built in the fourteenth century by Sultan Feroz Shah Tughlaq. On 8–9 September 1928, many revolutionary groups, including Hindustan Republican Association, met here and emerged as the Hindustan Socialist Republican Association.

First War of Independence (1857-1859): A two-year-long rebellion, waged against the British East India Company, the nominal ruler of India. The war was lost, but in its aftermath, Britain dissolved the East India Company and instituted the direct rule of India under the British Crown.

Ghadar Movement: Ghadar is a Punjabi and Urdu word derived from Arabic, which means to revolt or rebellion. This movement was organized in the second decade of the twentieth century by Indian immigrants. It originated on the West Coast of the United States and Canada but soon spread to India and the Indian diaspora worldwide. The aim of the movement was Indian independence through armed rebellion.

Ghadar Movement (1857): Another name for the First War of Indian Independence.

Granthi: A Sikh religious official trained in reading sacred Sikh texts.

Gurmukhi: Ancient script used by Sikh gurus to write the sacred texts of the Sikh religion. It also spread to become the script of the Punjabi language in India.

Guru Gobind Singh (1666-1708): The tenth Sikh Guru, who institutionalized various aspects of the religion, including the way Sikhs were to look (uncut hair, short breeches, and so on). He also led the Sikh resistance to the encroachments of the Mughal Empire into Sikh territories.

Guru ka Bagh agitation: An exemplary, prolonged non-violent struggle, part of the agitations undertaken by Sikhs under the Gurudwara Reform Movement in the early 1920s to regain control of the Gurudwaras from the corrupt practices and hereditary control of the Mahants, who were often backed by the British regime. From 9 August 1922, for months, hundreds of non-violent protestors were assaulted and terrorized by the police to keep them from collecting firewood for the langar. The protestors' capacity for suffering and resistance was put to test. Finally, the agitation succeeded on 17 November 1922.

Gurudwara: A Sikh place of worship and assembly, it also serves as a community centre, distributing free food, among other things.

Havildar: Sergeant.

Hindustan: Another name for India.

HRA/HSRA: The Hindustan Republican Association and Hindustan Socialist Republican Association. These were radical nationalist organizations favouring direct and sometimes violent opposition to British rule. They opposed Gandhi's insistence on non-violence, especially his abandoning the Non-cooperation movement after the violence at Chauri Chaura in 1922. Although it must be noted that members of these organizations often cooperated with the Indian National Congress led by Gandhi. The HRA was formed in 1924. Once Bhagat Singh and other socialists joined the HRA, the organization became an openly communist-like group, pushing forward an ideal of an independent and socialist India. In 1928, the anti-British sentiment within India after the arrival of the Simon Commission was at its peak, and the HRA became the HSRA, reflecting the socialist ideals they followed.

Holi: A Hindu festival that signifies the triumph of good over evil.

Jallianwala Bagh Massacre: On 13 April 1919, a largely peaceful protest demonstration against the British against the arrest of two independence activists took place in Amritsar at the Bagh, which had once been a garden and was then an area of rest for those visiting the nearby Golden Temple, a Sikh Gurudwara. British general R.E.H. Dyer ordered his troops to fire on the crowd, resulting in the deaths of hundreds of people and injuries to over one thousand. Today, a memorial stands on the site in honour of the dead. This horrific slaughter was a seminal event in deepening Indian resentment of British rule and the drive for independence.

Janeyu: The 'sacred' thread worn by brahmins in Hinduism.

Ji: Indian honorific, applied to both persons and inanimate objects. A sign of respect, as in Gandhiji.

Jaito Morcha: The agitation of Jaito was an Akali agitation that took place in February 1924 for the restoration of the throne of Maharaja Ripudaman Singh of Nabha. The British had forced him to abdicate in favour of his minor son because they were irked by his support of the Guru-ka-Bagh Morcha, his contacts with the Indian nationalist leaders, and his involvement in other popular causes.

Kakori Train Robbery: On 9 August 1925, an HRA-organized train robbery took place in Kakori in Uttar Pradesh. HRA members robbed the train to fund the organization with money stolen from the British rulers of India and to bring public attention to the intent of the group to drive the British from India. The robbery, arrests, trials, and sentences (including death), and subsequent hunger strikes of the imprisoned led to widespread protests in the country.

Kamagata Maru: To protest restrictions by Canada (a British colony at the time) on Indian immigration, in April 1914, an Indian businessman, Gurdit Singh Sandhu, arranged for a Japanese steamship to travel with a large number of Indians, mainly from Punjab (and overwhelmingly Sikhs), to Canada, via a circuitous route with the final embarkment point in Japan. Upon landing in British Columbia, the ship was denied entry. Riots and deaths occurred in British Columbia and later at Calcutta, where the ship landed in India. This incident spurred the Ghadarites in Canada and the United States to press forward with violent efforts to expel the British from India.

Karmkshetra: The field of action.

Kanpur: It is a northern Indian city in Uttar Pradesh. The British called it Cawnpore. It was the site of the 'Siege of Cawnpore', a massacre of British civilians during the 1857 Rebellion.

Kesari: Radical newspaper founded by Bal Gangadhar Tilak.

Kirpan: A curved sword or knife carried by Sikhs.

Kuka Revolt: The Namdharis are a distinct sect of the Sikhs, and the word Kuka emerges from the *kook* or high-pitched shrieks they emit while reciting the Gurbani. The Kuka rebellion against the British, led by Satguru Ram Singh, started in 1849. They evolved the earliest practices of Non-cooperation and the use of Swadeshi as political weapons.

Khalistan Movement: A Sikh separatist movement seeking to create a homeland for Sikhs by establishing a sovereign state called Khalistan in the Punjab region.

Kirti: Kirti, meaning labourer, was a Punjabi Marxist periodical started by Ghadarite Santokh Singh. The first issue of *Kirti*, a newspaper dedicated to farmers, labourers and the working class, was published in February 1926 in Amritsar. *Kirti* enjoyed cult status till the end of World War II. From the Wikipedia entry: 'The newspaper's offices were often raided, and the newspaper was sometimes banned, but its editors never bowed to the British'. Bhagat Singh also served on its editorial board.

Jats: The Jat people are a traditionally agricultural community in Northern India and Pakistan.

Lahore: It is the capital of the Punjab province in Pakistan. It is the largest city and the historic capital and cultural centre of the (pre-partition) wider Punjab region. It was the capital of the Sikh Empire in the nineteenth century. It holds an important place in the life and death of Bhagat Singh. He was enrolled at the DAV School and National College in Lahore. During the anti-Simon Commission protests, Lala Lajpat Rai was assaulted and died in Lahore. The murder of John Saunders (later known as the Lahore Conspiracy Case) and the subsequent imprisonment and execution at the Lahore Central Jail took place in the city.

Mahabharata: It is one of the two major Sanskrit epics of ancient India, the other being the Ramayana.

Matwala: A biweekly Hindi-language literary and political magazine between 1923-1930. The magazine was founded by Seth Mahadev Prasad and headquartered in Calcutta. And. One of the contributors was Bhagat Singh.

Minto-Morley Reforms: Formally known as the Indian Councils Act of 1909, it was an act of the Parliament of the United Kingdom that brought about a limited increase in the involvement of Indians in the governance of British India. Named after Viceroy Lord Minto and Secretary of State John Morley, it introduced, among other things, separate electorates per the demands of the Muslim League.

Nankana Sahib: The city now falls in the Punjab province of Pakistan. It is named after the first Guru of the Sikhs, Guru Nanak, who was born in the city and began preaching here. Nankana Sahib is the most important religious site for the Sikh religion.

National College: In 1921, in response to Mahatma Gandhi's non-cooperation movement, Lala Lajpat Rai founded the National College, Lahore. The motive was to encourage Indian students to shun schools and colleges subsidized by the British Indian government. Bhagat Singh joined the college in 1923.

Naujawan Bharat Sabha (trans. Revolutionary Indian Youth Society): The NBS was a left-wing Indian association that sought to foment revolution against the British Raj by gathering workers and peasant youths by disseminating Marxist ideas. It was founded by Bhagat Singh in March 1926 and served as a public face of the Hindustan Republican Association/Hindustan Republican Socialist Association. The NBS comprised members from the Hindu, Muslim, and Sikh communities and organized lectures, public meetings and protests. Attendance at its public meetings became particularly popular after the killing of John P. Saunders in December 1928. The association was banned in July 1929 when the government imposed Section 144 to control gatherings as public support burgeoned for the imprisoned Singh and his fellow hunger strikers.

NCERT: The National Council of Educational Research and Training. Established in 1961, it has been a centre of controversy. The past and present right-wing government's have accused it of promoting leftist bias in school textbooks, while themselves being guilty of historical revisionism with an extreme Hindu nationalism agenda.

Non-Cooperation Movement: The movement begun by Gandhi in 1920 to encourage Indians to refuse cooperation with British rulers. They would no longer support British 'reforms', withdraw labour from any activity supporting British rule, including schools, boycott British goods, etc. With the aim of attaining self-governance. Gandhi ended the movement after the violence of the Chauri Chaura incident in February 1922.

Pagri Sambhal Jatta: It refers to both a movement protesting anti-farmer laws in Punjab begun by Ajit Singh (Bhagat Singh's uncle) and others; and to a famous poem and song of the same name written by Banke Dyal. It means, Take care of your turban, O peasant. The turban represents the dignity of the common person

Panchayati Raj: It is an ancient system of local government in rural India consisting of a village council of respected elders. Gandhi liked this system as a good model of decentralized government.

Pandit: (abbreviated Pt.) is an individual with specialized knowledge or a teacher of any field of expertise. The term generally refers to Brahmins specialized in Hindu law. However, today the title is used for experts in other subjects, such as music.

Paris Indian Society: It was an Indian nationalist society founded in Paris in 1905 by Madam Bhikaji Rustom Cama, Munchershah Burjorji Godrej, and S. R. Rana. The Indian diaspora played a prominent role in the Independence movement.

Pratap: It was a Hindi revolutionary newspaper founded by freedom fighter Ganesh Shankar Vidyarthi in 1913. Bhagat Singh wrote for it.

Public Safety Bill: It was enacted in 1928 to suppress socialist and communist organizations and activities. It was one of the bills protested by Bhagat Singh when they threw bombs into the chamber of the Central Assembly in 1929.

Punjab Region: It is a geopolitical, cultural, and historical region in South Asia, in the northern part of the Indian subcontinent, on the Indus Plain. In its long and complex history, in the nineteenth century, the Sikh Empire was established here. The Second Anglo-Sikh War drew the end of the Sikh Empire and brought Punjab under British Rule. As the largest provinces under British Raj, anti-British sentiments and agitations began soon enough. Along with Maharashtra and Bengal, Punjab shaped the Indian independence movement and Indian nationalism by contributing significantly towards the struggle. As the struggle for Indian independence drew close, Punjab witnessed competing and conflicting interests. With independence came the partition of the region between India and Pakistan. Bhagat Singh was born in the Lyallpur district of Punjab, British India, now called Faisalabad in Pakistan.

Quit India Movement: The Quit India Movement (also known as the August Kranti Movement) was launched at the Bombay session of the All India Congress Committee by Mahatma Gandhi on 8 August 1942. After the failure of the Cripps Mission to secure Indian support for the British war effort, it demanded an end to British rule in India. Gandhi made a call to *Do or Die*. The British immediately imprisoned most of the movement's leaders.

Ramayana: It is one of the two major Sanskrit epics of ancient India, the other being the Mahabharata.

Rasa: In Sanskrit, it means flavour, sentiment, or emotion. The Indian concept of aesthetic flavour is essential to any visual, literary, or performing artwork that can only be suggested, not described. Each rasa is assigned a colour. For example, the colour of heroism is saffron.

Round Table Conferences: They were a series of three peace conferences between

1930 and 1932 organized by the British and some Indian leaders to discuss a more significant role for Indians in government. The main motive of the British was to contain the movement for immediate independence.

Sardar: It is a Persian word which means leader or commander, also used previously as a title for nobility. The term was also used by Sikh leaders and generals who held important positions. The title is still commonly used by Sikhs today, and along with Singh, signifies a Sikh male – as in Sardar Bhagat Singh.

Satyagraha: It means holding firmly to the truth. It is a form of nonviolent or civil resistance popularized by Gandhi in the struggle for Indian independence. It has inspired leaders, like Martin Luther King and Cesar Chavez, in their fights against systemic and state oppression globally.

Shaheed: A word of Arabic origin, adopted by many Indian languages, including Punjabi. It means both a witness and a martyr. It is used as a posthumous title for those considered to have accepted or even consciously sought out their death to bear witness to their beliefs – such as Shaheed Bhagat Singh.

Shuddhi: Sanskrit for purification. A Hindu revivalist movement that the Arya Samaj started in the early 1990s in Punjab and which later spread to other parts of India. This socio-political movement aimed to reconvert or 'purify' Hindus who had converted to Islam and Christianity. This often became a flashpoint between the communities, thus fuelling communal tensions and disrupting communal harmony.

Sikhs: They follow Sikhism, a monotheistic religion that originated in the fifteenth century, in the Punjab region of the Indian subcontinent, based on the revelation of Guru Nanak. There are about 30 million Sikhs worldwide, with most living in the Indian region of Punjab. Sikhs were often dedicated and militant nationalists. Bhagat Singh was born to a Sikh family.

Sikh Empire: It was a state originating in the Indian subcontinent, formed under the leadership of Maharaja Ranjit Singh, who established an empire based in Punjab. The empire existed from when Maharaja Ranjit Singh captured Lahore in 1799 to when it was defeated and conquered in the Second Anglo-Sikh War in 1849. The Wikipedia entry for the empire states: At its peak in the 19th century, the Empire extended from the Khyber Pass in the west to western Tibet in the east, and from Mithankot in the south to Kashmir in the north.'

Singh Sabha Movement: A Sikh movement that began in Punjab in the 1870s to halt the decline of their religion. Due to the proselytizing activities of Christians, and Hindu and Muslim reform movements, mainstream Sikhs rapidly converted to other faiths. It aimed to propagate the true Sikh religion and restore Sikhism to its pristine glory. In modern terms, it was a Sikh identity movement.

Subedar: An Indian military officer.

Swadeshi Movement: Formally started from the Town Hall at Calcutta on 7 August 1905 to curb foreign goods by relying on domestic production. It promoted Indian self-sufficiency, that is, the substitution of domestic for British production. The self-sufficiency movement was part of the Indian independence movement and contributed to developing Indian nationalism. Mahatma Gandhi described it as the soul of swaraj(self-rule).

Swaraj: As used by Gandhi, it means home rule, that is, India's independence from foreign domination. Gandhi also suggested a more expansive meaning of a stateless society – a decentralized government without a national hierarchical state.

Tabligh and Tanzeem: Movements for the communal consolidation of Muslims.

The Indian Sociologist: It was a radical nationalist journal founded in London by Indian journalist Shyamji Krishna Varma in 1905. It moved to Paris in 1907 – it was an important part of the struggle for Indian independence waged by the Indian diaspora.

The People: A weekly in Lahore, founded as the mouthpiece of Servants of the People Society by Lala Lajpat Rai. Some of Bhagat Singh's writing was published posthumously in this paper.

Tilak: Keshav Bal Gangadhar Tilak, an early independence leader, was the most prominent in India before Gandhi.

Trade Disputes Act of 1929: Among other restrictions, this law curtailed the right of Indian workers to strike. It was partly in protest against this Act that Bhagat Singh and B.K. Dutt threw the bombs into the chamber of the Central Legislative Assembly.

Uttar Pradesh: A state in northern India where the town of Chauri Chaura is located. It was called United Provinces during British rule.

Vande Mataram: See Bande Mataram.

Vasudev Kutumbakam: Sanskrit phrase meaning the whole earth is a family.

Yagyopavit: Hindu ceremony of wearing the sacred thread.

Yugantar: Jugantar or Yugantar (*New Era* or *Transition of an Epoch*), was both a Bengali revolutionary organization and a radical Bengali newspaper. Barindra Kumar Ghosh founded the newspaper. The Yugantar association, like Anushilan Samiti, started in the guise of a suburban fitness club. Several Jugantar members were arrested, hanged, or deported for life to the Andaman Cellular Jail. The San Francisco headquarters of the nationalist and revolutionary Ghadar Movement, established by Indian immigrants on the West Coast of the United States in the second decade of the twentieth century, was named Yugantar Ashram.